PAPA'S PORCH SWING STORIES

By
Robert Bryan

Copyright © 2022 by Robert Bryan
All Rights Reserved
Printed in the United States of America

ISBN 978-1-7376384-8-3

All Scripture quotes are from the King James Bible.

No part of this work may be reproduced without the expressed consent of the publisher, except for brief quotes, whether by electronic, photocopying, recording, or information storage and retrieval systems.

Address All Inquiries To:
THE OLD PATHS PUBLICATIONS, Inc.
142 Gold Flume Way
Cleveland, Georgia, U.S.A.

Web: www.theoldpathspublications.com
E-mail: TOP@theoldpathspublications.com

The names in these stories have been changed to protect the identities of the persons involved.

DEDICATION

I dedicate this book to Jesus Christ my Savior, who sought me and delivered me and saved me from sin and self. And to the heroes he sprinkled heavily upon my path through this life. I used to think heroes were imaginary characters who wore outlandish costumes and had supernatural powers. But I discovered that concept was totally in error.

When you wake in the night from a screammare, real heroes wipe your face; they hold you close. They say it's okay, you're here now. Real heroes cry and they help you shed your tears. Real heroes never mock you; they don't accuse you. Real heroes pray. And when they don't understand, because you don't understand yourself, they love you anyway and encourage you. Real heroes pick you up. They take a kid off the street from under a bridge. They take you into their home and into their hearts. Real heroes love. When you have a meltdown and you don't know why, and everything is dark, their example is a light of hope in your dark world. You promise yourself that if you live through this, you want to be like them. Real heroes tell you the truth about yourself, even if it breaks their heart. Real heroes feel your pain. They don't notice your scars. They don't see your quirks. They never stare. Real heroes have selective sight loss.

It is a great privilege to know a real hero and I have been miraculously blessed to know several. Some wore aprons, others wore jeans, some wore tennis shoes, some wore glasses. All wore scars.

They understand. Real heroes look like people but live like Jesus.

From earliest childhood to adulthood, I was surrounded by heroes. Even when my world was breaking and shattered, heroes would somehow find me and help me pick up the pieces and keep me going!

When I married, I soon discovered I had married a hero. The things I went through in coming out of the darkness, she went through with me. Her love broke through and never failed.

There are still many heroes today. They don't advertise or boast. But their life is a testimony to the character that's within.

Heroes are not born; they are made. Made from the love they bear and the choices they make every day! Thank you, Lord, for sending the heroes into my crazy world!

TABLE OF CONTENTS

DEDICATION 3
TABLE OF CONTENTS 5
WHY PORCH SWING STORIES? 9
   Coming Out of Hiding 13
   Behind the Scenes.. 16
VOLUME I: STORIES 21
   #1 In the Beginning, Where It Started: 4 Stories 21
      Introduction to the Abby Story...................... 21
   #2 The Abby Story, Where It All Started...................... 24
   #3 Wisdom My Sister, Understanding Kinswoman 30
   #4 Darkie 34
   #5 It Came Down the Stairs 40
   #6 "The Granny Story"... 45
   #7 The Revelation... 49
   #8 The Victory... 50
   #9 Fishing on Cedar River 55
   #10 Angel by the Bed 59
   #11 Bad Water 61
   #12 Bath Time in the Ozarks 66
   #13 I Don't Believe in Baths 70
   "The Power of the Shower Song"................................. 74
   #14 Being Moved up the Hill....................................... 75
   #15 Billie Jean and the Can Lid 77
   #16 The Black Bull and the Gray Slick- Haired Dog 80
   #17 Bro. McKee's Farewell.. 88
   #18 Bus Ride in California 89
   #19 Chain Rattling, by Robert Bryan 94
   #20 The Church Guest 95
   #21 Some Call Him Lord! 96
   #22 Crazy Harry and the Chicken 103
   #23 Macho Harry 106
   #24 Dad's Farewell 108
   #25 Dad's New Cadillac.. 109
   # 26 Dark Warriors vs. Faith...................................... 113
   #27 Defeating the Devil in Montesano 115
   #28 Drought in Missouri 117
   #29 The First Church of Foreigners 124
   #30 Giving Little Jake a Ride! (Hillbilly Happiness) 127

#31& #32 The Go Cart Stories 130
    #1 The Goat Hill 130
    #2 The Manure Spreader 134
#33 The Granny Story 140
#34 Clans at War! 143
#35 Too Old 151
#36 Landing on the Moon 152
#37 Granny's Threshold 153
#38 Ginger the Monkey 154
#39 James and Martha Saiders 160
#40 Hauling Water 162
#41 Frog Gigging at Frog Lake 163
#42 Escaped Prisoners 166
#43 The Football 167
#44 The Fight in the Corn Bin 169
#45 The Bluff 170
#46 The Blizzard 173
#47 Big Wind 181
#48 The Outhouse and the Dirt Clod 183
#49 The Dug Story 184
#50 Leaving James's Farm 186
#51 Returning 186
#52 I Say Old Chap! 187
#53 Lee Lee and the Outhouse 191
#54 KXEN With 1000 Watts to Serve You 197

Music **203**
#55 Music 203
#56 Music Lesson #1 203
#57 Music Lesson #2 204
#58 Music Lesson #3 205
#59 Music Lesson #4 208
    The Mechanical Church 208

Unusual Experiences **213**
#60 An Unusual Experience 213
#61 The Fjords of Hell 214
62 The Vision of Hell 215

My Visits to Heaven **219**
63 My First Visit to Heaven: God's Throne Room 219
#64 The River of Peace 220
#65 God's Library 222
#66 One Drop of Heaven 224

TABLE OF CONTENTS

#67 Walking With Jesus for One Week 225
VOLUME II: MORE STORIES.................................... 227
   Ships at Sea 227
   Time Warp Road 228
   You Sleep Here 233
   Visiting with Aunt Bess 236
   A Dream? With Dad... 243
   Having Company!.. 247
   Church Helper!... 252
   All Things.. 257
   Married to a Foreigner 259
   Truly God Works in a Mysterious Way!...................... 263
   The New Bloomfield Discovery 265
   The Hidden Tomb.. 270
   The Slave House 274
   Visiting the Vogels... 276
   You Can't Fly Out of Hell 278
Gold Country Lessons... 282
   The Herman Nelson Story 282
   The Ghost Town Bear 282
   This Story I Call "Being Drowned by a Grizzly!" 285
   #1 Quick Sale 286
   #2 Dark Cloud 287
   #3 Firepower 287
   A Funny Story Involving a Hand Truck 289
   The Anaconda Gold Claim 290
   Herman's Last Trip 296
   Farewell to a Legend 301
   UNDERSTANDING FORGIVENESS................................. 307
   What Forgiveness is Not: 308
   Complex Forgiveness... 310
   The Process of Complex Forgiveness 310
ABOUT THE AUTHOR.. 319

WHY PORCH SWING STORIES?

In the summer, the front porch was the favorite place to "visitate." It usually held three-legged chairs (*that was a long time ago!*) taken out of the kitchen and front room, maybe a bench, a porch swing, and always a rocker or two. The front porch, being raised a foot or two off the ground, always provided much seating. The handrails were very wide, which allowed sitting on, placing your dinner plate on, or lining up the tea bucket (a three-gallon galvanized milk bucket) with sweet iced tea to the brim, and Ozark China, (mason jars for gulping down the tea!). Listening to the katydids , the whippoorwills, the bobwhites, the crickets, and other outside night life was a welcomed and favorite pastime in the south. Of course sweet iced tea and southern fried chicken, fried potatoes, homemade biscuits with chicken gravy and corn on the cob still comes to mind when I remember those front porch dinners, even to this day!

There are memories of kids playing hide and seek or red rover while the adults were on the front porch chewing on toothpicks and swapping stories. Sometimes the stories got out of hand. The scary stories would separate the men from the mice. If the story was scary enough, there would be a major evacuation of the front porch. Everyone just "happened" to go inside about the same time, and "somehow" ALL the lights in the house would be on! Meanwhile the kids, out in the dark and not hearing the scary story, would be left to defend themselves from whatever sea monster or boogie man had chased the adults inside!

Another favorite porch swing memory was the family hoe-down. Everyone brought their musical instruments and joined in on the fun. The musical instruments weren't always musical. Sometimes spoons, or water jugs, or other improvised percussion instruments showed up as well. Banjos, guitars, fiddles, accordion, harpsichord and such like, were the norm. The songs included everything under the sun! If somebody thought of it, then everyone would likely join in.

The front porch was also a place of private solemn reflections for those sad times that we all faced. Those times were met with deep inward soul-searching and many changes were brought about by the porch swing "altar."

Sometimes when trouble came our way, as it did so often to each family, there was the, "let's go outside and talk" meetings. Those stiff and sometimes painful truths that we can't see in ourselves are presented with the painful facts that we are sadly aware of. And yes, there is a direct path from the front porch to the woodshed. Not all "woodshed" experiences involved going there. Sometimes it was the crushing weight of our actions that brought about the needed repentance. Our shame was the taskmaster, and it was our hurt to others that laid the stripes across our own hearts. I called those times the "woodsheds of the heart." Those front porch consultations were brutal and much needed. Repentance and healing was the norm from "the front porch chapel." No preacher could ever match the painful words spoken from a broken heart of the one who loves you so much. And no congregation was ever more attentive than a wayward youth that was seeking acceptance and direction. They were painful then; they are priceless now.

Perhaps the most enjoyable front porch stories were with those "sparking their gal." Today they call it dating. But as the couple went to the front porch to be alone, and yet seen, many a kid went into hiding! Some

WHY PORCH SWING STORIES?

went under the porch, or around the corner, in the bushes, or on the porch roof, all with ears tuned in like radar. They didn't want to miss a single mushy statement that could produce a blushing when repeated later (when the parents weren't around of course)! Sometimes even the adults would just happen to wander outside at a very "interesting moment" when things looked like somebody needed a reality check!

The porch swing was also an escape; a place of refuge when things in the house got too lively, too fussy or just too crowded. Or, there were times when the house just got too hot. The summer heat had a way of driving you outside to sit on the porch swing, in the shade, and feel the welcomed breeze! And, of course, sweet iced tea was always in the spring house or in the ice house, loudly calling your name!

The quietness of the front porch was always a welcomed place of rest.

While laundry, washtubs, dog baths, clotheslines, and water fights were all taking place off the back porch and out of sight, the front porch never lacked activities to provide family entertainment. Even today when I drive past a house with a large front porch and a porch swing, it brings back a flood of wonderful memories. I wonder what they would say if I asked permission to enjoy their porch swing for a while?

I trust these porch swing stories will somehow benefit the reader. I know times have changed, but human nature has not. We all still need those porch swing chapels, or those wonderful memories of sparking our gal, or even those soul-searching moments that strengthen our perceptions of who we really are. But wherever we are, and no matter what we have faced, and no matter how good or bad we have done, we all need those porch swing experiences to strengthen us and encourage us to be what we wanted to be in the first place.

This paragraph is my attempt to explain the "why" and the "how" to the stories that seem completely out of this world. It's only my opinion, but it's the only answer I have for these experiences. Only God knows the real explanation. Certain regions of the south are known for "outside of the box" living and experiences. It's no wonder those coming from these areas are very reluctant to share their experiences, especially in a place where those things don't usually happen. It puts them in an awkward position and often in a bad light. I wrote my experiences knowing they would make waves. But they had to come out. I needed "debriefing" and healing...so I wrote.

At the time of these experiences, Missouri was a very dark place spiritually. It was run by superstitions, fear and ignorance. Demonology and witchcraft were rampant at that time and many worlds were crashing together. The weird, the supernatural, and the darkness seemed to be fighting for dominance. Technology was starting to come in and many households were getting electricity and phones. Radios were becoming very popular. Running water was becoming available and creating a new rural lifestyle. Many old cabins were being rebuilt and upgraded to the modern ways of living. At the same time, there was the old school mindset that trusted in superstitions and feared change. It was as if two different invisible worlds were at war. The physical manifestations were only the symptoms of that war, but extraordinary episodes became a daily occurrence in the lives of many. Some with the old order mindsets, with their séances and spells and spirits, were fighting the coming changes. Many clan wars broke out between families due to the unrest and fear. The rough crowds said that "the world was coming to an end." My experience with "Time Warp Road," was not unique and I was not the only one who experienced such things. It seemed like everyone had their own collection of stories and tales they feared to talk about. I have met many who have had similar experiences. The only difference between any of us is this, that "I dared to write about it, and tell others." Someone said, "if we don't learn from the mistakes of our past, we will repeat them." The greatest weapon we have to keep the darkness at bay is to expose it to the light. It's no wonder darkness has fought so hard against my exposing it to the light. Today most of these types of experiences have passed away. While there are many who remember those dark times and their own experiences as well, they agree that it's no longer "that way," or certainly not as bad. So far I haven't met anyone who misses those dark and troubled times.

Coming Out of Hiding

My experiences were not even close to normal, so I started keeping it all to myself. But the Holy Spirit kept putting his finger in my back, and saying, "I want you to write about your life." So I would try to write about it. But as each memory and each event came up, it brought with it the darkness, the heaviness, the anxiety and the fears. I would be sitting there trying to write but the emotional and mental storms would come sweeping over me, and I had to stop writing. Then I would go back and tear the paper up. Sometimes, it would take days to get rid of the heaviness and darkness that came over me due to my writing the stories. So I would refuse to write. And the cycle would repeat, with the Holy Spirit saying, "I want you to write."

Then one night, while we were at a friend's house with many people there, this guy speaks up in front of everyone and says "Hey Robert, I read a book about this kid who's life was so wretched, he ended up dying from his parents abuse. The parents went to prison. It reminded me of you. Maybe you should write a book too?" I was so furious at the man, I said to him in front of everybody, "What right do you have to bring up my past and meddle in areas that are none of your business?" His response was this, "If you do not write, then your life is a failure. You have been through hell so many times, nobody can even count them. Even your family back then, is amazed that you're even alive. And yet you're here, free and safe. There are so many who are still in their living hells, if you don't write and show them the way out, then God will find somebody else to write, and your life and your road to victory, will have been for nothing."

This really rattled my thinking. His words had set off a flood of memories and I, once again, began re-living the nightmares. I knew I could never write to help anyone if I couldn't help myself enough to even write about it. I was really torn between two worlds of trying to write, and suffering for trying to do so. It was horrible. I knew Yim was right but finding the path to do it was a different story.

My world of friends was very small on purpose. I could not handle any close friends. If they got to know me, then the questions would start and the memories would start with them. After voicing their unbelief and shock, then the accusations would come. When that happened, I would immediately abandon that friendship completely and go back to being a loner. My friendship with Yim was different. He knew my past, but never attacked me because of it. When he said something about it, it was after much thought and consideration.

WHY PORCH SWING STORIES?

It was never intended to hurt. But when he did say something, it was a truth I did not like. However, he loved me enough to tell me anyway. Even if he didn't know the answer either, he knew what needed to be said. He loved me enough to say it.

There were other well-meaning people who knew me and they also encouraged me to write. But I could not stop the nightmares. Finally, after many years of this cycle, something happened that changed everything. I learned that forgiveness was the key to victory. But I could never get past the storms long enough to consider such a radical concept as forgiveness. At that time I didn't want to forgive. I wanted vengeance. But God was still working on me.

Then God stepped in and performed a miracle in me. It was this miracle from God that allowed me to forgive. Suddenly I could write without the inward/internal backlash that would normally follow. Praise God for his wonderful mercy to me!

But the battles were not over completely, there was still work to do before I could reach the mountain top.

There have been many hurting people who have had experiences very similar to mine. Coming out of hiding with my experiences has given them hope. They were afraid to tell their stories because of the persecution they faced from well-meaning, but unwise people. Once my stories started getting around, those who were rejected and hurting saw a light of hope and realized they were not alone. Someone knew, someone understood, someone cared, someone stood up for them! And they saw that there was Victory ahead for them as well!

Whether they come out with their experiences or not is irrelevant. But if they have been strengthened to find their way to God and his peace, that's everything!

Behind the Scenes

When God gave me the victory to write these stories, he would sometimes wake me up in the night and say, "Go write." Somehow I always knew what story he wanted me to write. So I went to my very tiny makeshift desk, turned on my ancient laptop, and started typing away.

I faced many giants in writing these stories. The fears would come back along with the darkness, and the anxiety attacks would go full swing. When that happened, I stopped, went straight to God, and poured out my heart to him. His amazing peace, somehow, would always find me, calming my terrible storms and comforting me with the phrase, "peace be still!". Then I could go back to writing the experience I was supposed to write about.

Some stories gave me serious setbacks. I pled with God for help but the struggles went on. Finally, at the end of the second day, His love broke through! The rapturous Glory that filled my soul I cannot express! I found myself wrapped in his presence as His peace flooded through me like waves of the sea.

I wondered if the angels were fighting their way to my rescue! But then Jesus came and the enemy had to flee. As He swept me up into his arms, I felt his "Peace be still!"

Some stories are funny, such as "Lee Lee and the Outhouse" or "Giving Little Jake a Ride." But I found that God was using these stories to help me debrief and

WHY PORCH SWING STORIES?

"reset" my mindset back to normal. I needed to vent but I also needed to recover from the venting

I found that writing about these experiences proved to be a great instrument in my personal healing. God was using the "pen" in place of the "scalpel." Writing them brought back many more terrors that had previously been blocked out, but in the remembering of them, there was also a releasing of them. If God was leading me to write that event, he was also preparing me to be healed of that event. It was of utmost importance that I ONLY write about what God wanted me to write about. I truly did not want to open anything that God did not want me to open!

There are some stories that I don't think I will ever have to write because they are damaging stories. They are dangerous. They cause more problems rather than expose them. One of these is "Time Warp Road." It's the only story that I felt led to write about from the list of "<u>Stories to never write about.</u>" I really struggled back and forth about including it anywhere. Surprisingly, that's the story I get the most feedback from! It seems several have had a similar experience just like that! I don't blame them for not telling their story! I struggled with writing mine! I still look back and wonder if I should ever have included it.

Another personal reason that I write is to leave my family a reminder of what God has done for me, He can do for them! They will no doubt face things in their lives when looking up will seem impossible. In my absence there is a reminder to always look up!

In the coming days, as the darkness, the wickedness and the injustice deepens, I expect these experiences will become the norm once again. But I can tell you, there is victory ahead for every child of God! We are NOT the victims! We ARE the victors! We must

,be like the servant of Elisha who had to look up to see there are more with us than are with them!

I would like to think these experiences would help people see that we live in a world that is far more spiritual than physical and perhaps increase their faith.

Like Peter, a lot of people struggle to look up. Keeping your eyes off the storm is a challenge by itself. But looking into the face of Jesus can calm our storms! Fear says, I cannot do it, but faith says, Jesus can! It's then that He reaches out to us and says, "Peace be still!"

I understand the act of reaching out to the unseen hand of God is not popular in a secular world filled with darkness. Satan and his forces are afraid of your faith in God. It's their total commitment to separate you from God and then to undermine your faith. It's only then that you are defeated.

Another tactic of darkness is peer pressure from the lost. Everyone wants to be accepted. For you to acknowledge God is to separate yourself from those who have rejected him. Acceptance is a powerful tool. It's easier to denounce the power of God's word and to "fit in" with the lost and be accepted, than to say something "out of the box" and be "mocked."

These experiences do not make you super spiritual. Just the opposite! They bring you <u>under attack</u>, especially from the religious world with its status quo of "just be nice and go with the flow." Speaking out can be a tremendous weight.

It's normal for people to accept what they know. Things outside the box frighten them; they feel threatened by them somehow. Fear says to keep accepting the darkness, don't look up. But there is a "still small voice from God" that's calling you, and it says to look up, see the glory that's calling you!

WHY PORCH SWING STORIES?

Staying in our comfort zone will feel safe for a while, but that feeling will collapse when the storms hit. Fear says to turn a deaf ear to that still small voice of God. But remember, not all chains are made of steel. Some are fashioned out of deceit, fear, ignorance, unbelief and even darkness.

When things are looking tight, and the storms are lifting their threatening waves, and darkness is shaking its spear at you, LOOK UP! YOUR REDEMPTION DRAWETH NIGH! Call upon the Saviour and see for yourself!

VOLUME I: STORIES

#1 In the Beginning, Where It Started: 4 Stories

Introduction to the Abby Story

These 4 stories have been placed together in sequence as they occurred in real life. They have already been written in other places separately, such as "The Granny Story," but it wasn't until I began to type up the list of experiences that I realized the casual reader may never see that these events actually went together, one happening or overlapping, right after the other.

The Abby Story, Wisdom My Sister, Darkie, The Granny Story, and Victory are in sequence.

There are other experiences that also happened together, but none so significant because of the path of destruction that followed, or the amazing mercy of God as he began to pick up the pieces from the aftermath of darkness.

There are other stories that I still cannot write. The brain responds to information flow and goes into shutdown mode for survival. I know people can't always understand this, but that's a different reality that some are forced to live with.

It has gotten to be very common for me to wake up during the night and feel the Lord's tug as he says to go and write about a particular event. When the Lord does that, it's usually a story that I have been avoiding; one that causes me a lot of trouble. One of these is "The Abby Story." I never dreamed in my worst nightmares that I would unlock those memories again. But the Lord woke me up and said to go write it. God helped me write "The Abby Story" very quickly that night. It had to go fast, or I would never have done it. But then it gave me serious problems the next day and a few days after that. I had a meltdown in a restaurant the very next day. I had to leave. My wife paid for our meal as I fled from the table. I was breaking all over again because I had unlocked another of my mysterious chapters and the quirks it brought with it. The next few days were very challenging for me. But it was God's way of releasing and healing me from another hidden episode that had lain silent and hidden. That is until God said that it had to come out.

Like a festering wound of the soul, it must come out or it will poison the spirit, and kill its victim.

I suppose before all this "story writing" is over, God will require even more of me. He will want exposed things I'm still afraid of, or ashamed of. But I know God never leads where he cannot keep. If I open these doors without God's leading, I will self-destruct. But God knows His own timing. And He knows how much I can take. He is extremely patient and merciful to me. He will not lead me, where He cannot keep me.

I realize there are others who carry their own stories, their own fears. They suffer silently, inwardly. But I happen to know those who love you see more than you are willing to admit. It's not hard to understand that they love you and want to help, but their hands are tied. They can't reach into a person's mind and undo years of torments or damage from others. **But God can!** However, we still have our part to do. We have a contribution to make that no other person can make. We may be the only ones who can communicate that meaningful insight that will encourage others to let go, and let God heal them too!

STORIES

So many families, so many loved ones have wept over my internal suffering. My dear wife has suffered much because of my own quirks. Church families have been so patient with me, and faithfully prayed for me.

Our kids heard most of the stories from their youth. When we moved back to my home state, they got a real surprise.

My wife thought I had a lot of odd stories. But when we moved back to my home state, she found I had not even revealed the tip of the iceberg. My family filled her in, showing her the places and pictures. She met the people in real life, and she was shocked.

I am thankful with sincere love and gratitude for those who have stood by me. My beautiful wife, our children, my close friend, Yim, the Lauritzen family, the James Smith family, the Hurlburt's, Ron and Rachel Beach, James and Martha Saiders, and, of course, Granny, are all examples of Christ's love in action during times of crises. They were a solid rock in my crumbling world.

At the time these experiences happened, I thought they were normal. Everybody goes through this, right? Little did I realize the actual atrocities of those events or the extreme weirdness of them.

There were many that did not understand such internal suffering, or simply could not comprehend the degree of suffering that a person may have to endure, either from their past or present circumstances. But their hearts were breaking for my release. Even when I clearly did not handle things very well, they were kind and tried to be understanding with me. When the tiny, littlest thing would happen that would mean nothing to others, triggered an unwelcome and fearful reaction from me, as I struggled with it they may have thought it was all so silly, but as time went by, they understood.

It was not a reflection on them but a mentally triggered response, a fiendish memory that haunts and mocks and cripples. God has grace for those crippling memories.

As God leads in each step of our own spirit-led recovery, there is a light up ahead. There is victory in the making. But we must do our part, to seek the Lord for his strength, and never launch out on our own making.

Prov 3:5-6 *Trust in the LORD, with all thine heart; and lean not unto thine own understanding. 6: In all thy ways acknowledge him, and he shall direct thy paths.*

These pages also address the tragic effects of shallow Christians, who for their own personal reasons, (whatever they were), incited all-out war against me because of my experiences. It was through their bitter hatred and darkness that I learned that forgiveness also means letting go. I do forgive and wish them the best. My sincere intent on writing was to unlock the doors of unbelief and indifference and to help those who ignorantly fight the devil's warfare because they do not know what else to do. They become afraid and strike out. There is a better way!

#2 The Abby Story, Where It All Started

"The Abby Story" came first. After my mind had snapped, then came Wisdom My Sister, then "Darkie," and finally, "The Granny Story." That is who brought the love and power of Christ into a very dark world.

Aunt Abby moved in with us. She was an alcoholic and her husband was an alcoholic though he never moved in with us, and seldom lived with Abby. Abby was has hard as it gets, as far as personalities are concerned. She drove a cab at night, caried a gun and a knife and was very skilled at both. She carried her scars like badges and often talked about the fights she got into as a cab driver, and what she did to protect herself. She taught her girls to be just as brutal and hard as she and her husband were. They took pride in their toughness, and in their standing together as a tough family.

My dad worked from early morning till late at night in town, several miles away. So, he was gone from home most of the day. He worked on weekends at another job, and was gone then also. Mom was left to represent the home. She was afraid of Aunt Abby, just like everyone else was afraid of Aunt Abby. Nobody wanted to stand up against Abby and her ruthless brood. Even her husband left because he could not stand against her and her cutthroat band of wicked, hardcore girls. They knew how to act, cry, accuse and fight. They knew how to lie and manipulate like cold-blooded dogs. They were the exact picture of a hardcore, fighting, negative, dysfunctional, brutal, violent family.

Around the age of 12, the most tragic tale of all started unfolding in my life. Aunt Abby moved in with us. She was my dad's sister. She and her brood of girls moved in with us while we lived in the haunted house described in the "Darkie" story.

I was the only boy in the house, except for Dad, who worked in town from before daylight to late evening, five day a week.

They brought to our lives a whole new level of hatred, bitterness, and deceit. From the very first day, the very first hour, the example was set that would be the new normal for my world. When they hauled their stuff over to our house to move in, they also brought a bicycle frame. It was only a frame with absolutely nothing on it whatsoever. It needed a seat, handlebars, pedals, a chain, wheels, brakes, everything! Of course, being a boy and always working on things, I started putting all the many missing parts on the frame. The bicycle frame belonged to the youngest girl named Elle.

Elle sat on the porch and talked with me the whole time I was building her this bicycle. I explained to her everything I was doing and how those parts worked together. When I was finished building her bicycle, I told her that I was going to ride it around the house and back to make sure everything worked well so she could ride it. I circled the house and returned to the front porch. When I got back to the front porch, Aunt Abby was there, Elle was there bawling her eyes out, and all of Aunt Abby's girls were there also. Elle was telling her how I had forcibly taken her bike away from her, and took off with it. Her sisters, who were nowhere around while I was building this bike, were all there agreeing with Elle on her awful story. Abby was extremely mad at me for taking advantage of her little girl and her bike. She threatened me several times during this discussion, and completely micromanaged my returning of the bike back to Elle, who promptly got on it, rode past me, and stuck out her tongue at me as she went by.

The whole event took me by such complete surprise. I had no idea how to mentally process what had just happened. When they returned and went into the house, I just stood in the front yard wondering, "what just happened?"

But that event was just the tip of the iceberg of what their presence in our lives was about to be like. Things got so off the chart insane very quickly.

Aunt Abby was a cabdriver in town at night. Her obligation when staying with us was to provide lunch money to her kids and my sister and I. Lunch was 30 cents per day, per child. She had Lori, Eve, Lois, Karleen, and Elle. Then she also was supposed to give lunch money to Sarah and myself. Every morning Aunt Abby brought home a canvas, zipped-top bag of coins that was always at least half full. This she said was her tips. Her pay was always in bills that she kept in her purse. But when she went to town, she usually put some of it in her bra, in front of everyone.

Right after school started, her kids told her how I was not using my lunch money. This was not true but, of course, they all consented to this lie. So the decision was made; Robert would not get any more lunch money as I was untrustworthy with it. So that stopped my lunch at school all together. This was made worse because my main meal was school lunch. There was seldom any food in the house and if there was, it was "their food." I couldn't touch it.

After a while, I went to my mom one morning, woke her up, and asked for some lunch money. I told her what was going on, so she got up and gave me 30 cents from her purse. I got to eat lunch that day!

It was decided by Abby's kids that anything I had was fair game to them if they wanted it. So they took everything I had, not because they wanted it, but because nobody would stop them. They would all agree to whatever lie they told, which always involved my somehow saying that they could have it. And so this went on all summer long and well into the next summer.

We lived not far from a dump. I would go to the dump, find something, bring it home, and clean it up. Abby's kids would see it, and it would be gone instantly. It didn't matter what it was, they took it because they could. I screamed my head off to Dad and Mom about all this, but they wanted to keep peace with poor Abby and her poor kids. So I was ignored on all points completely. Of course Abby's kids drummed up some kind of lie to defend themselves, and as always Abby backed them up saying that her kids were victims of my anger and lying accusations.

One incident was the final straw to my sanity. All this took an extremely heavy toll on my 12-year-old mind.

My sister always took sides with Abby's kids because they gave her whatever she wanted in exchange for going along with whatever they were doing. I really think she went along with them for her own safety.

This particular occurrence involved a high school class ring. None of us were in high school so I don't remember where I even got the ring. I probably found it in the many boxes of junk I went through at the dump. (By the way, you can find a lot of good things to eat at a dump!)

So, I got this ring that looked like it was something real and expensive. I knew if anyone saw it, it would be gone instantly, so I kept it hidden. Looking back today it was probably a piece of real junk. But that didn't matter at the time. So, Lori discovered my ring and took it. Of course a big lie was told as to how it became her ring. On this occasion, Sarah Lee decided to get involved and backed up Lori's story on who's ring it was, and how I had stolen the ring from Lori, and Lori was merely getting her ring back.

Lori decided to wear the ring on a chain around her neck where I could always see it. She would walk past me, lift the ring and say, "It's mine now, just try and take it, see what happens to you!" Her sisters and my sister, Sarah, would laugh at her, thinking it was funny, and, of course, this would make me mad, and the hatred and bitterness would sink to a much lower level. This is only one example of hundreds.

Somewhere during all this mental abuse, lack of food, lack of dignity, lack of privacy, lack of justice, physical abuse, threatening, the many punishments for my unacceptable behavior, my having to bow down to their every wish of their tyranny, plus the endless line of trouble at school they caused me, my mind snapped. They would tell kids at school some lie about me and everyone would then surround me outside of school or in the gym and persecute me mercilessly for whatever stories Abby's kids and Sarah would tell. Anything I said was clearly a lie, trying to get out of what they said I did, no matter how immoral it was or how stupid.

Another tactic they thought was so funny, was if they knew I wanted something, no matter what it was, if they could get it before I did, they would wave it around in front of me and say I had to beg for it. Bark like a dog, whimper little doggie! Of course I refused to beg them for anything. So they would keep it, destroy it, or hide it. Sometimes they would just lay it aside and watch me very closely, just so they could mock my attempts to get it. It never ever mattered whose it was, or what it was, as long as I didn't get it.

To say my life was a living hell would be a great understatement. This went on for the rest of that summer, and continued until the end of the second summer.

There is a limit to how much a 12-year-old can take. I reached mine. The episodes of mental breakdown started coming in rapid succession. Some called them emotional breakdowns, or nervous breakdowns, or mental breakdowns, or whatever. I called it hell. I was filled with intense hatred, anger and bitterness.

My mind and body could take no more. I broke and broke repeatedly. During this time, Abby and her kids never let up. They attacked me with their antics and hateful words no matter where I went to escape, or what I did. They were there to exaggerate and re-enact my trembling, stuttering, or whatever other quirk manifested itself. They would mock my words and laugh at my brokenness. "BA BA BA Bark little doggie"

Meanwhile my aunts, Lil, Polly, Abby and others banded together to convince Mom and Dad to have me committed to the Fulton insane asylum. My cousin was there already. They told me how wonderful it all was. But I knew from that same cousin that it was hell on earth there also. The pressure to put me there was very great from most of the family. But Dad and Mom steadfastly said no.

#3 Wisdom My Sister, Understanding Kinswoman

Pro 7:1 *My son, keep my words, and lay up my commandments with thee.*

Pro 7:4 *Say unto wisdom, Thou art my sister; and call understanding thy kinswoman:*

This experience happened to me while going through the very darkest time of my entire life. It happened during the Abby Story, when my mind had snapped. I simply must leave it at that explanation.

This experience is one of those things that is always with me, sometimes daily, sometimes weekly, but it is always there. I only vaguely related it to Jovanna. But like an onion peel, it comes off in layers.

STORIES

This is one of those layers. I'm very thankful for this constant companion that's always there.

Many years ago while I was reading the book of Proverbs I came upon this section of scripture. And as always, I took it literally. My beloved Granny had been reading Proverbs to me to restore my mind. (This explains why I repeat myself so much and think in contrasted comparisons. My kids didn't appreciate it because I wasn't balanced with it, but I am what I am.) As I pondered the message of the text, I saw right away I didn't want another sister. I already had sisters (I wanted a brother very badly) and they were typical examples of sisters growing up in the harsh realities of the Ozarks. Why would I want another one? But the example before me painted a clear picture of biblically perfect sisters whose names were Wisdom and Understanding. Then I thought, what a wonderful friend sisters like that could be, and, at that point, new friends entered my life. Wisdom and Understanding! As I presented to them the various situations I faced each day, they started talking to me. And everything they said was a quote from Proverbs! Now their voices were not to be heard with the ear, but with a still small voice somewhere in the mind. And thus the book of Proverbs took on a personality. It had a voice, a face, a perfect memory, and it was a constant companion, ever faithful to my best interest, even when I didn't always like the truths it was presenting. It also had a perfect understanding of me and my problems. Sometimes I didn't like what the Bible said about me, so I'd argue with Wisdom, and then I'd ask Understanding for her opinion, hoping she would back me up. But she never did. Her way of presenting the problem to me always made me see the rightness of what Wisdom was saying. Sometime I rebelled at what they both were saying to me. Then they would go away. I could not find them anywhere! If I went to the creek that was so quiet and peaceful, (for they often spoke to me there) they were not there. If I woke up in the night and slipped outside in the moonlight on the porch, they were not there. If I went to see Granny and tell her of my dilemma, she always said the same things that Wisdom said, so I knew she was right. Then I'd go and ponder those things and guess who would show up! My sister, Wisdom and my kinswoman, Understanding! How glad I was to see them again! Howbeit seeing them was not with the eye, I always sensed their presence and somehow I always knew they were there. But if they weren't there I couldn't see them. It's not like you could imagine them into existence. Try as hard as you might, you could not force them to show up. Then afterwards, when they would return, I'd feel bad for my actions, they'd forgive me, and we were together again.

One day I was reading in Proverbs and came upon Proverbs 8. This chapter denotes the existence of Wisdom as a personality that grew up before God, like a child grows up before his father. And again I took it literally. Proverbs clearly depicts Wisdom as a personality. It also depicts strange women as a personality. I have seen many strange things, but have never met the "personality" who is the strange woman. I'm not convinced I want to! Scripture has a lot to say about various personalities. There are people that are real to heaven, but vague to earth, such as Melchizedek, Wisdom, etc. I am convinced they are real. However, they are not revealed to everyone, but only to those to whom God reveals them. God knows. As time goes on, these personalities seem to fade into the background of everyday life. I can't explain to you the "spiritual science" of how these things work out. I just don't know. Neither am I willing to say that Jesus had several spiritual sisters in heaven, like wisdom, understanding, discretion, prudence, and beauty. Scripture seems to imply such things, but it would be very hard to produce concrete evidence. Today, I still go to the book of Proverbs and it still has a personality to me. The book of Proverbs is a very dear book that Granny used to bring me back to the world of reality. And The Holy Spirit speaks to me in the still small voice. Jesus walks with me daily, and he is ever so near.

I remember these things and still ponder them in my mind from time to time.

Then one day God gave me a vision that was an answer to a question I had asked. And there before were my old-time friends, Wisdom, Understanding, Discretion, Prudence, and Beauty! I saw them in my vision and instantly recognized them. How my heart did leap! These "sisters" of mine helped me through the most terrible times any human could endure. Naturally, they were very dear to me. And there in that visit to heaven was someone I knew from earth (Salone), walking in the midst of them. They were on a white flagstone path, following a winding line of tall marble columns. There they all were, laughing and talking excitedly as they went, in those beautiful gowns they always wore. I shall never forget that beautiful heavenly scene. But one day.....By God's grace and to the devils surprise, I shall walk that path again.....with my sisters! In that visit I never knew where they were going, but now I think I know. They were on their way to see our Savior and King and thank him for all the wonderful things he has done. HE DOETH ALL THINGS WELL!

Now consider all this and understand that after I had snapped and was just an empty shell of hate and darkness, they wanted to get rid of me. They could break me no further. It was then that the pressure was on to have me committed and it was then that "Darkie" showed up. And that story began to unfold.

#4 Darkie

This story of Darkie unfolded while Abby was still living with our family. "The Abby Story" came first followed by "Wisdom my Sister," Then "Darkie," then "The Granny Story." Granny, who brought the love and power of Christ into a very dark world.

This is a very dark experience. You may not want to read it. Stop now if you have any doubts. Some will rightfully say, "You were the victim, why did you get possessed? Shouldn't they have gotten possessed?" I tell you, they were possessed long before they ever moved in with us. Theirs was not the same dark spirit that possessed me. Theirs was a spirit of destruction of soul. I call it a controlling, destroying spirit.

This illustrates perfectly how one can open doors in their soul, but cannot close them. The adversary of the soul knows the where and why's and how's of starting the process leading to your destruction. It will take God to close those doors that have been opened. Only God can close them. We can't even try. And it will take holiness to keep them closed. Being conservative, having zeal, love, good intentions, and even faith cannot close them. Faith can cry out to God, but God is the only hope. All the "self helps" and "faith" groups are helpless when God is silent.

It all started in the attic of an ancient, dilapidated mansion that was, at one time, a farm house in the Ozarks of Missouri. Our family lived there. There were so many manifestations of the supernatural, we should have moved away instantly, but we didn't. The results were tragic as you will see. We moved into that house like any young family, with the joy and the happiness of a "new" place in the country. There was a very large lake just 5 minutes' walk away. It was a private lake owned by the same people who owned the house. It seemed like a beautiful setting but that was soon to change. There were many good times in that house and life seemed to be getting better and better. But all the while there were events taking place that were unexplainable at first. As time went on, we got accustomed to the strange and eerie. We were becoming callused to them, and as we did so, the events became more and more frequent and more intense. I'll try to relate this experience by speaking in general terms, trying to avoid the specifics. Specifics can be dangerous. But there are a few happenings that must be told. After a year or so, we were so hardened and calloused to the supernatural, that we became amused by these incidents. We considered them as entertainment. Looking back now, it's beyond staggering recalling the events that unfolded in that house. So far to date, not even Hollywood has copied it. Neither does it need to. Somehow we never put together the horrid life we were living, with all its atrocities, heartbreaks, and tragedies with our presence in that house.. We just kept on living there and sinking lower and lower, becoming harder and harder. I suppose we blamed and found fault in everything, trying to discover why our lives were in such a mess. But obviously, in our darkened state we could not see the light of truth. We didn't know about demons and evil spirits. It was only a phrase we had heard of. BUT THEY KNEW ABOUT US! We called them ghosts and told ourselves they could not hurt us. WE WERE WRONG! WE WERE **VERY** WRONG!

As things began to unfold and build up, something happened I will have to tell you about because it's a turning point that was spiritual murder. My bedroom, if you could call it that, was the attic of this dilapidated mansion. There was no flooring in the attic to cover the plaster and lath ceiling below. There was a boarded walkway across the center of the attic to get you to the end of the attic. At the end was a small area about 4 feet wide by 8 feet long area where there was an improvised floor. This was my bedroom. Next to my bed was a window. Looking out of this window I could see the side yard of the house. The mercury vapor light in the yard shone into that window and that was my only light. My ceiling was the bottom side of the nail infested roof. There was no insulation. In the winter it froze and in the summer it was blistering hot. At night, as I lay in my makeshift bed, the light shining in from my little window darkened until there was no light at all in the room. It also became shivering cold. This was VERY unusual considering the heat of the summer nights in Missouri. As I peered into the darkness of the room, trying to figure out what was going on, I saw something that really surprised me. There was something standing just off the foot of my bed in the darkness! It was so terribly dark in the room already, and the only reason I could see it was because it was many times darker than the darkness that surrounded it. I watched it silently move around the room. It came closer to my bed, not just at the foot, but it came around to the side of the bed, next to me. I could see it in the darkness very well. The room was freezing cold. It would move around in the room, but it always came back to stand beside me as I lay there on the bed. I was so scared. Having lived in that house for so long, and having seen so much, and becoming so calloused to many things just like this, did not prepare me for this creature stalking around in my room. Finally, I covered my head with the blanket. All was perfectly silent, and distressingly cold.

After a while I peeked out from the blanket that was covering my head. The creature's face and eyes were less than an inch from mine. It was staring at me nose to nose. (if it had a nose). I stared back into its eyes. They were much darker than its body and seemed to be sunken and tiny. So now I've got this stare-down going on with this horrid creature. Finally I covered my head to keep from seeing it any more. I sensed it there. I knew it was there, and it was. After what seemed like a VERY long time, I felt the room becoming warm again. I actually felt the light coming in from the window. I knew it was gone, and it was. I was badly shaken from that encounter that I could not explain. Unfortunately, this event repeated itself almost nightly. Soon I got used to the sequence of events and knew what was coming. Not wanting to repeat the stare-down, I covered up my head and stayed that way until I fell asleep. In the morning it was always gone. But during the night, the darkness, the coldness, the evil presence, the fear, all lasted for what seemed like forever. After this event repeated itself for an extended time, suddenly it stopped. It stopped as unexpectedly as it started. I don't know why it started; I don't know why it stopped. I do know it stopped. And I was glad. I thought it was over, but it wasn't. Little did I know, but the worst was yet to come.

It was during this time many horrid atrocities took place in that house, most of which I will not relate. But as a result of those experiences, I had what they called a nervous breakdown. Later another event caused what they called a mental breakdown. And yet another event caused an emotional breakdown. I don't know how much a person can take before death delivers them. Somewhere, I had definitely crossed that point, but death did not come. Instead something worse came. It was also during this time of many breakdowns, (I had them often. Just as soon as I began recovery from one nervous breakdown, another would follow.) my mind snapped. It would never be the same again. Normalcy was gone from my life forever. It still is. Reasoning was not a part of my planet. Some people wanted me to be committed to the insane asylum in

Fulton Missouri. They said I was dangerous and I was going to kill everyone in that house. Everyone was terribly afraid of me. I'll not relate why, but they all had good reason to feel the way. Today, I don't blame them.

One time a teacher in school (before I was not allowed to go to school anymore) took me into the hallway and asked, "What is going on in your home?" So I told her! I held nothing back! She put her hands on each of my shoulders and shook me as she said, "Never tell anybody what's going on in your home!" So I didn't. I felt ashamed of what was going on in our home, and I didn't want to be ashamed anymore. So I didn't. I thought she was right, that she knew what to do. But, she was very, very wrong! Then things got worse. I thought I had problems before, but they were about to worsen. One Saturday morning, as my parents were having a knockdown, kicking, biting, stomping, screaming and cussing fight, (mostly in the front room), all of us kids scrambled to our favorite hiding places. My hiding place was on the front porch. If anybody came out there, they usually would see me and go back inside. If they didn't, I'd run. NOBODY could catch me when I was running. It was almost supernatural; it might have been. Something happened that I will not relate, and as a result, and because of it, I made the decision that "love was an emotional weakness." And I would never love again! There was no love in my world, and I had none to give.

As I stood there making that decision out of bitter hated, something happened. That dark figure that had been staring at me in the attic, entered my heart! I cannot tell you how I knew this. It wasn't something you could see with the eye, nor anything you could put your hand on, but it happened and I knew it happened. From that point forward, I had no emotions, no feeling, no compassion, no expression. I was totally without any expression or feelings of any kind. My presence totally unnerved people. I didn't have to do anything. All I had to do was stand there and they would literally panic. At the time I didn't know why, but they were leaving me alone, and that was best for everyone. I still didn't like violence. But I hated compassion. Even pets, especially dogs ,would cower and howl and run away from me. On one occasion somebody sicked their dog on me. The dog came running out of the house, took one look at me and started running the other way with the usual panicked dog "ARF ARF," like it was shot. I started after the owner who slammed the door and bolted it in panic. I didn't run through the door crashing it in like I wanted to, and could do, but I didn't. I do not know why I did not, but I didn't. So I left. For the most part, people stayed far away from me. Nobody ever bothered me. Walking down the sidewalk, people would see me and quickly veer away to one side or the other. Some would turn and run into a shop to get out of my way. It was weird. On one occasion, I was on a side street where there were houses and kids at play. As I stopped to see these little kids playing in their yard, the front door suddenly burst open and a woman came running out screaming at the kids to get inside, NOW! Hurry! She grabbed one and drug the other into the house as fast as she could run. I was startled by this whole affair and wondered what she running from. I looked around to see where the problem was, but saw nothing. I thought that was very odd. I left.

    I said earlier that I didn't like violence. I still didn't. But if someone made me mad, I would fly into this shocking, brutal, cruel and hateful rage. It would happen almost instantly. And, at the same time, I found that I had supernatural strength. I could do amazing things. Things I won't relate. Living in the heathen darkness that I did, I never heard the word, "possessed." And even though I never heard it, it was very clear that I was. You don't have to go to Africa to find darkness.

#5 It Came Down the Stairs

One day after certain events had happened and my dad was getting threats from the family, another dramatic and terrifying event took place. That event was so intense, it even terrified me, and I was running. Before, if I were running I was after something, usually somebody's dog that sincerely needed to die, or somebody. But that day I was the victim, and it would be the climactic event. The things that happened after that event would start a change that only God could have brought to pass. It was time to bring Robert back from the world of the living damned, called insanity. (If the previous experiences bothered you, DONT READ THIS!) It happened at that same house of course. I don't remember the day. It was summer and evening was approaching. My parents and siblings were gone somewhere. It was not unusual for them to go and visit somebody and leave me at home. That was the safest and accepted way. Being in that house alone toward evening was not the place to be. And, to be there with me was even worse. I was a part of the problem. I was somewhere downstairs, I think I was in the kitchen. I heard something in the house and went looking for it, but saw nothing. I looked outside, and nothing was there. Again, there were MANY manifestations going on daily in that house and it wasn't a house just anybody could walk into. The word was out about that place and people stayed far way. I distinctly heard something in the front room, but not finding it, I returned to the kitchen. What I was looking for isn't the same as what somebody normal would have been looking for; not in this house. So I'm in the kitchen again and I hear something upstairs. I thought I knew what it was

STORIES

because I had seen it many times before. But now it was making sounds, and I thought that to be strange, for normally it was silent. Then I heard it again, and I could tell it was moving toward the stairs coming down from upstairs. This meant it was right at the front door.

If you stepped inside our front door, you would be standing at the bottom of the stairs. But there was a door to the right that led into the front room. So I made my way to the front living room to see what was coming down the stairs. As I hurried around the corner and through the door that put me at the bottom of the stairs, I was met by the most terrifying, shocking, and dreadful creature I had ever seen, EVER! In that house we saw many manifestations. But NONE were anything like this. I'll not describe it, though it's image is branded in my memory. It was looking at me, and I knew it was coming to get me. I had paid the dues, and it was coming to collect. This creature was unprecedented in horror! Even people that are possessed will often encounter a stronger demon then they possess. And when a rival demon shows up, he is many times stronger and more dangerous. Even the spirit that possessed me was terrified at this newcomer! The race/fight started. My mind immediately snapped and I started laughing hysterically and uncontrollably as I started running, grabbing things as I went and pulling them down to slow the progress of my pursuer. My flight took me directly to the kitchen, which was very unfortunate. It was a dead end! As I ran past the counter I grabbed this huge butcher knife. Suddenly I was cornered in the kitchen and horror was in control. I couldn't stop this heinous laughter but I was crying at the same time. I slammed the kitchen table up against the doorway coming into the kitchen and backed away into the corner, waving the butcher knife wildly in front of me. I heard the footsteps of something as it was coming through the house toward the kitchen. Then it stopped just around the kitchen door, out of the line of sight. My laughter had become even more heinous; uncontrollable and louder. My mind had snapped. I saw it's shadow on the table and on the floor. It wasn't just coming to get me! IT WAS HERE! The table was being moved away and it was coming into the kitchen!

My parents had gone to visit somebody, and they had returned home without my knowing it. That alone was very unusual, for I normally sensed someone's spirit before they ever showed up. But this time I didn't sense anyone; probably because I was in the middle of another event. My dad later related this part of the story to me. They had returned home and knew immediately that something was very wrong, but they didn't know what. Dad told everyone to stay in the car and not make a sound. Quietly he slipped out of the car, being mindful not to close the car door, lest a sound be made. He moved quickly and silently through the darkness of the night to the front porch. He knew not to step on the porch as the groaning floorboards would reveal his presence. He did not know what was wrong, or who was in there, but he didn't want anyone waiting for him that he didn't know about. He said he heard the sound of running feet and crashing furniture coming from the house. He also heard blood-chilling laughter that struck him to the bone. He peeked over the bottom of the front door window and saw the furniture flying and a chair spinning wildly. He did not see the creature at all. He had seen many a creature in that house, as we all did, but, fortunately, he didn't see that one. He paused on the front porch just long enough to open the front door and as quietly as possible, he slipped inside without being detected. He was mindful not to bump or move anything lest his presence be known. He could tell that the heinous laughter, that sounded like a mad man, was coming from the kitchen. He moved very slowly through the house on his way to the kitchen. Before he reached the kitchen door, he saw my reflection in the side kitchen window. Being dark outside, and light inside, it was a perfect mirror. He saw me waving the butcher knife and he knew the horrid blood-chilling laughter was coming from me. He could not see what was in front of me that I was fending off and he couldn't enter the room without giving his presence away because the table had to be moved and that would be a dead giveaway. So he stood there for what he said was a brief moment. Then he started calling my name, softly at first, then louder. I could not hear him. He knew his shadow was on the table and on the floor so that anybody in there would easily have seen it. His presence was now known, so he started pushing the table away. He was still calling my name but I was not in his world, nor was he in mine. He pushed the table far enough away that he could slip through. Now he stood in the kitchen and I saw him. The creature was gone. It left possibly a split second before Dad came into view. Dad was standing across the room from me, calling my name. I saw his lips move, but couldn't hear him. I didn't know if it was really him, or the creature had changed its form. I couldn't stop laughing. I couldn't stop crying. I couldn't stop swinging that butcher knife. I couldn't stop anything. I was in a world of horror and I was completely out of control. Dad continued to call my name until the tone of my heinous laughter started changing. He felt then that perhaps I may be coming back from that world of horrifying hell. When he could, he moved closer. I saw him, but I still could not stop my frenzied movements or my bone-chilling screams. After a while, he positioned himself directly in front of me, but out of range of the wild knife. He was yelling my name but I couldn't stop! I wanted to stop, but I couldn't. I wanted to die. But I couldn't. I just stood there, wildly waiving the butcher knife with my dad standing there dangerously close, calling my name.

Then it happened. Something unsnapped. Something changed. I threw the knife down and hurled into his arms. We stood there. Now I was out of control, sobbing and blubbering. I thought I was talking but it was just a bunch of mixed up eerie sounds. He continued calling my name, though he no longer had to yell it. I don't know how long we stood there but my speech came back. My mind was trying to. My body was shaking violently. Somewhere amid all this, we had moved out of the kitchen. My dad felt that I needed to change the visual surroundings and he led me like I was a little child into the next room. After a while, reality began to set in once again and I was able to talk. I related the event to him and he understood perfectly well as there had been many events in that house. That night Dad made the decision to move out of that house. I wasn't around when that actually happened because that event was the breaking point. I needed protection from an unseen sinister world and all that was in that house. I needed help that no doctor on earth could ever give.

Meanwhile, my dad had contacted Granny about my condition, and wanted to know if she would take me in and see what she could do for me. Far away from that house and all that was in it, living in a one room house way out in the country, beyond Guthrie Missouri, was an elderly woman who walked with God. Everyone who knew her called her, "Granny." Granny would take me into her home, and into her heart. She would also take me to God. It was a very uncommon match! A demented boy, violent and cruel, filled with hate, and a seemingly helpless old lady, full of love, who walked with God. The battle lines in a spiritual world were being drawn.

STORIES

#6 "The Granny Story"

This part of "The Granny Story" continues this chain of events from Abby, to Wisdom, to Darkie, to Granny.

Granny was Dora Agnus Wolfe Bryan. She was the head of the entire Bryan family clan. The stories of her childhood, living in a covered wagon, crossing the rivers and wooded lands with her parents and family, always received my keenest attention. The way they lived and how they did things, kept me spellbound for hours. That's why I call her the last of the pioneer women. She really was! Granny was Granny to everyone. And she often said I was her pick of the whole bunch. We were extremely close knit. But, as this story reveals, things in my life at home, away from Granny, were changing very rapidly for the worse. My life had reached an all-time low of spiritual darkness, breakdowns, unprecedented abuses, and a personal holocaust of the mind and soul. The mind snapped, and would not come back. The world it left me in was from hell. How could I ever come back?

Granny was called upon to deal with that impossible, dangerous, and lengthy task of bringing me back from the world of insanity and possession. Fortunately, Granny had God, and it would take a miracle from God to release me from that demonic place. Here is the story.

There was certain young man about 12 years old that had become possessed with a spirit of hate, anger and bitterness. His mind had snapped and left him in a world that was unreachable by anyone but God. He had been accused of killing one person already, and was well known for his acts of violence and rage. Many had warned Granny not to have anything to do with that mess. "If you get him out here to your place, they will find you dead, Granny! He's insane, he's violent and nobody has been able to stop him. He's got some kind of supernatural strength, Granny. You can't stop him. Don't do it! It's not safe and nobody will come way out here to see if you're all right."

But Granny said, "bring him out," and it was settled right then. They would bring him out to Granny's little house in the country, drop him off and leave. Then everyone would wait and see what was to happen.

Far out in the country, in a little house in a hill, the stage was set. The characters were an ancient sage who walked with God, and a possessed boy, full of the devil. If there was ever a modern-day Mt. Carmel, it was surely on that hilltop right then. Invisible faith meets visible darkness.

One of the first things Granny said was, "Proverbs lays the foundation of our mind and Psalms shapes our spirit." So we started several times a day reading Proverbs in God's word. I would sit down on the floor and massage her feet, for she had bad circulation in her feet. And as I rubbed her feet, she read chapters out of Proverbs. We would talk about what she read and she would explain it to me in very simple terms. Then she would continue reading, stopping often to ask, "Robert, do you understand that?" When I didn't understand it, she would say, "Well, you just hang on to it and some day you will." This was repeated several times a day, and sometimes far into the night.

Sometimes she would stop reading suddenly, even in the middle of a sentence, and start praying earnestly, tears running down her face. Her face would light up like it was glowing.

I knew she was talking to her Lord. Somehow, he was there, but I couldn't see him. There was this sense of peace that accompanied those times.

Her reading would sometimes send me into fits. My mind would lose contact with the things of this world. I saw things, I heard things, I felt things. I always fought back against the creatures I saw, and their attacks on me. It would become violent and brutal.

When this happened, Granny would pray with much authority, and the creatures would flee. My fighting was intense and vigorous and I was always terrified. But Granny was never afraid of me or my invisible enemies. If I was having an attack, she would start praying and the attack would cease.

To my amazement, she sometimes saw the same creature I saw. But she was never afraid, and they would never attack her. We had some long talks about those experiences.

As time went by, the attacks lessened. My mind was starting to separate the spiritual, the imaginary, and reality. I was learning to think rationally, and my sentences were beginning to make sense.

Once Granny said to me, "It's time we do a little reading in Psalms." So she switched to Psalms and I cannot explain or put into words the wonder and refreshing joy that filled me when we did. I soaked up as much as she could give. There were many late night sessions of Bible reading, prayer and rejoicing together.

She sometimes went back to Proverbs, but it depended upon how I was doing mentally. My face lost the wild look and my actions became more natural. My reasoning was returning. She was now working on my spirit's foundation.

This lasted the entire summer. Word got around what was going on out there at Granny's. People started driving all the way out to see it for themselves, usually finding Granny sitting in her rocking chair and me in my most treasured position, sitting at her feet! The shock on their faces was evident, but at the time I didn't see anything to be shocked about. To me it just another day at Granny's house. But the Power of God over darkness has never changed, and it never will.

One day deliverance came in a most unusual way. Granny's prayers were touching heaven and my soul was stretching to escape hell. God was working. I can't say it was salvation. But it was a deliverance from the darkness. I still needed to get saved. But "saved" was nowhere in my world at that time. I was not there yet, but God came and broke the darkness. Now I was set free from my tormentors, but I had to learn how to live without them. The decision was up to me, Just like any normal sinner. No more were dark sinister spirits calling the shots. The light had shown into my darkness, and the light had won! I made a deliberate decision to never go back into that world of darkness. I wanted whatever Granny had. I wanted to know her God. God was waiting for that moment, and He let me chose my path. I chose God's mighty and merciful ways that I had just experienced that summer; the extreme contrast between light and darkness. Now my darkness was gone, and I wanted light! God was that light!

Note, at the end of the great deliverance while at Granny's, I was returned home. The family had moved out of that house during my absence. Abby and her hellbent kids were gone. It was a new beginning for me in many ways.

STORIES

#7 The Revelation

In the car on the way home, Sarah started to act out what Abby and her kids had taught her. Dad and Mom were in the car and they both heard it and saw it. Dad was driving. We were on a gravel road. It was daylight. Dad literally stomped on the breaks, bringing the car to a very sudden stop. He got quickly out of the car, went to the back door where Sarah was sitting, opened her door, grabbed her by the arm pulling her out of the car, and gave her the beating of her life! I was shocked! Then he threw her back into the car and gave her some very explicit instructions on how she was going to treat me, what she was going to do, and what she was not going to do, and what was going to happen to her if she even considered doing anything other than what he had said!

I saw it, but I could not process it. It was still too much for me at that time.

It seems they knew all along what was going on. I will never know why they allowed it to happen. The instructions Dad gave her spelled it all out. They had known the whole time.

It was about 18 months from the time we moved into that haunted house, till the day I was returned home from living with Granny. There are many things that I will never understand from those times. But I find it hard to relate how I felt when the first sign of justice and protection and hope appeared on my dark horizon.

The experiences related in these stories left a definite impression in my spirit and in my mind, and my soul was bitter. For over 50 years following, I carried the scars. The quirks, the haunting memories, and the bitterness and hardness that was produced affected my life, my marriage, my kids, my jobs, my friends, and my character. Everything was touched by its darkness. My faith was broken and rebroken many times in my struggle to find God. I was considered a problem at church and in social circles. I could not have any close friends, and if I did, they would not last very long. I could not take the pressure of it. They would find out too much about my past and the questions would start. Then the memories would return, bringing their problems with them.

If you read the Granny story, and how her faith in God brought me back from the world I was in, you will see God's miraculous hand working in a way that words cannot express. It's a story of deliverance, of healing, of hope and sanity. It's a story of the power of God's word and his wonders to perform, of his love and mercy. It's a story of faith, patience and prayer.

But, I want all to know that it's also a story of forgiveness. Forgiveness from every direction. Throughout life, when the memories start, forgive. When bitterness attacks, forgive. When you're made fun of, ostracized, mocked, and misunderstood, always forgive. Forgive the offenders, including the simple minded who cannot accept your experiences; the guilty as well as the innocent. Forgive the well-meaning, but misdirected. Forgive the sincere as well as the mockers.

#8 The Victory

The life of victory is a life of forgiveness; the life of forgiveness is a life of victory, and forgiveness requires compassion from God. It's only by walking with God that we gain the strength to forgive, to love, and let go. An intellectual understanding of forgiveness will not do. That is like a blind man describing color. He's heard about it, he can repeat it, but it's not in his heart and he has no personal experience with it. But to take

STORIES

our broken hearts to God, confessing our part, and surrendering ourselves to his care, will bring the healing, deliverance and compassion we need to forgive, and to live again. Granny taught me to forgive and how to be forgiven. She lived by the example that humility is stronger than pride, and love is stronger than darkness. Forgiveness is stronger than hate. Obedience is stronger than vengeance or selfishness, and faith is stronger than reality. God is God over all!

Some of the characters in these experiences have long since passed from the scene. I totally forgive them; every one. For those still living, I wish them the best. I very much desire that they find God and his peace. I sincerely want them to find God's forgiveness. I may never know all the "whys" of what they did. But I know what God can do if we ask Him!

Forgiveness involves a lot of things. But above all, it's letting go of something and giving it to God. No matter what. It involves no blame, no justification, no acceptance and no excuses. It's simply letting go of it, (ALL OF IT!) and all the feelings and memories that go along with it. It becomes God's domain and He will sort it out. We are no longer a part of it. THEN we are free to heal!

Forgiving others is the first step to being forgiven.

Forgiveness is not a one-time act. It's a lifestyle of keeping the past on God's altar and not taking it back; not even to rehearse any parts of it.

Even when we have to face it every day!

It was shortly after all this that my parent's life also fell apart, and there was the divorce. Even after we had moved away from the haunted house, and Abby was no longer a part of our lives, everything continued to spiral downward. When the divorce was final, I was kicked out of the home altogether. I was told that I was too much like Dad, and I had to go. I think I had just turned 13 years old. So I hit the woods, and then hit the streets in town. I lived on and off the street from that time until I was 17 years old. By then I had returned to my former darkness. It was my hiding place from the hell-bent life on the streets. Life on the streets is brutal. I lived under bridges, slept in doorways, ate out of dumpsters, fought with dogs for food, and froze in the snow and slush of winter. It was by the mercy of God that my darkness never ever reached the same proportions as before. However, I had become possessed with hatred all over again and bitterness was my daily fare. It was during my street time that I stumbled into a real church for the first time!

It was in the winter of 1974 when I found my way into a navy recruitment office looking for warmth, that my un-voluntary services were hijacked into the USN.

I didn't see it at the time, but looking back, it was the best thing that could have happened to me. God was working on me, and I did not even know it! Praise His name forever!

I needed the structured, organized, disciplined, mannered, training and obedience required to make it through boot camp and in real life. God knew just the place to get me off the street and back into the real world again!

Boot camp was one of the finest places I ever lived! Life had never been so good! I thought I could stay there forever! But again, God knew best! And God was still working on me!

Forgiveness was the start to being forgiven. Bootcamp provided me with the training to function in

STORIES

society, but the lessons learned from Granny stuck with me even as I struggled with the bitter life of being a hobo. It was her prayers, faith, and example that brought me back out of darkness the second time.

I have more stories about Granny and her great faith. Some I'll tell as they come out in other experiences that are waiting to be written. I've included some here before I forget them, and also to help the reader to get a glimpse of a pioneer woman's faith in her wonderful Lord. Also, the power of a mighty God whose love can conquer hatred, and whose light can conquer the darkness!

<u>Learning to see God's wisdom in his directions is all part of learning to love him, regardless of our circumstance.</u> Learning to love God is very important to learning to forgive. Everyone has their battles and their giants they must face. None are encountered by accident or coincidence, but are all divine appointments. There are many things we must learn in the dark times that we can never learn in the bright times. God knows exactly what we need to make it to heaven. And he has placed each test and trial in our pathway by his loving and wise decisions. It's all part of his desire to see us in heaven. He is giving us the "classes" we need to get there!

The greatest weapon against bitterness, fear or depression, is to accept our trials and testing as from God, by his loving care, to get us to heaven. He will never allow more **on** you, than what he has put **within** you. And he stands by your side the entire way, every step, every inch, every crossroad! He is there. It really does not matter if we see his face, sense his presence, hear his voice or feel his hand. God is still there! That's not faith; that's the reality of it. No one can take us from our father's hand!

When we fall, He is there to pick us up.

When we fail ourselves, He is there to encourage us.

When we are overflowing with gratitude, He embraces us.

When we are weak, He is there to strengthen us.

When the storms hit, He is there to hide us.

When we are confused, He says, take my hand.

When we are afraid, He picks us up, holds us, and we feel His breathing.

Again, nothing can take us from our father's hand.

He is there, turning stumbling stones into stepping stones.

STORIES

#9 Fishing on Cedar River

Fishing isn't my favorite pastime. I know nothing of the sport, and don't have the time to find out. However, there have been times when I ended up going because somebody made the way for me to do so. My first experience with fishing was at a preteen age. I went to a lake by our house and discovered my dad was there, fishing. I didn't know he ever went fishing! So I joined him on the bank of the lake. He pointed out the Red and white thing floating in the water, called a bobber, and told me that if it started slightly moving, it was because there was a fish examining my bait. But if the bobber suddenly took a dive, then I was to jerk my fishing pole and set the hook, (whatever that meant). Sure enough it all happened just like he said, so I jerked the hook. However, it may have been a tiny bit too hard because the fish came flying out of the water, smacked me in the face, flopped around on the ground, flopped back into the water and swam away! I seldom saw my dad laugh as hard as he did that day! Fishing wasn't for me!

Many years later, my son-in-law wanted me to go fishing with him. He was a tour guide for fishing and hunting groups. He knew everything there was to know and he had all the equipment for both. He was very good at it. I tried to convince him I knew nothing about fishing, but he assured me that it would be okay, so the date was set and off we went, fishing on Cedar River.

The first sign of trouble came when he had me put on a pair of fishing onesies. I later found out they are called waders. They looked like a pair of bibs with rubber boots attached, and everything was made of some kind of rubber. I should have known to empty my pockets first, but I didn't know about that yet. Unfortunately, my small 8-inch, triple A flashlight came out of my pocket and fell down across my booted right ankle. It looked like my ankle was grossly broken, but in reality, it was just the flashlight making it look that way.

We went to the fishing area, packed up our gear and equipment, and followed the path through the woods that led us to a river. The problem was, the flashlight was still across my ankle. It didn't take long for it to start feeling like it was a cactus with a hose clamp around it. I kept stopping to move it, but it went right back. I found that stomping my foot sideways would do the trick without stopping each time, so I did that frequently. This location was a little downstream of a fish hatchery and provided an abundance of fish.

My son-in-law and daughter were casting and reeling their lines on the bank of the river, but not catching anything. I decided to go upstream a ways and give them some space. I found a place on the bank where the water had cut a small harbor-looking area. There were piles of fish coming to the top, rolling over and going back down. Across the river from me were some fisherman casting their lines over to my side, trying to catch some of the fish that could plainly be seen. They didn't like my presence there and made some very derogatory remarks to me. I ignored them.

I was standing on the bank about two feet above the water level, so hanging my baited hook in front of the noses of the fish coming to the top was easy. But they were not interested in it at all. I decided to cast my line out a little to see if the fish would try to get it. Everyone I saw that day was casting for fish. Maybe I should try it. So I cast out, and immediately caught this one single limb hanging over the water. It wrapped up tight. I also succeeded in snagging a huge birds nest and rats nest in the reel I was supposed to be turning. I couldn't get either one undone so I left it hanging by the branch and proceeded with makeshift plan B. I waded into the river and could feel the many fish bumping against my onesies and coming to the surface right in front of me, so I started grabbing fish and throwing them onto the bank. This worked well enough to produce a large volume of cussing and screaming from the fishermen across the river!

The problem was that the bank was sloped, and my fish kept flopping around and getting back into the water. So I started throwing them far up onto the bank where the brush and grass would stop their return. It worked very well.

I had two big fish stuck up there when this guy in brown Carhartt's showed up and started watching me from the bank. I didn't know he was a game warden, or that my fish were the wrong ones, or that it is illegal to catch fish that way. He never asked me for a fishing license, but that's okay because I didn't have one anyway.

About that time my daughter showed up and started talking to me like I was some kind of retard saying, "Daddeeee, are we ready to go hooooome yeeeeet?" I wondered what her problem was. About that time my tour guide showed up and started talking very quietly to this guy in brown Carhartt's. The two of them quickly disappeared down the path to their truck.

I didn't know what that was all about, but it was obvious that it was time to leave for some reason. I thought it was bad timing because I was just getting started and I was starting to like this fishing thing.

So I climbed out of the water and got my fishing line out of the tree branch by pulling it till the line broke. Then went to get my fish. Now I have a problem. How do I pack the fish back to the truck? I had to carry the birds nest fishing pole with the line trailing behind it, the tackle box, and two very large fish. I also had to stomp sideways a few times to move that flashlight. Everything was too long and too heavy to pack very far. Plus, the fish were very slick. I saw people carrying fish with their fingers in the fish's mouth, but those fish were dead. These fish were still alive and flopping around. I know fish can bite. I had heard many times that fish were biting that day. So, sticking my hands into their mouths was NOT going to happen. That was when I had an idea. The coat I was wearing had a hood. The hood had two drawstrings on it.

Problem solved! I made a loop on each drawstring. Kneeling down between the fish, I put the sliding loop around each of their tails and stood up! It worked great! The fish extended from my shoulders to just a few inches from the ground. I hoped the onesies were thick enough if the fish tried to bite me. So with fishing pole, bait box, and two fish tied around my neck, side-stomping as I went, I started up the trail. The guy in brown never said a word to me, but he looked very confused or maybe he wasn't feeling well. He just looked odd. When I came to the place where he was standing, he backed way off the trail into the stickers. I went by, but he never said anything.

I made it all the way to the truck, stomping and carrying my stuff. When I got to the truck, my son-in-law and daughter were frantically motioning at me to GET IN! Hurry up! Let's go! I really wanted to get the flashlight out, but apparently there was something of great importance going on. So I tossed my stuff and fish in the back of the truck and jumped in the rear door. They went screaming out of there like they had just stolen the truck. Meanwhile they were laughing so hard the tears were rolling, and trying to talk at the same time. Daughter says, "DAD! Do you know what you just DID? Did he say anything to you? What did he do? What happened?" I told them what had happened, the whole story, and they roared with laughter. But I really didn't know what was so funny about any of it. They finally told me who the guy was, why he was there, what I had caught and how he could take their truck, their fishing gear, give huge fines, and maybe put me in jail. Not to mention the anger of the other fisherman who weren't really impressed with me. Somehow that was funny. The game warden was Indian and we were fishing on reservation land. The Indians have a superstition that if you touch or harm a crazy person, that evil spirit will enter them also! Well, I may have put their belief to the test that day! But he sure didn't say anything to me and stayed way back. Honestly, I thought I had done very well for someone who knew absolutely nothing about fishing.

It was said in the truck before we got home, "The next time I take your dad fishing, we will take the boat, he stays with us, we watch him closely and keep him under adult supervision!" I got four giant fish fillets, and they got a bucket of fresh fish eggs. Somehow they were very happy to get that. But we all got off easy and had a wonderful time! And yes, when we got home, I got the onesies off and my flashlight back!

#10 Angel by the Bed

Some time ago, before I learned you don't put curses on people, I put a curse on somebody at work. He sincerely deserved it more than most. But God had dealt with me about putting on curses. This guy was trying every hate trick and stunt he knew to get me mixed up in a big physical fight with a mob of several people.

I knew his tactics very well. You instigate the fight and stand back and laugh at those who get victimized by it. It gets bloody, violent and cruel very fast under those conditions.

Every day he was building it, and people were starting to bite. I was his intended victim. It made me sick to see it unfolding as it was, and seeing the tragic fallout as it began to build. So I did my fighting in the spiritual realm before it came to a head. I put a curse on him to stop him. It was after this that God gave me a burden for his soul because I knew where he would be in just a day or two. He would be in hell.

That may seem like a severe price for him to pay, but so what? He was the one demanding it. I had reached the end of my rope and so I did it. Very early on his fatal day, I was awakened by a presence standing by my bed. It was an angel, who had a sword in his hand and he asked me a question. Evidently he knew about God dealing with me on that very subject. He had come to carry out that curse and his question was, "Do you still want me to do it?" I thought to myself, "Larry has a soul, and he knows not God, nor what he is bringing upon himself." I felt sorry for him and where he was going to go that day. So I said, "No, don't do it." Immediately the angel left and I lay there pondering what would happen that day. This would be the day Larry would start his last instigation and people were in a frenzy. Larry was pushing it. The time had arrived and I had just spared his life and put his eternity on hold. Did I do the right thing? I guessed I'd have to face one ugly fight today and it made me sick again. I was a fighter in my foolish youth and didn't want to go back. So okay, here goes . . .

When I got to work that day, the usual strife and elevated tension was not there. But I knew that it could be hidden and could arise without warning at a very unfortunate time that was usually planned beforehand.

STORIES

All day I was watching my back. Nothing happened. Larry was acting as though the entire event had been erased from the earth. Those he had instigated into a hateful anger and pointed that anger at me were acting as though they had never even been involved. Everything was quiet and peaceful. That was a bad sign.

I was very nervous and felt that way for a good reason. But nothing ever came of it. I don't know how that angel completely stopped the coming storm, but I'm glad he did it. It seemed as if he had erased the whole thing in everyone's mind. I have no idea how he did it. It would be difficult to tell how glad I was about it. One day in heaven I hope to see that angel again and thank him! I stopped putting curses on people. It is biblical and it works a devastating blow, but I'll not put another curse on anybody unless God tells me to do so!

#11 Bad Water

Many years ago when I was just a small child, our family moved into this old farm house. After we moved in, we found that the water was bad. It was kind of off-color and had a foul smell to it, but as we continued to drink it, we got used to it. In time we didn't notice the smell anymore and didn't notice the taste and got used to the color.

It's truly amazing what a person can get used to if they keep doing it long enough!

People would come over and make comments about our water and many wouldn't drink it. But we were used to it; it didn't bother us. We must have had the immune system of a cast iron stove.

One particular summer, we had another drought. The heat was up in the triple digits, hanging around

110°. Of course everything was just hot and drying up. The grass was all brown and the trees were dying. The creeks went dry and the rivers were shallow and muddy.

It was at that time Dad decided we were going to clean out our cistern. So we went to town and rented this big water pump to pump the cistern out. A cistern is a large concrete container in the ground that rain water runs into for storage and water supply. Many times a well will dry up and somebody will turn it into a cistern.

After we had pumped out all the water we could possibly get out of it, we lowered a ladder down into the cistern. I went down the ladder wearing rubber boots that leaked badly. The muck was about two feet deep, and about 15 feet across in a round circle. The side of the cistern was hand-laid flat rock, held together by cement. The bottom was also flat rock, mud, and cement.

I had several 5-gallon buckets that I would shovel about halfway full and Dad would pull them up with a rope and walk away to empty them. Meanwhile I would fill the other buckets. We had this rotation going on as I continued to shovel things out.

At the bottom of the cistern were all kinds of dead creatures of various sorts. Skeletons of rodents and rats! There were dead mice floating around in the shallow water; rotting carcasses floating in the muck.

While shoveling, I began to find what I thought was gravel, but it soon turned out to be just more bones and skeletons in the muck and mire, that had sunken into the mud. We had killed and skinned about every type of creature you could think of, but there were bones down there I didn't recognize. Some of them I'm sure could've been in a museum somewhere.

STORIES

Of course after I had exposed the stuff while digging it up, the smell began to rise up and it was very rancid. I began to realize that all that stuff I was seeing was also in the water we had been drinking. It seemed odd that we didn't notice it! The deeper I dug the more junk came up. After several hours, I began to get to the bottom of things and there it was really bad!

Getting to the bottom of things isn't what it's cracked up to be. It's usually worse.

When I had shoveled out all I could, Dad began lowering down 5 gallon buckets of bleach water. I rinsed down the sides and bottom, scrubbing them with the water. Then I mopped it up, and continued to re-wash and re-mop until we had it very clean. Finally it was as clean as brand-new! There was no more bad smell and the only thing you could smell was fresh water and bleach!

Dad then called this fellow in town who was to fill his giant water truck and bring it out. The water he delivered was clear and icy cold. He brought that big truck down our narrow lane, which was no small task, and backed it up to our closed-in back porch. Inside the porch, at the far end of it, was the lid to the cistern. We strung this big black hose across the back porch all the way to the well top and lowered a few feet of the hose down inside the well.

I stood at the well and yelled to Dad that I was ready. My job was to stand on the hose to keep it from coming out. Dad yelled back to the guy at the truck and said we were ready. So he opened the valve and started the pump. When he did, that hose came alive! It jumped around like a mad snake as the water came gushing through it. The end of the hose was swinging wildly and fanning out this avalanche of clear, fresh water. The mist of that water came rising up out of the well. It felt so good. It was like a cool fog on our back porch. Outside it may have been 110° and everything dead and dying, but on the back porch we had a fog of cold fresh watery mist that filled all the house. It wasn't long until everybody was on the back porch laughing and rejoicing and soaking up all that cool water. There seemed to be no end to it and it felt so good. He emptied his whole truck into the cistern, which mostly filled it. Even Dad and that man outside, standing in the heat, could feel that mist coming off the porch. They were enjoying the cool fresh mist also, laughing and cutting up like a couple of kids playing in the water. What a good time we were all having bringing this fresh water into our house.

Once the well was all filled up, and the hose all rolled up, Dad turned on the water pump to the house. It chugged and jumped around a little bit because air was in the line. Then the old water started coming out of our faucets. It was all murky and blackish, and Dad said, "Let everything run until it flushes out good."

And flush it did! We realized the gross black water coming out of the lines was what we had been drinking all along! We had just gotten used to it. But now with the fresh water coming out, giving us a direct contrast between the two, we saw very clearly what others had been telling us about that we did not recognize.

Once we had seen the good clean cold fresh water coming out of those faucets, we had no desire to ever go back to what we called the dead water that used to be in our well. We wanted to wash everything; clothes, dishes, windows, floors. We all took baths and drank all the fresh water we could hold. Something about that good clean water made you want to drink all you could hold. After that we were always very careful to make sure that the top of the well stayed on and

STORIES

always monitored what was in it. We had found a good treasure and we didn't want to lose it.

That's the same way it is when God deals with a person's heart. You will do things you wished you hadn't done, you will say things you wished you had not said, you will think of things that make your spirit heavy and the atmosphere heavy. You will always have a lot of regrets.

Others may come and talk to you about what you did, but you can get so used to what you do, and what you have become, that you don't see what's wrong with it anymore and it won't bother you.

Let me tell you, your view of things, looking outside, isn't the same as the view of others looking inside! It's like a bug in a jar. The bug sees eyes and noses of all the kids looking at him! But the kids see every intricate details of that bug and every move he makes!

When the Holy Spirit begins to nudge you about things in your life, it can get pretty hot, dry and murky in your soul. At that point you have a choice. You can just keep on going and live with the filth of your life, or you can clean up your heart. Once you've pumped out all the trash of your heart and begin to realize what's in there, it'll make you want to keep digging right down to the bottom of yourself. You won't want any of that stuff left in there. You will find all kinds of garbage and trash in your heart you did not know was there. You'll be glad you started and you'll be glad you finished.

This is the picture of a soul getting saved. God will come and clean you up better than bleach water! He makes everything new again! That's a real good start, but you are not done yet!

You have not yet been flushed or filled! You can get on the prayer line and call God up and ask him to come over and fill up your place with his blessed spirit. But if you haven't done your part in cleaning things up, he may not be very excited about dumping a truck load of good water into your septic tank. Works can't save you, but it sure can get you ready! And what a time of refreshing and rejoicing that will be, not just for you, but everybody in the whole house will be glad you got some help. They will all be coming out and rejoicing in your victories and be so thankful for what God is doing for you. And as good as that is you're still not done. You need to start flushing out some "old water" and change the way you've been doing things. If you don't, your "well" is going to become contaminated all over again.

The choice is yours, you can be eating Manna or maggots, and you can be drinking in salvation or sewage. Nobody is going to force you, the choice is yours.

Sooooo........What's in your water?

#12 Bath Time in the Ozarks

These experiences of *Bath Time in the Ozarks* are true experiences of the writer; they were not copied from anywhere but the memory of them. I wrote them in a comical form because, looking back, they are very comical. However, at the time, there was nothing funny about it.

I hope this brings back good memories for those who read it. Also there are two experiences to come, that if you didn't understand what "bath time" was like, then those stories won't make sense. So here it is, "Bath Time."

Living on a farm in the Ozarks had many benefits, but it also presented some slight disadvantages, such

STORIES

as no running water, no showers and no hot water, just to name a few.

Bath time was a summertime event. Winter baths were a complete chore. Summer baths involved a creek and a bar of soap. And many a time the soap was optional. You didn't even need a towel because by the time you got home, you'd be completely dry. And sometimes possibly needing another bath! A good creek nearby was an essential part of Ozark living.

In the winter, baths required heating water in a five-gallon bucket. All buckets back then were metal. There was no such thing as a plastic bucket. Actually, I don't remember a plastic anything!

Having lots of buckets was a rich man's privilege. We had one bucket, so heating water took a very, very long time. By the time the wash tub was full, the first water was already cold. So lukewarm water was the best anybody could hope for.

The next obstacle was the tub; it was normally to small and too shallow. No matter how full you got it, after you got in you had half as much as you started with. You were lucky if you had enough to cover your feet.

Then came the pecking order. It was always baby first. If baby had a problem, you disposed of it before anyone saw it. But some things just weren't noticeable until too late. Then came the rest of the pecking order. Girls were always first. I didn't know why, but they were. I hated it. At the end of the girls turn, came Mom, and then it was the guys turn. If it was the girls turn, it was the youngest first. But for the guys, the youngest went last. Whoever started equal rights must have lived on a farm in the Ozarks!

However, I needed some equal rights! Or at least I thought I did. I was the only boy in the family. That made me by default, the last one to get a bath, if you could call it that. It was more like a baptismal in the county lagoon. Why anyone would get into bath water that you could almost "walk on" is beyond rational thinking. The biggest reason you even did it at all, especially if you were last, was due to the repercussions if you didn't! My Dad believed in "the laying on of hands," and anything else besides hands that happened to be close by. So you jumped in and out faster than you could say "I didn't step on "nothin'."

The next problem with baths was proximity. That's a big word for where you put it. In the summer, it was the back porch if you couldn't use the creek. In the wintertime, it was the kitchen. If the kitchen had a hand-powered pump mounted at the end of the sink, then the tub would be placed there because that's where all the water was. If the kitchen didn't have a hand pump, then the tub was placed in the front room next to the wood stove, because that's where all the heat was. If you tried to use the cook stove in the kitchen for the heat, you could burn up all your kindling trying to heat up bath water, and still not have any hot water. The small kindling used for the kitchen stove burned way too fast to be practical.

Proximity also created another problem. It seemed no matter where you put the family bathtub, almost without fail, (possibly because I was last), long before you ever got done, every neighbor and cousin in the whole county would drop in! Just walk right in and start talking to you, like it was normal to just sit around in a tub of yuck while you carried on a wonderful conversation.

My aunt had 7 daughters, and I am totally convinced she waited down the road till somebody gave her the signal, and then they'd all come marching through like "ducks following their mama," asking very

STORIES

important questions that obviously they needed to know right NOW! Like, "How's the weather?" Or, "Is that really water?" Or, "Are you taking a bath?"

Of course very important questions like that need equally important answers, like "The weathers dark and cloudy," or, "no, it's not water, it's Avon skin conditioner," or "I was soaking my feet and fell in."

And if all the above problems weren't enough, think of what happens when somebody walks in on your so-called bath, and you grab all your clothes and try running away. Trust me that won't work! Somebody will always lock the kitchen door between the kitchen and the front room, so you're pulling the doorknob frantically before you realize that it swings the other way. Then you go running through, only to discover your wet feet and the stairs are a really bad combination. After you land on the bottom of the step the second time somebody will ask, "Are you hurt?" You answer, "No, just my pride so far, but I'm trying real hard to break a bone or two."

The next problem you had to conquer was emptying the so-called water. It took at least four people to lift the tub. But there was room for only two. This meant that most of the water went on the floor long before it ever went outside. Then you'd dump it off the end of the porch and get a "bird's eye view," not to mention "a pig nose experience" as to why you should NOT have dumped it off the porch. Of course there was always an alternative to this type of abuse. It was called "a sponge bath."

It was many years later before I encountered my first real bathtub where the water actually came right out of the wall! It was like there was a serious water leak somewhere. And I know it sounds amazing, but it was already heated! And if that's impossible to figure

69

out, think about this. It was in its own little room! AND the water just went right out the bottom at this big hole that nobody had to patch!

I realize in this big day of technical advancement, many rituals of the past have gone to the wayside. And many a folk have no idea what yesteryear was like. When they do a common everyday task, they seldom realize just how well and easy they've got it.

Sometimes it would be good to look back and count our blessings and be thankful for the day and its benefits.

> The good ol' days, the good ol' days,
> We all so fondly speak of,
> That if they ever should come back,
> No one could stand a week of.
>
> Author Unknown

#13 I Don't Believe in Baths

Many years ago, when I was a about 10 or 11 years old, I decided that I was done with taking baths. That exercise was no longer in my vocabulary. Since Dad was gone for that summer, I got away with it. What a coincidence of timing! Mom couldn't make me take a bath, and after a few attempts, she stopped trying. I suspect she knew this "new horizon of independent thinking" would be very self-correcting. She was right!

The program worked like this: I'd go to the city dump and pick up all the clothes I could find and wear them at the same time. Then as the outer layer became unacceptable, I'd peel it off and have a "new" layer underneath! This had to be the master plan of a lifetime and I didn't know *why somebody hadn't thought of it before.*

So, I set in motion by my own wisdom this wonderful plan of deliverance from the bathtub. I made it through most of the summer looking like a refuge from the city dump and smelling like it too. But since it seemed to be working so well, I was pleased to keep it going. Then the unthinkable happened!

As I was strolling up the gravel road through town one day minding my own business, I had a certain air of distinction about me. When I approached Aunt Sue's house, guess who just happened to be standing at the gate watching me come up the road! Aunt Sue! Now Aunt Sue wasn't your normal aunt. She was an ex-truckdriver turned drill sergeant, ex-bar bouncer, and ex-human, who went by the alias of Aunt Sue. She had a nice modern house, was raising three kids, took no guff from anybody, and, worst of all, she was a clean freak! Her kids weren't even allowed to chew their food with their mouths open, or wipe their noses on their sleeves, and everything they did, they had to pick up after themselves. This lady was a terror to any fine outstanding bona fide hillbilly, if you know what I mean.

So here I am, minding my own business and enjoying the nice fresh air of summer. Aunt Sue is waiting for me at the gate, next to the road. It never even dawned on me that anybody who saw me could easily have called Aunt Sue and said, "He's coming toward your house, be ready."

She invited me in for Oreo cookies and milk. She knew my weakness! So being the fine outstanding citizen that I was, I naturally accepted. It was almost fatal! I had no sooner gotten into her house and seated at the table when she said, "I'll be right back!" She left me in the kitchen expecting milk and cookies, but what I got was something else!

SUDDENLY, out of nowhere comes this screaming mad woman! She has this leather razor strap that she is waving around wildly, and screaming something about a pig in her house, and a skunk! Well, I understand very well why you wouldn't want either in your house, but why was she chasing me around the kitchen with this razor strap? I didn't bring them in! But she would not be comforted about my sweet innocence. I was running around her kitchen like a chicken, trying to avoid the lash of that strap she was brandishing wildly, and she was screaming at me like I was about to die for something, but I didn't know what. Finally I saw my chance to duck into the parlor. Now Aunt Sue kept a spotless parlor (or sitting room) where you entertained important people. And I knew I was not allowed in there. But if I ran in there, maybe she would stop waving that strap around and start explaining things in a mild and humble fashion.

Well, it didn't work. It got worse. Now I was afraid of breaking something. The parlor is no place to be chasing somebody! Finally, I headed for the hallway, but she must have seen it coming and cut me off at the rocking chair. I was doomed to die at this point.

So here I am leaning way, way backward over the coffee table by the rocking chair and Aunt Sue was waving that strap around in my face, telling me what a skunk and a pig I was! Image that! Me! I hadn't done anything wrong to her, except a few things she hadn't found out about yet, like sneaking into her garden, and here she was treating me like was some kind of criminal against society.

Now at this point she did something I never had happen to me before! She grabbed me by the ear and started off down the hallway! I made an amazing discovery; if somebody leads with your ear; you're very

STORIES

likely to go along with them. So I went along so as not to cause any division with my ear.

Unknown to me, she had this modern-day bathtub all filled up with hot water and soap suds! It was all ready and waiting for SOMEBODY! Then she began to give very clear instruction as to what was going to happen to that somebody if they didn't get into that tub! I was horrified! Anything but the bathtub!

I sort of stalled, or paused at this point and she let go of my ear without removing it. She stood there, blocking the doorway with her arms crossed and staring at me! What should I do? It was comply or die! She had made that very clear. Apparently she couldn't stand the pausing (or the smell) any longer so she informed me that if I didn't get into that tub, she was going to undress me herself and drown me in that tub! By this time I was beginning to see the light. I had this strange and uncontrollable desire to throw myself into the bathtub! Finally she agreed to step outside the door and allow me to get into the tub for myself. BUT I had better hand out to her every stitch of my wretched clothing or else she would come in and take possession of them herself! Terror and fear just took on a face that closely resembled Aunt Sue.

Needless to say, I promptly obeyed. The soap suds lasted about a minute, and the bottom of the tub felt like a creek bed from all the sand and gravel that somehow got into it. After this "dignified" bath, she came in and gave me some new, clean clothes that fit like she had picked them out with me in mind. What a coincidence?

But then something else happened that REALLY alarmed me. When I had gotten out and dressed, she came in there like she owned the place, and said, "It's time for an inspection young man!" She looked behind my ears and shouted, "Look at this! There's enough dirt back here to plant potatoes!" I think she just found out who had been in her garden, but I wasn't going to confess anything! She began scrubbing behind my ear with something that felt like a wire brush or sandpaper. I really wanted to see what she had in her hand. I was scared that there were potatoes behind my ear. I hadn't felt anything there, but I couldn't see to be sure. So I believed her and really thought there were potatoes there, and was glad she was helping me get them out. That would be so embarrassing.

After the drill sergeant inspected my ears, hands, scalp and arms, she turned me loose and we headed for the kitchen where she made good on her invitation to milk and cookies. However, there were many instructions like, sit up, close your mouth, don't do that, etc, etc.

I survived the ordeal, and I must admit the new and modern bath was the way to go. It had none of the problems of the conventional style. And I actually felt much better. I never went back to my "new program." And, I think I learned a valuable lesson, namely this: STAY AWAY FROM AUNT SUE IF YOU STINK!

Years later, as an adult, I wrote this song about the ordeal. I would sing it in the shower. Then one day, somebody asked me about the song. So I told them. It will NOT be a church special!

"The Power of the Shower Song"

Chorus

The power of the shower, Makes you smell just like a flower.

And that's the way a shower ought to be (ought to be!)

If I don't take a shower, I won't smell like a flower, And everyone will be avoiding me!

Verse 1.

Once I had the notion, I was quite content, I'd never take another bath as long as I would live.

I made it through the summer, making quite a stew, Until that dark and fatal day I ran into Aunt Sue!

Now I sing......Chorus

Verse 2.

I made it to the kitchen thinking all was well, When suddenly she appeared, and she began to yell.

She waved a strap into the air, with threats of death and pain, I hit the floor and tried to run, but it was all in vain.

Verse 3.

She pinned me in the parlor. Cornered by a chair, she grabbed me by my little ear, that filled my heart with fear.

She had a tub awaitin', filled with soapy suds, If I valued life at all, I'd best get in that tub!

Now I sing.... `Chorus

#14 Being Moved up the Hill

This happened when I first started logging in Washington, the summer of 1980. I had signed on with a logging company called Weyerhaeuser. They sent me out to start setting chockers. I had never done anything in the logging industry, and so had no idea what I was getting into. If I had known how tough those guys were, I'd have never attempted it, for I was expected to keep up. (yeah right!) This is a good time to place a "stupid" sign on my head.

Anyway, I showed up and got a wonderful education. These guys were tough in fact, they were more than tough. The hills were so steep that I had to hang onto things to keep from falling down the hills, but they would run down the hills. Then they'd grab steel cables about half the diameter of a golf ball and 40 feet long, and drag them in every direction to do what I would call "lassoing" logs, before running like deer to get in the clear before the whole thing exploded into a massive avalanche going uphill to the "landing." Meanwhile they were watching for any "widow makers" that might be coming down the hill without any warning. These could be stumps that got uprooted or logs that broke loose, or pieces of the "turn" that blew out, or log jams the "mainline" would send avalanching back down the hill. No time for daydreaming or carelessness. You watched everything or else! These guys did this every day, all day long, often without breaking a sweat. I had just started and was as soft as a house cat. They'd be talking about the next turn; I was talking about needing oxygen. I was breathing so hard it hurt. My whole body hurt. My heart hurt. If there was ever suicide in slow motion, this had to be it. You don't take breaks in logging camps and I was trying to start a new trend. They did feel sorry for me and would let me skip a turn or two just before I passed out. By the end of the day, I knew this job wasn't for me. But I'm not a quitter. So I stayed with it.

At the end of the day they said they were impressed with my grit and hoped I'd come back the next day. So as the whistle blew and we all started the long walk/climb out of the canyon, I was very happy to go home and possibly swing by the hospital and pick a bottle of oxygen or two. Somewhere about the halfway mark, my lungs and body finally gave out and I could go no further. I fell into the soft dirt on all fours. I was so weak I couldn't get up. I couldn't catch my breath, my head was pounding, my lungs were on fire, and I felt like I was suffocating. My face was on my arms in the dirt. If the crew left me there, so be it. At that point, spending the night there sounded like a real good idea. I don't know how long I stayed there, but it was a long time. Long enough to breathe without fire, for my heart to slow down, my ears to quit pounding, and my sweat to start again. It was a long time. Finally, I felt like I should at least make an attempt for the landing. They would be waiting for me and probably yelling for me or looking for me. When I stood up on my weak knees, I froze! I was just below the landing! It was just a few feet away! How'd I get here? I looked back down into the canyon and I could see that I was at the halfway mark, sure enough. But now here I was at the top! It sort of rattles your thinking! I just stood there looking around. Did this really happen?

Yes it did! I recalled how somebody in the Bible was moved from one place to another by the power of God, but now I had just experienced it for myself! I walked to the crew bus right behind the rest of the crew as though I had kept up the whole way! And they never even knew it! But God did!

#15 Billie Jean and the Can Lid

Granny's house was situated on the edge of the goat hill plateau. The top area of the goat hill was really a very large area containing many acres. The road up was extremely steep. Once you broke over the top of the hill, you were right on the edge of that area. Granny's house was located right at that edge. Consequently, at the back of her house, the land fell away very quickly for a long way.

Unfortunately, the outhouse was a very good distance down that hill also. So, the front of her house was level with the ground but the back of her house had the rear basement wall exposed completely. Somebody in years gone by built a back porch off of the top story. This arrangement made a nice covering for the entrance to the basement. It created a very high commanding view of the valley behind her house, for there were very few trees on her side of the valley.

Many of us kids would head for Granny's house every time a storm came up because you could see for miles and the lighting strikes in the distance put on a very amazing display. There were many a tornado that came and went down that valley. You would find us kids and sometimes adults, all congregating on Granny's back porch to see the tornados and marvel at their power.

Sometimes one would cut across the valley and head straight for us. It was a thrill to feel such wind and hear the roar it made. At the last we would all go running for the basement, half scared and half excited over the ordeal, only to come out afterwards and brag about how close it came and who was the chicken that ran first.

So, one day I'm standing on Granny's back porch when out from beside the house comes my cousin, Billie Jean. She was headed for the outhouse that was a good distance down that hill. I watched her go down the hill and realized she didn't know I was up on the porch. So, wanting to get her attention, I looked around for something to throw down the hill, to get her to know I was there. But the only thing I saw was the top of a tin can that somebody had opened and left there. Now, we saved all cans; the tops, bottoms and sides. They made excellent covers for plugging holes in the floor or walls when the knots would fall out. And the sides, when cut, would flatten out to cover the really big holes or cracks that would appear as the lumber or logs dried out. So my throwing away the top of a tin can was not the norm.

I picked up the lid and threw it as one would throw a frisbee. And it acted like a frisbee acts. It went far out to the right like it was going somewhere and then made a wide sweeping curve back to where I thought I was throwing it in the first place. As this speeding and spinning lid made its way down the hill, it was obvious it was going to land somewhere near her and she would see it. It went somewhere near her head and I saw her grab her ear and start screaming bloody murder. She turned around and started back up the hill in a real fast hurry, crying, holding her ear with blood covering the side of her head, down her arm and down her side. What a terrible sight it was! It scared me more than it scared her!

She came in the front door of the house bawling and bleeding profusely. The house was full of adults and they all kicked into action at once. Her mom, (Aunt Anna) grabbed her and made her stop running. Somebody else showed up with towels and washcloths. Somebody else asked what happened. Someone said that she had gone to the outhouse. Several of the dads bolted out the door to find the monster and the culprit who had done this. Soon enough, Granny had her doctor's bag and was working with Billie Jean. Aunt Anna asked her what had happened, and she told her story of just walking down the hill when she saw something shiny next to her head and then hit her in the ear. She didn't know what it was. But it hurt so bad and bled even worse. She ran to get away from whatever it was and saw me standing up on the porch as she came up the hill. I was standing next to Granny at that time and they asked me if I knew what it was. So I told them what I had done with the lid and how it all played out. Meanwhile the dads had followed the blood trail from down the hill and found where it started. And not far from the trail, was this shiny lid. They had pieced together what Billie Jean had said, noted where I had been and was wondering if I had thrown that lid! Granny told them I had just said that very same thing, how I had thrown the lid and what had happened. I felt terrible for Billie Jean, and apologized profusely, for it never was my intention to hurt her in any way. She forgave me for the incident and we both cried together and hugged each other and soon enough we were all patched up together and friends again. We were both about seven years old and had always been chums.

I was drilled with many questions from almost everybody there, but it was obviously a freak accident. I should not have thrown the lid, but the chance of it playing out as it did, was almost impossible.

I promised never to do that again (and I NEVER did). But the talk about how impossible that was kept on for some time, along with how it could have been so much worse if it had been a little lower. By the time they were done I was petrified. I didn't get a spankin' for it, but I got a beating from my conscience.

#16 The Black Bull and the Gray Slick-Haired Dog

This is a true experience that clearly proves the divine grace of God working in the life of a sinner who doesn't even know who God is!

We moved into a farmhouse located on 200 acres. It was several miles from town, but three mobile homes were located nearby. These homes all housed close family; Uncle Peter and Aunt Lil, Uncle Herman and Aunt Polly, and Uncle Red and Aunt Harriet. Taking the road to their house was a 15-minute walk, but by cutting through the woods, it was about 5 minutes.

The house we moved into was situated on the brow of a long gentle hill that overlooked the "bottom land" of the creek and its adjoining pastures and fields. The creek was very winding as most creeks are. And scattered along each bank were several large trees of various types. The banks of the creek rose and fell. Sometimes the bank was high and very steep where the water had cut and meandered into the hill side. Sometimes the banks were low and gently led into the water. As always, there were scattered clusters of various brush and small trees along the banks. For the most part, the creek was about knee deep but there were places where the creek got about chest deep. In most places it wasn't very wide.

I had a special place I liked that was about 1 foot deep and very wide. My favorite pastime was laying in the creek at my special place, looking up at the trees and clouds overhead, and daydreaming about just about everything.

One day, unknown to us, somebody rented the 200 acres for pasture and put a large heard of Black Angus cattle in the fields. We didn't know the pasture had gotten rented out, and we definitely didn't know there was a very large and dangerous bull in the herd. This bull was known for seriously hurting people. (Something we found out later!)

So here I am, laying in the creek and daydreaming, when I heard something snorting and stomping! That had my attention! I sat bolt upright and saw, about 100 ft. away, this giant black bull snorting at me and stomping the ground! This is what they do just before they charge.

Every farm kid in Missouri was well acquainted with that scene and I was no exception! I literally bolted out of the water and made for the trees! This bull was hot on my trail! I climbed the high bank to the top in record time. But the bull couldn't get up the steep bank. I was at the top with this mad bull just a few feet away trying desperately to climb the loose dirt, and steep bank.

When bad-attitude bull realized he couldn't climb the bank, he charged downstream to the low ground and came back with an even worse and very serious attitude! But while he was going downstream, I was making fast track upstream! I got to another high bank with trees on it and stopped. I knew I couldn't outrun the bull to the next high spot. The trees were all saplings but provided a good hand hold. I didn't have to wait but a few seconds when here comes the black demon on hoofs. I jumped down the bank and started upstream again but the bull couldn't come down the bank without falling end over end, for it was a very high drop off. So Bad-Attitude ran down stream again to get back into the creek. Meanwhile I wasted no time getting back up on the high ground again and continued my mad dash upstream. I took advantage of the fact that the steep edge ran for several hundred feet.

Bad-Attitude soon showed up in the creek and discovered I was back on top again! Not being the brightest bull in the creek, he turned around and headed back down stream again, to get back on top! If he had gone upstream, I'm sure the outcome would have been much different!

I saw for the first time what it means when you say the bull's eyes were bright Red in rage! I had heard that phrase but never knew it was for real! So I bailed off the ledge again! Now the bull was getting the picture of how this was working out for him. He stood at the very edge of the bank, just above me, and was swinging his horns and bellowing in a rage. I didn't know if he was going to try jumping down or not, but I moved upstream very quickly, keeping an eye out for him. If he came down, I was going up! But the bull backed away from the edge and I couldn't see him. I didn't know where he was. There was no sound, so I made a fast run upstream, staying close to the bank. Suddenly the bull comes screaming down the bank like a falling bag of rocks! Obviously, the bank had given away under him. Judging from the way he was twisting and kicking, I don't think he was expecting it.

I wasn't expecting it either! But it left no question as to where he was! He was about 30 ft from me, with both of us in the creek! While he was trying to get up, I may have set a world record on steep hill climbing! He was up in a flash but was just standing there! He may have been dizzy after rolling down the hill. When he spotted me at the top of the bank, he started trembling with rage, something I had never seen before. Then he exploded upstream looking for a way back up. One of us wasn't having a good day. I noticed that the bank turned around a small bend and then the ground was low again. It was sort of shaped like a horseshoe, only a very BIG horseshoe! There was a stand of large sycamore trees at the other end of that horseshoe bend very close to the water. I knew bad company wasn't far away, so I cut across the "horseshoe" and made it to the sycamore stand before Bad-Attitude made his arrival.

Sure enough, here he comes! I could jump from my elevation above the creek bed and into the first tree. That would put me well out of his reach. But what then? Nobody in the whole wide world knew where I was or the trouble I was in. However, when the bull came up out of the creek bed and was back on top again, he automatically turned and went the wrong way. He went downstream looking for me. He must not have seen me standing amongst the brush at the edge, trying to decide if I should jump for the tree or not. I watched him go charging downstream for quite a ways before he stopped and looked back. I didn't dare move as he made several trips to the edge looking for me. I think he fully expected to see me standing down there somewhere, and he wasn't about to give up the chase. I saw him throw a royal fit of stomping and snorting. He was truly mad.

But there was a problem. That sycamore stand was the last place of refuge along the creek for a very long way. And I was still a long way from home. The fence of the pasture was right at the edge of our back yard and I was almost directly in line with the house, except there was a very long ways uphill in order to get to that fence. The distance in city terms was about two long city blocks. If Bad-Attitude had anything to say about it, I wasn't going to make it up that hill.

I waited for a long time to get my breath and I wanted that bull to be very far away when I took off and hopefully he wouldn't see me right away. He seemed to have settled down after a while and gradually started grazing and looking for me at the same time. When he got to where our initial race had started, he went no further. I had hoped he would cross the creek and be out of sight when I started my last run, but that wasn't going to happen. So when he turned and faced away from my direction, I bolted up the hill. Somehow he knew when I took off and he came full speed! I was in the open with nowhere to go.

Needless to say, I was running for my life. I could hear the bull's thunderous hoofs as he approached and didn't have to look back to see where he was. He was right behind me!

Suddenly it happened! There was a loud burst of barking and growling right behind me! I kept running but turned to see this very large gray slick-haired dog biting at the bull's flanks! The bull had turned and was fighting furiously at this fearless intruder! I kept running!

Then I heard it! Those thunderous hooves again! Here he comes! My lungs were bursting and burning and my legs felt like rubber. I could see the house now but I knew I wasn't going to make it! I was still way too far!

Then it happened again! That large gray slick-haired dog had caught up with the bull again and resumed his attack! The bull had been close enough for me to hear its forced breathing. It was sweating through its hide and breathing foam when that dog attacked. I felt like I couldn't go any further but I kept running. My stride must have looked awful for I was so weak and breathless.

This time the dog kept the fight up long enough for me to get some distance, but I had to stop or collapse. I stood there bent over, with my hands on my knees. I was sweating profusely and breathing harder than I had ever done before. My heart was pounding in my ears. I could see the dog giving that bull a vicious fight. The bull was bleeding and the dog wasn't. I took that as a good sign!

Long before I was ready to run, I started again for the house. It was still so far, but I kept running. It got very quiet behind me for a second, and I wondered what had happened. I didn't have long to find out as those thunderous hooves were behind me again! This time I thought for sure he was going to get me. The house was a lot closer, but so was the bull! Then came the dog again! But now I had another problem. I was close to the house but if I slowed down to climb the fence, it would easily rip me to shreds! Then came the dog! Just one more time Doggie! Go for it! Sure enough, the fight was on!

I made it over the fence, though I don't remember how I did it. I could see the dog and the bull still going at it just on the other side of the fence. That was still too close for me, fence or no fence. I crossed the yard and literally fell through the back door of the house. I was safe, alive and in one piece, which was a lot more than I thought I was going to be.

But the story didn't end there. Several weeks went by and I didn't see any of the cattle again. I did see tracks where somebody had brought a truck and trailer through the yard and into the pasture. I thought they had taken them away, but that was not the case. So, one fine summer day, I decided to soak up some water in my special place again. This time I stayed close to the fence and followed it as far as I could. This was the long way around, but it was a lot safer.

I'm lying in the creek again, but listening very carefully! Sure enough, I heard a cow bellow and, jumping up, I spotted Bad-Attitude. He didn't know I was there so I ran undercover downstream as far as I could. Then I saw Bad-Attitude coming full speed ahead! This time he wasn't between me and downstream. Downstream, and not very far, was a fence and a road. I made it to the road in plenty of time. But I got away from the area very quickly because if the bull broke through the fence, I didn't want to be there.

One day somebody showed up with a truck and cattle trailer at our house and I went out to see who it was. It was the rancher who owned the cattle, so I told him his bull almost got me one day. He told me that bull had a bad history of seriously hurting people, something

I didn't question one bit. He also said he was taking some of them out and moving them back to the farm (wherever "farm" was). So I assumed he did just what he said. WRONG IDEA! He may have taken some of them back, but he didn't take the bull!

So again, several days later, I was in my special spot, soaking up the creek and daydreaming, when I heard this snorting! I flew out of the creek and made it to the top of the bank before Bad-Attitude charged! I didn't have time to go downstream, which would have much easier, so we repeated this choreography until about halfway to the sycamore stand the gray slick-haired dog shows up! Somewhere in heaven I hope there is this gray slick-haired dog waiting for me! I want to take him to Jesus and tell him all about it!

By this time the dog had the bull pretty much figured out. And the bull knew he was going to lose. They fought only for a while when the bull gave up the chase and headed back across the open fields with the dog in hot pursuit. I wasted no time in getting out of there and up the hill to home. I stayed out of the pasture after that.

Late that summer, on a beautiful night, we had a whole house full of people. At least a dozen trucks and cars were sitting in the yard and driveway. People were everywhere. Bad-Attitude decided he wanted to charge the gate, break it down, and get somebody! If you know anything about the south, there were enough guns and happy gunners to make a war. He made quite a showing getting through the gate, giving several people more exercise than they had previously been accustomed to. But it didn't last long until the hot lead followed by more hot lead returned the favor. Bad-Attitude was more Red than black by the time he decided to return through what was left of the gate. He had stirred up a hornet's nest and found it to be very unfortunate for him. He didn't die from it, but he was completely broken of crashing through gates! Dad called the owner that night and they had a little discussion over the phone, if you know what I mean. A few days later they came and took the bull away.

And yes, I returned to my special place several times after that. I retraced my path and the crazy ordeal that had taken place there. It seemed like an impossible feat. But I was living proof I had made it. Some of the marks were still in the ground, and the memories were still alive and well.

Looking back, I realize God had intervened in the entire matter. I could never have done it in my own strength. I was 13, strong, fast, and had plenty of fear to motivate me. But it would have taken more than that to have survived it. It was a merciful God looking down on a sinner who never had any idea who God was. But God knew who the sinner was very well. Some would say God doesn't accept sinners. But I believe God is working in everyone's life, even if they don't know him. I know he was working in my life that day.

#17 Bro. McKee's Farewell

While living in Springfield, MO, our pastor was Bro. Phillip McKee. He was no doubt the best pastor we had ever had. His spiritual depth was amazing. He seemed to clearly understand the spiritual aspects of spiritual living. He was a warrior in the faith. While we were there, as he was to undergo a hip replacement, he was given some medication to take the night before his surgery. He took it the night before as instructed, but the medicine they gave him was not the right medicine. By the morning light it was evident he wasn't going to make it. They rushed him to the hospital, but he died there. We attended his funeral, but it wasn't like any funeral I had ever heard of. The glory of God filled that place like it was the rapture in progress. It was more like a camp meeting when God moves and there's no altar call, than it was a funeral. If ever there would have been a resurrection during a funeral, it surely would have been then. I was watching EVERYTHING! I'd never seen anything like it before or after.

After the funeral service we went to Bro. McKee's house for a meal. It was primarily for his family and some church people. I was standing by the front door just inside the living room when it happened. Suddenly there was a strong presence of Bro. McKee. It was very strong and very real. I looked around, fully expecting to see him, but he was not there. I walked around the house looking in the rooms for him as his presence was clearly there. Other people were looking around also. I wish I had asked them what they were thinking or looking for, but I felt it a strange question to ask at a time like that. His family was already grieving over his death and it was no time to start asking those types of questions in that atmosphere. It was the first time I had ever experienced such an event, though later there would be similar experiences.

#18 Bus Ride in California

In the summer of 1974 I was stationed on board the USS England, DLG-22. It was later Redesignated as CG-22. The ship was home-ported in San Diego, Calif. I was still single, had no prospects of any dating possibilities, and bored stiff. Sailors do a lot of really strange things to fight off boredom. Most of the guys just drank themselves into oblivion, but that had no attraction for me. I did however go to almost every decent movie in town. I saw "The Hiding Place" three times in a row. You can get involved in a lot of groups that range from A to Z, but like all distractions, they soon fade into the background, and before you know it, you are looking for something to do again.

On this particular Saturday morning I had taken the city bus from the navy base to downtown San Diego. It was called "the Square." It was a 24/7 vanity fair. Nobody was safe there, not even the police. I had learned long before to get off the bus a few blocks before the square, walk a couple of blocks to catch my outgoing bus, and avoid the square all together. On this day, for whatever reason, I did not get off the bus early so I changed buses at the square. Not really knowing what I wanted to do, or where I wanted to go, I looked at the bus routes posted at one of the bus stops. There I found a route that went many miles away and back again. I had my answer. I would take this long route and spend the day sightseeing out the window. That sounded like just the thing to do; spend the day sightseeing the countryside, in California.

I went to the right bus stop and only waited a few minutes before my bus appeared. I got on, paid the fare for the round trip, and sat down where I could see the countryside go zooming by. I saw it go by for a very, very long time. I looked again at my map for the route and sure enough, this route returned to the square. So I thought I was okay. The bus traveled for hours and many miles went flying past. I began to feel that something was not right. By now I was the only passenger on the bus and I was somewhere out on the backside of some desert. The road had started out as highway pavement, then it turned to blacktop at some turn off many miles behind us, and now we were on a totally dirt/sand road. There was nothing to see but desert and dirt as far as the horizon. It was almost 4 pm. NOW I was worried. I went to the front of the bus and asked the driver about the return trip and he pulled over right after I asked him. I thought something was very wrong as he said that was as far as I could go and I would have to get off but the bus would make the return trip in the morning, bright and early. He said he lived down the road a few miles away and he takes the bus home at the end of each day.

I looked at him in disbelief! Surely someone would say something about this route dead-ending on the back side of some desert, with no way back! But alas, I had to get off. The bus disappeared into a cloud of dust and when it settled, I took inventory of where I was, and what I was surrounded by. This last stop was at an intersection of two single-lane dirt roads, completely surrounded by desert as far as you could see. Not even the tax collectors knew about this place! There was only one thing to do; start walking back!

I walked for hours. I walked for miles. When it started getting late in the day, I could see far off on the horizon the bright lights of a city lighting up the sky above it. It was so far away that the hue of the lights seemed almost imaginary. The bus had been air-conditioned but the desert was not. I was thirsty as thirsty could be, but there was nothing but darkness settling in, and the stars were coming out. By the mercy of God, there was a full bright moon, so I could see the road very well. And if something were on the road, it could also be seen. There were times when things ran across the road in front of me, but I wasn't afraid of any of it until later that night. Still walking, things began to get bigger as the night wore on. Some of those critters were very large and I wondered what they were. They moved with lighting speed and did not seem to be bothered by my being there. It made me nervous when I came to the place where they had just crossed the road. Again God was watching over me. As the night came on and the stars came out, the air-cooled way down. At times it was almost cold.

Somewhere during that night, I came to a crossroad. I did not remember any crossroads previously, but the lights shining in the distant sky led me to go that way. I hadn't gone far beyond that crossroad, when the road began to be much wider and much more even. It was still barbaric desert, but the walking conditions were much better. A few times I came to a little lane that left the road, and up that lane I could see the lights of a house. My thirst was saying to go ask for water! But something inside me said do not do it. Whatever it was, I did not want to regret finding out. Occasionally I heard a dog barking that sounded close. But they never got closer; they stayed off in the distance. Sometimes a house stood dark and silent close to the road. Then a dog would bark. But I never left the road and kept my focus on the lights of the city ahead. It was definitely getting closer. A few times a car could be seen far off in the distance coming my way from the direction of the city. I thought of flagging it down, but my gut feeling said, "hide." So long before they ever got close, I would walk off the road, squat down among the tumbleweeds and put my back to the road so they would not see the white of my face standing out in the darkness. After they had passed, and the dust had settled, I would resume my journey. Eventually I came to this little town. I say "town" because it had about three or four houses in it. They were all dark and silent. All had cars in the driveways. Fortunately there were no dogs to call attention to my passing. It was there where the dirt road I was on intersected the black top. And again, the light from the city ahead was my compass. The blacktop was not any wider than the dirt road, but it felt like I was nearing civilization. I felt like I was making progress, and the city was getting brighter.

I walked for several miles on this lone and dark road. I could see no other signs of civilization. I expected to see a road sign that would give me some idea of where I was, but there were none. Finally I came to an actual town. It was a very small town, but it had streets lights, and a small park. There was a bus stop where the bus would come by in the morning. Searching around I found a water fountain that worked, and I made a serious attempt to drink all the water in that town! I drank until I sloshed. I washed my face, wetted my hair and combed it, and washed my hands. It felt so very good to sit down on a bench and rest my whole body. It seemed like I was not there very long before I needed more water. So I returned to the fountain and repeated the whole scenario over again before returning to the bench. I could see, down the lighted road, that this town came to an end just a few blocks away, but the road went on. I thought about continuing my walk, but my exhausted body said to wait a few more minutes.

As I was sitting there, this big full-size, white Cadillac highway cruiser appeared and stopped beside me. The dome light came on and revealed an elderly man in the car. He rolled down the passenger window and asked if I needed a ride. I said, "Yes, I do!" He asked where I was going and I told him to San Diego Naval Base. He told me he was going to San Diego to work so he would take me as close as he could, if that would help.

On the way, he asked how I came to be so far out of town. I told him what had happened and he thought it was extremely funny. At that time there was nothing funny about it to me. We talked some more and I offered to happily pay him for his gas. But he refused it and said that he was going that way anyway.

Later, as we approached San Diego, we continued our conversation. It was revealed that this guy was wicked beyond measure; the vilest of the vile.

I knew we were approaching the base by this time and that made me feel a little safer, and he did drop me off right at the main gate of the base, where we went our separate ways. I walked to the pier where my ship was tied, and drug my carcass back up the gangplank. The sun was starting to break on the horizon as I was crossing the quarterdeck of home.

I can look back and see many allegories in this experience. But the one that stands out the most is that when you think you're almost home, the devil will still try some kind of wild shot to hit you. We can't let our guard down, even when "relief" or "help" comes along. Until you hear the quartermaster of the old ship of Zion say, "Welcome home," can you say, "I'm home at last!"

#19 Chain Rattling, by Robert Bryan

You tell me that you've changed,
that you've been born again.
That Jesus Christ has set you free
from the yoke and chains of sin.

But tell me clearly brother,
you've made me all confused.
If you have been so set free,
why use the words you do?

You said you've been delivered
from the chains that held you fast.
But every day it seems to me,
you're living in the past.

You like to tell the stories
that tell a worldly tale.
You talk and dress and seem to walk
on a road that leads to hell.

You often sound so worldly;
your spirit seems so dark.
You're often at the altar
seeking oh, so hard.

And every day you struggle
to keep the old path straight.
Always blaming others
for your walk that's not by faith.

If you want to keep the victory
and stay away from sin,
Don't keep going back again
to rattle all the chains.

Christ has set before us
a race that we must win.
But we'll never cross the finish line
by turning back again.

#20 The Church Guest

While preaching in Burlington Iowa, I saw Jesus come into the church sanctuary. He stood in the back of the church as I continued preaching. I was overwhelmed with glory and emotion. He stood in the back of the church for some time and finally, after a while, I could not be silent about it any longer. I wondered if others could see him also. So, daring to make myself look like I had lost my mind, I asked the congregation to tell me who was standing in the back of the church. EVERYONE turned to see! But no one saw him! He was still there, but they could not see him. He never spoke, he just was there watching. I did not know what else to do, so I went on preaching. I do not remember what I was preaching on, but I never forgot the guest that came!

Then several years later, while visiting in South Dakota, I was asked to preach on a Sunday night. Again, while I was preaching, Jesus came into the services. Again, I could see him, but I knew no one else would be able to. I alluded to Jesus being there with us tonight, but never came out and told them <u>why</u> I knew he was there. I COULD SEE HIM! I remember the message: *Are You Willing to be Broken?* Over the years, I have seen Jesus several times and talked with him several times. But I have learned that not everyone can accept this experience or even believe it. That's to their loss, for if they would only trust Him to come, He would!

#21 Some Call Him Lord!

I've always had a problem with the word, "Lord." There was always something about it that I did not like. I read it in the scriptures and heard it used, but very seldom did I ever use it my vocabulary. It was a word that had no meaning to me. There was nothing I could relate it to. I didn't like the word but didn't know why I didn't like it. So I avoided it. At times I even became embarrassed when others used it extensively.

Years went by and one day I got a call that my dad was dying. The doctor told me if I wanted to see my dad alive again that I had better come fast, and there was no hope that he would even last that long. I went on the 2,300-mile flight as soon as I could get the ticket.

I arrived very late in the night and found him alive and hanging on by a thread. I fully expected to lose him before sunrise, which was just a few hours away. I had heard that he had gotten saved. He was in and out of consciousness, but while he was alert, he prayed and <u>Oh, how he prayed</u>! I had never seen or heard my dad pray before and I was deeply touched. This man had come up in the old school. He was hard. I had seen him say and do a lot of things but praying wasn't any of them, so I was so surprised to hear him pray! His love and intensity were amazing. I had never heard a prayer quite like that, of such simplicity and openness.

He wasn't just saying his prayers knowing God would hear them because God knows and hears everything, and perhaps someday God might answer back. That's how I prayed. But this man was talking to God and God was talking to him and they both knew it! The radiance! The spirit! were obvious.

I was humbled and very thankful that he had come to have such a close relationship to Christ. It really made me wonder where he learned to pray like that. I had gone there wondering if somehow I could get him to turn to Christ in his last hours, only to discover the conversion he was having was very real to him, and that I was the one who needed to do the catching up.

He repeatedly called Jesus as Lord and the love and truthfulness of his praying convicted me. It was the first time I had heard the word, "Lord" used in a manner that carried with it such depth and love as I had not known.

Later on that same night/morning when I went to prayer and began to ask God for direction in his will concerning Dad and how I should pray, God made it very clear to me that "God was my God," but "Jesus was not my Lord."

In my understanding, I had acknowledged God as the Father of the trinity, the Godhead, the creator, the great I AM, MY creator. But that's where it stopped. I saw Jesus as the lamb of God who takes away the sins of the world and my sins. But that was only that I might know God. My Christian faith was wrapped up in knowing God and being blessed by God. Jesus was the instrument used by God to bring me to the Father. After that, Jesus was put on hold till I needed more help. Then I would go to the Father seeking the Father's help to get Jesus to do what I wanted. I envisioned God as the supreme ruler of eternity that was closely watching everything that I was doing. Therefore, I had to live by his laws of doing what was right and living righteously that God might bless me. As long as God was just a God, I could live my life however I saw fit as long as I stayed inside of God's boundaries, so that God would bless me for my righteousness, like Abraham.

This wrong concept caused me so much trouble. If my salvation was based upon my righteousness of right and wrong, then being and doing right was everything!

If anybody from the pulpit to the pew started doing anything that I felt was wrong, then it was my Christian duty, yea, even my salvation, to straighten things out. Then I could go to God and expect his blessings for my sacrifice and efforts. I had a nervous breakdown trying to "convert" everyone and I was considered a troublemaker in the church. Leadership thought I had a problem with leadership, but in reality I was afraid of losing my soul over someone else's inconsistency. From the pulpit to the pew I found issues that I felt threatened my salvation. I wanted God's approval more than anything and would go through anything to get it. Standing up for right meant standing up for God, and standing up for God meant getting God's approval. I was so sincere yet so wrong.

But if someone mentioned the word, "Lord," then I would cringe. The word "Lord" implied rulership. I didn't want anybody to be in control of my life. They might lead me in ways that would put me in bad standing with my God and/or my comfort zone. I didn't like the word "Lord" and wondered why it was ever applied to Jesus. It was a word used to be polite, kind of like being called sir, or mister.

That day I heard the words of a "died in the wool, hard as stone, never back up, go down fighting, Dad"..... my hero! He raised his hand in the air and prayed with such intensity as I had not known, calling on Jesus as Lord with such tears of love running down his face, which was almost glowing in admiration, and he meant every word of it! I was shocked! Speechless! Yes, speechless!

Who said an "old school" hillbilly can't teach a young hillbilly anything!

I added my little feeble amen at the end of his prayer and feared he would say to his religious, used to be pastor, "I am here to help you get saved, Son. Pray and try to say something intelligent."

What could I say? I knew Dad had found something that was real in this word, "Lord," and I wanted to find it too. But how? He was drifting in and out between worlds just a few feet away and I began asking God to spare him that I might find what he had and how to get it. Jesus as Lord? How could this be? But the evidence was overwhelming and the conviction was on full blast.

Now, in the Old Testament, righteousness came by keeping the laws and doing right. But the Old Testament laws couldn't change the heart or the spirit. And if the "laws" didn't help anybody back then, they surely couldn't help anybody today. But I was sincerely trying, with every grace that I could get, to resurrect righteousness by works and trying to use the New Testament to prove it. It wasn't that I deliberately set out to do this but looking back, I see it very clearly.

After all the aforementioned problems, I gave up on all of it and walked away from the church. I resigned from everything, except membership, and quit. Gone. It was over. The pastor I had at that time was a hireling and didn't know how to pastor. He ruled his family with an iron hand and tried to run the church the same way. He was all about control and image; image was everything to him. He didn't care who he had to push out of the way to get what he wanted. All in the name of God? I felt he too was on the wrong road, and I thought we might help each other. I really wanted to help him. Perhaps by helping him, I could get help also. But he wasn't going to be told anything by anybody unless he was forced to. This caused me more anguish than before, so I walked out.

The devil was using the problems in the church to keep me from seeing the truth that I was seeking for in Christ. After much soul searching and prayer, I started seeing glimpses of what Dad saw. Going to God empty handed is the only way! Jesus said, "No man cometh unto the Father but by me." I was using Jesus as a bridge to get to God but had not understood that Jesus was God in the flesh.

Everything that I wanted God to do for me came from Jesus. My life could never be pleasing to God because all my righteousness of "fighting for the truth" was contaminated by my carnal heart and was considered as filthy rags in the eyes of God; the very God I thought I was pleasing.

Only the righteousness of Christ would suffice.

It's one thing to know this in your head but another to keep it straight while it's there. If Jesus was truly in control of my life, through the Spirit, then Jesus would lead me out of all this mess and turn things around to what He wanted and I sought after.

So with renewed energy and armed with this new concept, I became REALLY dangerous. After trying to let Jesus be Lord of my life, that Jesus might make me and conform me into His image and that I might be found acceptable to the Father, I found another problem in my thinking. And again it was that word, "Lord."

Following Jesus simply for the sake of God's approval is a very miserable road indeed. If I really wanted to follow Jesus it would have to be from the heart and not the head. This could not happen until I went to Christ and saw Him as He is. But doing this made me see myself as I was, which led me to being broken and humble. Soon I was crying out for mercy. I was expecting his wrath, but he gave me his love. Jesus once was a bridge, then He became my master, then He became my Lord!

This led me to the next problem. And again it was that word, "Lord." After all I had been through and learned, you would have thought by now I would have gotten it straight. But I wasn't through proving how mixed up a guy could get, or so it seemed.

I discovered that what I wanted Christ to do for me was out of harmony with reality. I found that God wasn't going to do more for me than what He did for Jesus. Everything Jesus did was done by His own choice. God never forced Him to do anything. But I wanted God to make my choices for me. Jesus did it because he wanted to,... out of love for the Father. I was wanting Jesus to fill me with His Spirit so that I could serve Him in great power and holiness. But what I found out was that Jesus would not do my thinking for me. I still had a will and I still had to make choices, and God wanted me to use that for His glory. I was hoping for a robot experience but that didn't come. My service to God after all He had done for me was now returned back to me. Not that I was seeking acceptance by my works, but rather for my obedience and surrender.

Works say, "I call the shots and God blesses me for it." Obedience says, "Jesus is Lord of my life and everything I do for Him is out of love for what He has done for me."

The word, Lord, is not truly Lord unless it's expressed out of love. Otherwise, it's still master. But the glory of God in us is from His Spirit within us. And this Spirit will not co-exist with my self-willed, intellectual spirit. Sincerity is never a substitute for purity.

And church is never a substitute for godliness.

I will stand before God and give an account on whether I took personal responsibility for my choices. I have found those choices are a lot easier when they are made in order to express my love for Christ for what He has done for me. If I lose sight of the Saviour, then the focus shifts to my "spiritual performances," also known as works. For lack of vision the people perish. And that vision is Christ.

Oh, the battle between "works of righteousness" and "acts of love!"

But how can you love someone whom you do not know, or have not seen? The answer is brokenness, humility, repentance and love. These are the tools of the Spirit as He tears down our altars of self-righteousness, vain ideas, procrastination, self-will, and plain old stubbornness. Those all are a very cheap brand of Holiness, and not one of them is willing to let Jesus be LORD! But the gentle nail-scarred hands of Jesus does not throw the clay away when it becomes hard and unyielding. Instead, He applies more pressure to just the right place to shape us into a vessel fit for His glory. And we don't have to wait to see the finished work before we decide if we want to let Him do it. If we can't trust Jesus to lead us and shape us, then He will not be our Lord.

Jesus was once my bridge, then He became my master, then He became my friend, then He became my LORD! And all along the way it wasn't Jesus that was changing, it was me.

#22 Crazy Harry and the Chicken

While I was living as a transient, I hooked up with another transient my age. (about 15). We were using the buddy system before there was a buddy system. It wasn't long before I found out why they called him Crazy Harry. He was the only hobo I ever met that was scared of the dark, and everything that wasn't in the dark! That's a real bad handicap when you're a transient. It did not matter where you slept, before long you'd wake up with somebody crowding you, trembling and shaking the whole time. It was Crazy Harry. You couldn't chase him off with threats because he was scared, and he wasn't leaving. His real name was Harry *******, but very few in those circles know your real name and you don't tell anybody either. You use a nickname. It's much safer that way. I was given the nickname "the kid" in the hobo camps because of my young age. One day Crazy Harry and I found our way into the next city along the tracks. It was Jefferson City, Missouri. Every hobo along the tracks knows just where to go to find a bite to eat at a particular city or town. They know just the right door to knock on and who to expect to come to that door. If you feed a hobo along the tracks, he'll mentally mark your house and tell everyone he knows about it. So I was reluctant to tell Crazy Harry about my place, but my stomach soon overruled my brain, my mouth took control, and my feet followed. Soon all of me was going and all of me was happy to do so. We had not eaten anything for several days and we both were absolutely hungry with capital letters. I said to Crazy Harry that I knew somebody in this town who would feed us and let us stay there too! Needless to say, Crazy Harry was all over that. So we made our way across town to "Granny's" house and knocked on the door. She welcomed us in with great joy to see us and immediately said, "You fellows look like you could use a bit to eat" She soon had us into the kitchen and was cooking up fried chicken that was fresh as any farm could get it, and hot from the skillet! Life was good and getting better. So here I am shoving fried chicken into my face at a high rate of speed, and here's Crazy Harry with one piece in his hand and staring at it. Finally, I had to ask, "You okay?" (I knew he wasn't if he's just starring at fried chicken!) So he asked one of his not so typical stupid questions. He asked, "Is this a city chicken or a country chicken?" Granny said, " I suppose it's a country chicken; we killed it this morning." So Crazy Harry puts it down and says, "I can't eat it!" Sure enough, I just had to ask, "What's the difference?" Crazy Harry, in his not so bright manner says, "A city chicken lives on corn, a country chicken lives on bugs and insects." I didn't want to ask him the difference

STORIES

between a bug and an insect. That would have been too much for Crazy Harry. I could not believe what I was hearing! Did he really just say that? So not to offend Granny, who was by now laughing so hard she was leaning over the sink, I did the only Redeeming thing I could think of. I said," I love buggy chicken!" and grabbed his plate of chicken before his brain woke up. I was chuckin' it down fast enough to impress somebody. I knew when Crazy Harry came back to earth he'd be wanting his chicken. I was determined to make as much of his chicken disappear before he realized who he was, and where we were. Not to mention what we would be eating when we left which would be NOTHING! That guy never did wake up. I ate everything she cooked and was mighty grateful to get it. Crazy Harry would not eat another bite. After it was all over except for the burping, I tried to explain to Crazy Harry that it didn't make any difference what the chicken ate. It all was turned into chicken, and what didn't, wasn't around no more to worry about. But he would not change. Granny fixed him something else to eat. I knew if we ever ate anything again, I would have to tell Crazy Harry it was a city product and it came in a wrapper. Granny's house did us much good, and we stayed for quite a while because she didn't want us to leave. Later, when I left, I went without telling Crazy Harry I was leaving because he wanted to stay and I wanted him to stay there also. It was a win- win. But I had to leave quietly or else Crazy Harry would get all worked up over it. I never saw him again after that. Sometimes along the tracks, you'll run into somebody again or hear of them, but it seemed Crazy Harry had just disappeared.

#23 Macho Harry

Some time ago, another hobo and I stayed at Granny's house. Granny's house had three rooms in a straight line. The first room was the living room where you entered her little house. The middle room was a small room where everyone slept. There was a small cot along the wall under the window where Granny slept and on the other side of the room was a much larger bed where Harry and I slept. When Harry and I lay in bed, we could see into the third room, which was the kitchen. On the wall in the kitchen was an electric clock that looked like a teapot. On the top of that teapot clock was a small Red light. While we were lying in bed that night, in the darkness of the room, Crazy Harry happened to look into the kitchen and see this little Red light glowing on the wall. So, out of the silence and the darkness comes this scream, "What's that??" I looked into the kitchen to see what he was looking at and saw the Red glow of that teapot clock on the wall. So I said, in a very frantic voice, "Harry! It's a Red eyed monster from hell coming to get you." Harry sat up in the bed and started fighting with the blanket and screaming, so I yelled at him to knock it off! Harry stopped for a moment and asked, "Is that really what it is?" I said, "No."

Harry then began begging Granny to make me stop scaring him. Granny who was awake and listening to this was covering her face with her hands trying not to laugh. Granny mumbled something about stop scaring him, and I promised to be good. The laughter in her voice was very noticeable. Now that everyone in the house was awake and listening, I struck up a conversation with Harry. So I said, "Hey Harry, did you know they're tearing down that old house on top of the hill? He said, "No." So I answered him and said,

"They're putting in a graveyard," stretching the word graveyard out into a long word.

That did it; that was the last straw for Crazy Harry. He jumped out of bed, turned on the light switch, and started bouncing around like a kangaroo with boxer shorts on, pumping his fist up and down in the air in front of him like he was trying to pump up a flat tire or something, and yelling, "Come on Robert, let's fight!"

Now, I have seen a lot of strange things, but I had never seen anybody that weighs less than 100 lbs. and 5 ft. tall, jump up and down in boxer shorts, waving their fists in the air and yelling, " Let's fight." I found that very amusing. The fact that Harry was as skinny as a noodle did not help his cause. Granny, who was laughing hysterically, had turned over to face the wall, trying to hide her laughter. But it wasn't working. The more she tried, the funnier it got. I must admit I was laughing also, which made Crazy Harry even madder. Finally, after Harry had jumped around for a while, he began to cool down. I apologized and told him I was sorry for scaring him. I promised to be good if he would go back to bed and try not to be scared.

Crazy Harry turned off the light, went back to bed, and tried to not be scared. You could hear the muffled sound of laughter from across the room, which made the situation even funnier. I was trying not to laugh at Crazy Harry because I had promised him I would be good. As the scene continued to replay in my mind, I found it very hard not to laugh. Eventually the laughter died down and everything went back to normal. Then out of the darkness would come another muffled laugh, and we both would be laughing and trying to stop. Fortunately for Crazy Harry, he never did find out why skinny people don't jump around in boxer shorts. I must admit of all the strange people I've seen, Crazy Harry had to be in the top ten somewhere.

#24 Dad's Farewell

When my dad passed away, it was a shock to everyone. Many times we had been told by some doctor that he wasn't going to make it and the family would be called together. As the only son, though I had four sisters, it was usually my job to tell him he wasn't going to make it. I'd go into his room and everyone would know why I had come in, and they would all leave while I told him. I would explain to him what the doctor had said, and he would look at me with a disgusted look and say, "That doctor don't know what he's talking about!" I'll walk out of here when I get ready. God knows when he'll take me home, and he ain't said anything to me about it yet. That doctor don't know nothin'." From that point on he would get better, the doctors would all be amazed, and he would walk out of that room just like he said. This happened on SEVERAL occasions. It became his norm. Something would happen, they'd take Dad to the hospital, and the scene would repeat itself. The last time it happened I went into the room and said something like, "Well, you know why I'm here." And Dad said, "Yeah I know, that doctor still don't know nothin'." Dad had many doctors during those times; They would all say he was not going to make it. But he proved them wrong again and again.

I was in Washington state, at work, when I got an emergency phone call from my sister, Sarah Kay. She started out with, "Well, you know why I'm calling," but I had no idea. So I said, "What happened?" She said, "Dad died this morning." I was shocked, for I didn't even know he was in the hospital. She said he wasn't, he was in the nursing home. My stepmom's sister and her husband from St. Louis were visiting him and they were talking, when suddenly Dad fell silent. He had the strangest look on his face, so she asked,

STORIES

"Marv, what's wrong?" But he didn't answer. He was looking all around the room, seeing something, but he wasn't seeing them. She asked again but he didn't answer. Then he fell back into his pillow, and he was gone.

There was no rushing him to the hospital, no family gathering in, no dumb doctors, no more, "You know why I'm here." He was just gone. God came and got him as Dad said that He would.

I made the trip to Missouri to attend his funeral. There were many things that happened during that trip and perhaps someday I will tell about them too. But I will tell this; my wife and I were in bed the night after his funeral service when I asked God, "Did Dad make it to heaven?" There was no reply and that worried me. So now here we are in bed after the funeral and it was nighttime. Guess who came a-calling! It was DAD! He stood at the foot of the bed. I did not see him with the eye, but his spirit and mine were totally in reality and present. He said, "You asked God if I made it." Right then I knew he had made it, and it was God's way of answering my question. Then Dad was suddenly gone and I knew he would not be able to come back. I sure missed him; there have been times when I sensed he was watching me, though I never sensed his presence or had any indication he was there. I somehow knew he was watching. After a while, those experiences passed away also.

#25 Dad's New Cadillac

One summer weekend, my stepbrother, Alan, and I went to a party. It was the kind of party where you go because you know it's going on, but nobody really invited you. And when you got there, nobody really cared if your there or not. Except this party was so far out in the country, you had to pipe sunlight to the place. It was amazing we even found it. And I have no idea how Alan even knew about it.

While this "party till you puke" was going on inside the house, the very elderly man who owned the farm and I were sitting on the front porch and visiting like we were two long lost brothers.

We seemed to hit it off very well and he had a lot to say. I was a good listener (believe it or not) but it seemed he had the weight of the whole world on his shoulders. He needed somebody to talk to, and I was too embarrassed to go inside. So, I was content to listen to the old man and his many adventures. I really enjoyed listening to him.

Somewhere in our conversation the question came up about the large "something" that was sitting in his yard, covered up with a tarp. He said it was a brand new 1963 Cadillac. His son had been drafted into the army some time back and he had just bought the car when he got drafted. So he covered it up, removed the tires, drained the water and other things like that, and put it in storage until his son got back. But he got killed in action, so the car was there for good.

The man had to pause several times as he told the story. Then he said "I want that car gone. It reminds me to much of him. I don't want to touch it and start grieving all over again. But nobody will take it away because they are too concerned about me." Then he turned to me and asked, "Do you want it?" I wanted it so bad I could have danced a jig. But I felt the same way everybody else felt. The man's heart was in his son and taking the car would be a bad idea. So, I politely declined. He said "I really do want you to get that car out of here, and you can have it. The title is in the glove box." We talked about his son and then our

STORIES

conversation moved on to other things. I know people will say things they don't really mean when they have been drinking. I supposed that was the case. I wasn't going to take advantage of the kind, gentle man.

Sometime later that night, Alan and I left and went home. I took careful notice of our location when we left. If Alan passed out, I would have had to drive. But he didn't, and I didn't need to drive, but I did get an idea of where we had been.

Saturday morning comes around and sometime later my dad showed up. He lived in St Louis but drove down to the farm on weekends. As we visited in the house, he said he needed to go to the junk yard and get some parts for his car. I hadn't noticed what he was driving when he walked in, so I asked him what he was driving. He said it was a 63 Cadillac. So, we went outside and looked at it. It was a faded, two-tone blue with what used to be white interior. But it was clearly in very bad condition. It was no surprise that he needed parts for it; probably a lot of parts.

I told him my story about this guy and his car that nobody would take away for him. Needless to say, that had my dad's attention. He asked me if I had looked at it and I said no, that there might be anything under that tarp. And I didn't know if it was the guys whisky doing the talking for him. So, Dad asked me, "Do you think you could find that place again?" "Yes, I answered." "It was a long way, but I think I could find it."

So, we agreed that he would be back the following weekend with tires, rims, gas, battery, etc., etc., and a tow bar. If I could find the place, he would be more than happy to take the car. I told him that I thought it would be good to make sure he was talking straight before we got any hopes up. Dad agreed and went back to St. Louis Sunday night. The following weekend, Dad showed up in his ratty, banged up, faded, two- tone blue Cadillac. It looked like a junk yard on wheels.

We started out, and sure enough we found the place. The man answered the door and I asked him if he remembered me. He said that he did, and he also remembered trying to convince me to get rid of the car for him. He reassured me that he was serious, and I really could have the car if I wanted it. I asked him if it would be alright if my dad could have it. To which he replied, "Anybody can have that car. I just want it gone."

Dad and I both thanked him for his kindness and headed for the car. When we pulled the tarp off, my mouth must have hit the ground. There, sitting right in front of me was a brand new, two-tone blue with white interior, 1963 Cadillac in mint condition! It had less than 100 miles on it. Dad was VERY happy about it, and I was trying to recover from shock. I kept thinking to myself, "I just gave this away?"

We put the tires on it, but later found the original tires in the trunk. After we had put in the battery, added gas and water, checked the oil, and stuff like that, Dad said, "Let's see if this thing will start." He primed it and it cranked over just fine. Then it started but died. He primed it once again and then it started and purred like a kitten! Dad said, "It needs to run for a while."

I think my dad could have done cartwheels about that time! He was clearly excited. Then he said, "I'm not towing this thing home, I'm driving it!" So, we hooked the tow bar to his rattle trap and towed it home. Dad was extremely happy about the ordeal; he was smiling "wide load" style all the way home.

Even though it was either 1968 or 1969 when we obtained this treasure, the inside of the car still had the brand-new smell to it. There was no mold or dust anywhere! It was really a brand-new car.

Dad drove that car for a very long time. he babied it and bragged on it till everyone knew the story. I, however, kicked myself many times after that. But eventually I found a deep joy in Dad having it. Recalling that day has been a joy to me ever since then; the day I gave my dad a brand-new Cadillac!

26 Dark Warriors vs. Faith

I use this phrase, "dark warriors" to denote any spiritual being that is not serving Christ! That includes all the host of hell's fiendish group, but also many people who serve them. It's sad to say, but there are people who serve Satan even without knowing it. Sinners serve sin out of darkness. It's in their hearts. But there are those who serve sin with their whole heart, soul and mind and they do it knowingly and deliberately. They know whom they serve! I have found the greatest number of people who serve sin do so out of ignorance or darkness. They have been deceived as to who and what the devil really is. I have seen devils and demons alike, many times. As a rule, I avoid them. They are trouble at its worst, and I don't need their problems. But if I am forced into the situation, I plead the blood and rebuke them like Jesus did. I stand upon the word, trust in God and plead the blood! I don't describe them unless I feel led to because when I do, it causes some people tremendous problems.

I've seen angels, but only on a few occasions. It is always a powerful experience when I do. One day not too long ago, the summer of 2014, I was home alone. It was night and I was going to take a shower and go to bed. As I was standing in the front room, suddenly the room filled with devils of every sort. THAT REALLY SURPRISED ME! I wondered why they were there. I pled for Jesus to come and get them out and they left, but came right back few minutes later! Now what do I do? I asked God to kick them out for good, and He did. So I went to take my shower. While in the shower, they all came into the bathroom. I could see their wicked shadows on the shower curtain. Then one with horns came and stuck his head into the shower with me! I rebuked him and he left. But the others stayed there in the room. I asked God to throw them out again, but he didn't! I pled the blood, but they stayed. I quoted scripture, but they would not leave! NOW I WAS WORRIED! I didn't want these creeps hanging around my place. I asked God why they wouldn't leave and God said that I was acting by intellect, not by faith! Everything I was saying and thinking and doing was correct, but only according to knowledge. I was not asking in faith. So, as I stood there thinking about that, I recalled how God had helped me in the past and I knew He was there, always. I recalled an experience in the navy when the devil personally came to destroy me. He really took me to task that time, but I remembered how God came to my rescue. Now my faith was soaring!!!! I stood as solidly on faith as I ever had before! My voice had a different tone and a certain ring of triumph that was not there before. The "creeps" went screaming out of there before I even started praying! They knew what was coming! They'd seen faith in action before and they didn't want any part of it! They were now gone for good and I thanked Jesus for his advice and victory again! I felt as if God was pleased with my faith in him. Faith is not an intellectual understanding or a knowledge about things or something, it is confidence in what God can do and that special unction

STORIES

that accompanies it! THATS FAITH THAT WILL MOVE MOUNTIANS! And "creeps" too!!!!

Don't ever get caught up in works or knowledge in your spiritual performances. Throw all that aside and grab onto Jesus and say help Lord, I'm sinking! Peter threw all his self-confidence away and trusted in Jesus alone. THEN HE GOT THE VICTORY! That's faith! He got out of the boat with knowledge of what Jesus had said, but when it turned to self-confidence, knowledge, or circumstance, he began to sink.

#27 Defeating the Devil in Montesano

We lived at 310 River Street in Montesano, WA. The kids were very young at the time. This house was built almost exactly as the house in Missouri where many of these stories were located, including "Darkie", "It Came Down the Stairs", and others. The color, floor plan, and everything else was almost the same. The two major differences were a bedroom that was not there and the back porch on the Montesano house had be walled in and turned into a bedroom. Also, like the Missouri house, this house had serious spiritual problems.

During this time I was having all kinds of flash backs and the problems that go with them. I know the mind blocks out certain things that overload the nervous system as well as the reasoning system. This house had been blocked out, but the daily sights triggered memories that were having repercussions. We went to prayer mightily and dealt with each problem as they came up. What I didn't know at the time was that God had orchestrated everything to deliver me from some of those memories and the quirks that they created. It's a long story that I probably will not write.

It was after several spiritual healings and much prayer that this "blocked house" became "unblocked." When it did, I thought I was going to snap with too much overload! But after understanding that God was using this place to set me free, my heart, mind, and soul was somewhat comforted. However, if it involved more of what we were already facing, than I wasn't sure there wasn't a better way for God to do this. But I wasn't in control of the circumstances.

Things got so bad in our bedroom upstairs, we could no longer sleep there. We ended up moving everything out of that room and secured the door. Thus, our bedroom became the front room downstairs. This is where the story starts.

My wife and I were sleeping on a hide-a-bed couch downstairs. This particular night everything seemed to be normal; at least "our" normal. We had pled the blood in a few rooms to get rid of some problems that were going on, cast out a few evil spirits, bound the strong man that didn't want to leave, and so forth, just so we could turn the lights off and go to bed. Our nightly routine of going to bed was so unreal. As we lay there in the bed, the streetlights outside were shining in through the window. It was hot that night and we really didn't need a blanket, so we used a sheet.

I soon sensed something was not right, but I didn't know what. I looked at the window and saw the streetlight coming through the window turn as black and dark as a cave or a tomb. I knew what that meant! We had company! Then the temperature in the room became frigid and I started shivering. There was an atmosphere of fear filling that room, and I knew it was back. But this time it WASN'T Darkie! It was Satan himself. He was furious(as always)! He pressed his ugly face right into my ear and started screaming! I instantly started pleading the blood. Then he grabbed the bed and started throwing it into the air like he was going to throw us out of it. He would not get out of my ear or face, nor would he stop throwing the bed around. I knew NEVER to try to talk to him, so I just kept pleading the blood. I also started screaming, JESUS! This went on for a minute or so. Then, suddenly, the devil left in such a fury of violent speed as I have never seen. The whole experience had been so different. I watched the light outside slowly come back into the room and the temperature became normal hot. All was eerily silent. I was still sitting up and when I looked around, everything was back to normal. I looked over at my wife and she was sound asleep. Not once did she wake up. She had no idea what had just happened. I sat there for a while, praying and thanking Jesus for coming to our rescue!

The next morning, I told my wife about it. She was VERY glad she had missed it. She felt that God knew she couldn't handle stuff like that so he kept her safely through it all.

I will confess, I don't always handle it real smoothly either. But I know Jesus my Lord and Saviour gives me the grace to endure such things. Praise him for his goodness!

If I remember correctly, that was a turning point in the many experiences we had there. It certainly proves the scripture, "If the Son therefore make you free, ye shall be free indeed!"

#28 Drought in Missouri

Several years ago, when I was about 13 years old, Missouri experienced one of those record-type droughts. It seemed every summer was a record breaker to us, but this one was a real scorcher. The ground was so dry it had cracks in it everywhere, and you could put your hand right into the ground most anywhere you had a mind to. It was like a big puzzle. The creeks were all dry, the wells went dry, and the ponds were empty. Even the springs, that were everywhere, were mostly dry, but not all.

Our place sat on the edge of a hill overlooking parts of the valley, so you knew the well would likely be very deep if it went down to the water table. But this well had a spring that fed it and wasn't very deep at all. For some reason our well didn't go dry, but it got to tasting really bad at times. Outside the house was the pump. It had a round top that covered the sprocket head that pulled the chain with the grommets that came up the pipe. It had a handle on the side that you cranked and the faster you cranked it, the faster the water came out. It was always teeth-hurting cold!

Most folks were buying store-bought water from town. The trees all looked dead with their brown, stiff leaves. The grass was dead and brown and mostly lay flat. If you stood and looked across the yard, the house and trees appeared to be shaking, but really it was the distortion from the heat waves. The humidity was zero. There was no morning dew, no clouds, and no dampness in the ground even if you dug down a few feet. Early morning coolness was early morning meltdown. For some reason even the whippoorwills were silent at night and the bob whites couldn't be heard. It was as if the birds had left the country for wetter places. Normally you could hear them in the woods at night, but not then.

For some reason (that I don't remember), I had to be somewhere that was several miles away. As always, I walked cross country. That was the norm for most everyone at that time. There were those who had cars, but I wasn't one of them. We usually had horses we could take, but if you had to cross very many fences,

STORIES

it was best to just walk it. Farmers didn't take to kindly to you cutting their fence to get a horse through and jumping fences with a horse isn't what it is cracked up to be. Boot Hill will never be empty as long as there are tight fences and slow horses. So I just walked it.

I knew the heat would be unbearable, so it would be best to start out early. It's always best to follow the creek anytime it went in your direction. That was always the norm. Creeks offered a variety of benefits, so staying with one as you traveled was the best bet. However, this stream had gone dry early on in the summer, so staying with it was more habit than practical.

I set out very early that morning to get as far as I could before the heat set in. I had gone several miles and was making good time. As the day opened up, and the fireball in the sky became like a furnace, the heat set in with a vengeance. I kept to high ground when I could, not losing sight of the creek and possibly a stand of water if it were there. Normally if it's very dry, you can smell water a good ways off. But most folks today don't know what that is.

I still had several miles to go when I began to get heat sick. Having grown up in the Ozarks, I was well acquainted and well accustomed to the harshness of that environment, but this year's heat was far above anything anybody had ever seen.

Turning back toward home after going so far didn't seem like a good idea, so I moved to higher ground hoping to get a breeze, but so far there was nothing but burning, stinging heat. I had already stopped sweating about an hour earlier, so I knew I had to get water and get cooled off fast. But there was none, and I knew I was in trouble. There were no houses around for a long, long way, but I did know of an abandoned farm just a mile or so away. As I started down the dirt road that led to it, the heat in the woods was becoming fatal, so I returned to follow the dry creek again. At least it was in the open, and that was several times cooler than being in the "heat-bound timber." I looked around in the shimmering heat and considered this day could very well be my last.

Everything was blurry from the heat waves, but I knew part of the blurriness was my heat sickness setting in. And again I knew I was in trouble. I decided to turn back for home. Little did I know the importance of that decision!

When I started out that morning it was hot. I was sweating and wiping the sweat out of my eyes and face. It didn't take too long until my forehead was raw from the wiping and the salted sweat. My face started bleeding at the pores. Wiping my face produced a Red handkerchief. It was normal back then in cases of thirst to pick up a small rock and start sucking on it as if it were a piece of candy. This was a good way to keep your mouth moist even when it didn't want to be. But it produced nothing at all. I tied the handkerchief around my forehead to soak up the blood that was blinding my eyes. I had gone a good way when I discovered walking in the gravel of the creek bed was better than the higher ground next to it. The creek bed itself was about 7 feet below the normal ground. I had been avoiding the bed thinking the gravel would be hard walking. But I found it was less hot, so I continued on my way staying in the creek bed. I got so hot I started to get nauseous. I had to cool off or die.

I found a place along the creek bed where the ground was shaded by the overhanging turf. I climbed under the turf and began digging into the very loose soil. After digging back far enough to get cooler soil, I covered myself with the cool dirt and stayed there till I wasn't nauseous and felt much better and much cooler. (That was a very bold move in snake country!) After staying buried in the loose cool dirt for quite a while, I felt much better and moved on.

I had gone a considerable distance when I smelled water! Suddenly I was excited and started following my nose. After identifying the very spot it was coming from, I began digging frantically into the creek bed. I expected to find water, but what I found was cool mud! How happy I was to find it! I packed my head and face and arms with it, laughing and giggling like a school kid. How happy I was for mud! NOW I really felt better! Just before that I had pretty much figured out I probably was not going to "make it." I contemplated where I should go to be found when they started looking for me. Finding the body of someone who died from the heat is a very sick sight, and I never thought I would be the one, but it was looking like the next one would be me. Then I found the mud!

Praise God for cool wet MUD!

After the mud bath, I felt very good and started my journey home. The mud was very cool but didn't stay wet or cool very long. But it was a great deal better, so I pressed on. I still had about 5 miles to cover and, in that heat, that was a very long way.

It wasn't long before the heat started working on me again. Some time had passed and I started getting weak and shaky and nauseous again, but stopping would be fatal this time with no way of getting any relief. So I kept staggering along. The nausea was really bad by now but there were no soft banks and no mud.

My vision was blurred and the red mud had started falling off my face. The heat was unbearable; I had no spit, my tongue was thick, my arms were just as Red as my face, and again I was reminded of how much trouble I was in. I have been in some very precarious circumstances before, but this time I had this sinking feeling of heaviness down deep in my gut. I felt like I was not going to make it anywhere.

I had lost track of where I was and didn't know if I had even passed our house or not. Now I was really worried. I knew when I got to the right place in the creek, I had to turn and go up the hill and the house would be about ¼ mile up the hill. But I was in the creek bed and couldn't see over the elevated sides of the creek, so I couldn't see just where I was. I really wanted to give up. I had done all I could and was ready to quit. I no longer cared. Surely dying would be better than this!

Then I smelled water again! It's amazing what that did for me! I knew I shouldn't try running, and really couldn't run due to my weakened condition, but I couldn't hold myself back, and was giving it every last bit of strength I had. I must have looked a real sight trying to run when I could hardly walk. I went around a bend in the creek bed and saw water glistening just below the top of the gravel. I looked to see where it was coming from and there just ahead was a spring emptying out into a dipping hole about the size of small wash tub!

On the edge of defeat comes deliverance! I went staggering and falling toward that spring! I knew dirtying up somebody's dipping hole was a good way to make trouble, but I didn't care! I plunged my muddy, bloody, swelling, salt-crusted head right into it and was happy to do so!

Let me tell you, I was laughing and shouting and crying all at the same time! I plunged my head into that now very ugly water, gulping it down as fast as I could, only to come up for air and doing it again, having a

STORIES

wonderful time doing it. At that moment I didn't have a care in the world. At that moment there was no such thing as bad water although there can be repercussions from doing that.

I stayed there for a good long while. I rinsed my clothes, washed up, and felt like a thousand dollars! I climbed up out of the creek bed to take a look around to see where I was and was shocked to discover I was just below our house! I had passed the turn off point by a few hundred feet, but otherwise I WAS HOME! In my delirious condition I didn't even recognize my own dipping hole! But finding it was a life saver indeed!

I don't remember where I was off to that day, but I'll never forget my return! By the time I had reached home, I was completely dry and all ready for another dip. We had a well outside our place that was spring fed. It had the new style pump where you cranked a handle instead of pumping it. I started cranking that well handle like I was trying to start an airplane! Then I'd plunge my head under that wet cold water and drink it down in great gulps! I knew I was acting foolishly, but I sure did enjoy it! It took me several days to recover from that ordeal for it left me very weak, but I had learned a hard lesson.

If I had stayed close to home in such dire times, I never would have had such a close brush with dying. That's the way it is when we as Christians run into trouble; we have a tendency to start going places that would be okay in normal times. But in trying circumstances it's always best to hold steady with God and listen to his leading. The thing that's acceptable in good times may not be so acceptable in bad times! Be sensible and stay close to God even when it seems okay to wander off into "safe" places. No matter how close to God you get, if you can't hear his voice, you ain't close enough!

#29 The First Church of Foreigners

Living in the Ozarks presented some unusual circumstances. This is surely one of them.

It was a beautiful summer Saturday. My gang of cousins and I were playing ball in the field next to our house and next to the road, when a van stopped nearby and this guy gets out and walks out into the field to us. ANYBODY coming by our place was always there by intent. We lived so far out in the sticks; a probation officer couldn't find us. (That had some really good benefits!) So, this stranger shows up. We knew that the minute we saw his clean van and his shoes with shoestrings in them that he was from town. This was his story.

He started a conversation with us by asking if any of us wanted a brand-new baseball glove. Another proof he was from town was that he wasn't real observant. Of course we all wanted a new ball glove. His offer was this; he would come back tomorrow morning, Sunday morning, and pick us all up for church. Now, not a one of us had ever been in a church before. We had seen them and saw lots of people going into them, everyone dressed up like paper dolls in a toy catalog. That was our full extent of our churchin'. What everybody did in there was a mystery, and how they got so many folks in there was another mystery. When they all were let out, it seemed like they would run right over the top of anybody in their way. We concluded since so many of them were in there, they were probably very happy to get away. If getting away was so important, why did they go in there in the first place? We all agreed we would be ready to go if he came back out.

He walked very cautiously in his shiny shoes all the way back to his clean van, being careful to avoid: (1) the many bovine deposits, (2) proofs there was a dog someplace, (3) flies in great abundance, and (4) getting tangled up in the barbed wire fence he had to cross. It was obvious he wasn't accustomed to doing fences either. But it sure was interesting to watch him act so dignified in a cow pasture!

I'm not sure how he found us, or what made him think we needed church, but a stranger showing up out there was a big news event to us! We concluded he must have gotten lost when he found us.

So the next morning Mr. Dignified showed up to pick up the whole gang of us. However, there was a problem as I was the only one who got up to go! But he was there, so I went. I probably should have told my parents I was going, but I didn't and it was too late to tell anybody now. They may have wanted to know some stranger showed up, promised us ball gloves, and left with one of the kids. Another day in paradise!

So there I was in town, which was about 15 miles away. Nobody knew where I was, in fact, I didn't know where I was. Then it got bad. I was seated somewhere near the back of the church on the end of this really long bench seat which had a back on it. When everybody stood up, I stood up too. The guy on the stage says, "Let's pray." I'd never prayed before, but I had seen others do it. You close your eyes, act like you're asleep, and start talking to somebody who ain't there. That's prayer! P.S. I had a lot to learn!

I wasn't closing my eyes for nothing. I didn't want to miss anything! Soon the guy beside me starts yelling something I couldn't understand, and waving his arms around like he was swatting bees. I started looking for bees, but there weren't any! I tried to find out who he was yelling at, but nobody was listening to him. I got the impression something went terribly wrong somewhere because now everybody started doing it! Then it dawned on me; this was a church of foreigners because nobody was speaking English! Truly amazing! I didn't know there were so many foreigners, but I guessed they had to go to church somewhere, and this must be the place!

I couldn't wait to see Granny again and tell her about this place. She had family somewhere across the ocean when she was a little girl. I wondered if she might know some of these people.

Then it happened! There was this big commotion up front, not on the stage, but on the floor in front of the stage! So I leaned way out to get a look at what was going on. There were two old grandmas rolling around on the floor! All I could see was the lower half of them. They were rolling all over each other. That only meant one thing! THEY WERE FIGHTING! I could not see the top half of them to see who was winning, but there sure was a lot of yelling going on. And if that wasn't shocking enough, NOBODY was breaking it up! They just let them fight it out right there on the floor in front of everybody!

Then this guy next to me stood up on the bench and really started yelling and jumping! I thought he wanted to get a better look, but his eyes were closed and his fists were flying everywhere like he wanted to hit somebody!

I always wondered what all those people did in those churches. Boy, did I find out! One thing was very clear; church wasn't for me and that was the last straw for this kid! I bolted for the door like the wind! I never slowed down to open it either! It must have shaken the whole building when I left. But I didn't look back and I didn't slow down! I knew none of them city folks could ever catch me, but still I ran with all my might!

I was several blocks away when I stopped and looked back. Nobody was in sight, not even a car or that guy's van. I darted down a few alleys and headed for the river. Sure enough, when I reach the river, I knew where I was in town. As it turned out, I found myself less than a mile from Uncle Tim's place in town. So I headed there, spent the night, and they took me home the next day. I told everyone all about the foreigner's church and what they do in them places. They listened and agreed nobody should ever go there!

I've often wondered what that guy did when he couldn't find that kid he picked up so far out in the country! Or what the adults back home did when they discovered I was gone. He never showed up at our place again and nobody suspected he would.

PS. DON'T EVER GO TO A FOREIGN CHURCH! THEY ARE NUTS!

#30 Giving Little Jake a Ride! (Hillbilly Happiness)

It was the usual extremely hot summer day in the Ozarks. The blacktop roads got so hot you could actually fry an egg on them. The oil that makes up the tar in the asphalt road will start to bubble. It was common for us kids to ride our bikes on those hot roads because it put a coating of that tar on our already bald bike tires. I was riding my bike down the hill in front of the school to recoat my tires and also to enjoy all the coasting down that long hill. At the bottom of that hill in front of the school, and also in front of Little Jake's house, was a gravel road. This road provided plenty of gravel to land onto the blacktop. So here was the scenario; ride your bike up the hill to the top, turn around and ride back down, pumping like crazy to coast a long ways downhill. When you got to the gravel on the road, slam on the brakes to see how far you could slide in the loose gravel. Then turn around and repeat the process without hitting another rider doing the same thing. (Hillbilly Drama)

So while I'm doing this, my cousin, Little Jake, who was about 5 years old, wanted a ride. So I said sure, hop on! So Little Jake comes out and jumps on the handlebars. That was the normal and customary place to ride. And of course, he was wearing the normal shorts. With no shoes or socks or shirts of any kind. This was what most boys wore at that time. So I rode to the top of the hill and started back down. On the way back down, I really started peddling hard and fast. I wanted to give Little Jake a fast ride and I DID! When I got to the gravel, I slammed on the brakes, but I wasn't quite in the gravel yet, so I stopped almost instantly. That was bad for Little Jake! He immediately got launched off the handlebars and landed bellyflop down on the hot asphalt mixed with gravel! He did this magnificent rendition of belly surfing on the blacktop while his bent legs allowed his feet to keep pounding him on top of his head. His arms that were spread out in front of him provided him with plenty of gravel scooping, so his open mouth was not lacking for an abundance of pea gravel, dust, tar balls, and other things you might find on the road. Now when you have done such an amazing stunt as this, you clearly have all the bragging rights you want because nobody else had ever done that before or seen anything like it either. (Hillbilly Bragging Rights) Little Jake's older brother, Ben, was right next to me, also witnessing this amazing feat of belly surfing on the hot blacktop road. He hadn't ever seen anybody ever do that before either!

Now, as I said, several kids were out riding their bikes at the time of the event, and we all saw it. (Hillbilly Entertainment) It was a real miracle that no one ran over him! But we all did stop and stare and talk about how bad that must have hurt, or how hot the road was. Of course, there was plenty of talk about, "how he didn't do that right." And of course nobody moved a muscle toward getting him off the road. (Hillbilly First Responders)

I must admit, it was extremely funny to watch. (Hillbilly Compassion) We finally decided maybe we should see if he was still alive because he ain't moved since he stopped swallowing gravel. (Hillbilly Wisdom) So we went over and rolled him over. We couldn't prove he was breathing, but he was bleeding real good, so we knew his heart was beating! Ben and I tried to pick him up but we were laughing too hard to carry him. Finally we were able to pick him up and pack him over to the porch of his house.

We laid him down on the porch and commenced picking the gravel out of him. (Hillbilly First Aid) When his mom came out to see what all the noise was about, and she saw Hamburger Little Jake, she panicked and started screaming at us. (Hillbilly Nurse) She took him into the house and started doctoring him up, like all moms do when their kids get a couple of scratches, (as to the bone, and from top to bottom.) Meanwhile, we went back to riding our bikes. (Hillbilly Debriefing)

Little Jake was out of circulation for quite a while. Nothing was ever said to me about the incident. (Hillbilly Norm) When I did see Little Jake, he was all bandaged up like a mummy and moving real slow but we treated each other like always before. It was just another day in paradise. Paradise, Ozark style.

#31& #32 The Go Cart Stories

#1 The Goat Hill

In Missouri, when I was growing up, a go cart was anything that had wheels and was not motorized or pulled by something, such as a horse, mule, goat, family member, cat or dog. If it was pulled by something, then it was considered a buggy. If it was motorized, it was a contraption of some sorts. A wagon was something you pulled and usually hauled stuff in. A cart was something you generally pushed, such as a grocery cart.

Being the creative and ambitious boys that we were, it wasn't long before walking wasn't getting us there fast enough. Most of us had horses. But horses and fast cars on the same road is a bad combination. Farmers get mad when you start cutting their fences to get through! And most of us had more than our share of cuts and bruises from riding the half-wild and half-stubborn beast we called transportation.

So the only solution for those of us who weren't old enough to "borrow" somebody's truck or smart enough to get a license, was to create, build and modify some of the most mind-bendin', chicken-killin', death-defyin' heart-stoppin', indescribable go-carts anybody ever saw. And needless to say, we succeeded in doing just that!

Looking back, I am quite certain we provided several guardian angels with combat pay and early retirement. But if any of us boys survived a genuine hillbilly master-minded go cart experience, it's truly a trophy of God's grace and mercy. I suspect some of those angels still talk about "do you remember when….." Here are just two examples.

STORIES

#1 One particular go cart consisted of three misfit 2x4's, four misfit lawn mower wheels, and a jump rope. Add to that mix two misfit hillbilly boys looking for something to and you've got a recipe for disaster. And sure enough it came.

You take the first 2x4 and put a lawn mower wheel on each end of it by driving enough rusty nails through the center of the wheel so that it won't come off the end of the 2x4. Then you repeat that again with the second 2x4. Don't pay any attention to the fact that none of the wheels match, or none of the 2x4's match. Just do it because you're not going to be walking. Then connect the two together with the third board, driving lots of nails into the back board so it won't pivot. You only put ONE very big nail in the front board, making sure to bend it over underneath. You want it to turn. Then you tie the jump rope to each end of the front board for steering, although you're actually going to be steering with your feet and using the rope for holding on when you hit a hole or a rock.

Then the next obvious thing was to find the biggest and longest hill in town. That would be the goat hill! Yes! The infamous goat hill! That road was built back in the heyday of the model "A" cars. It was so steep you couldn't keep gravel on it, so the county paved it. The newer cars couldn't climb the goat hill so a bypass road was built that switched back and forth up the hill. But EVERYBODY took the straight DOWN road when leaving the goat hill, usually with all the kids screaming in excitement and all the adults shouting in fear; the brakes screeching metal to metal.

My cousin and I took our newly made go cart and tried it out in front of Granny's house, which was at the very top of the goat hill. It worked good there but it made a loud squeaky sound as it rolled along.

Well, the bully of the hill, Justin's older brother, Smittee, heard us and came out to see what the noise was all about. He decided he wanted our go cart and took it from us. We waited till he was in the house for a while before we quietly went into the yard and picked up our go-cart and packed it out as fast and quietly as we could. But just as we got to the road, we heard the screen door slam and looked to see "Smittee" coming out of the house at full speed! So we made our fast, and almost fatal, get away!

We threw the go cart down, Justin jumped on it, and I started pushing and running from behind. When I couldn't run any faster, I jumped on. I stood on the rear 2x4, leaning over and hanging on to Justin's shoulders by way of his bib overalls.

We were at the top of the goat hill and already moving faster than anybody could ever run. Not even a dog could have caught us, and a chicken could not have escaped us. In only seconds, we were going so fast our bib-overalls were pressed hard and tight against us. The pointed tips of our collars on our shirts were making sore spots on our faces from flapping so fast and hard. Our eyes felt like they were being inflated. Then it got scary.

That squeaky noise had become a loud shrill "death-like" scream. Then the front 2x4 exploded into the ground! Right away the whole thing flipped over and exploded and we both went flying and tumbling with all these boards and nails and ropes and wheels and rocks and blood and screams and lots of new sounds we never heard before and never wanted to hear again. Sounds like boards grinding and cracking, and voices yelling, sounds like hail stones in a storm, and bullets zinging past, and moans and groan of the deepest despair! Then we discovered those moans and groans were ours! The whole world was in a big blender of light and cartwheels, belly flops and back flips, body slams and sounds of banging gravel, smells of dust and sweat, mixed with ouches and more ouches and confusions! All of which you have no control over what-so-ever! But you're going to pay for them later in payments of hurts and pains and scabs and bandages and regrets and moans and sleepless nights, just to name a few of the minor things.

After what seemed like forever, everything came to a stop. We were at the bottom of the goat hill approximately 1/4 mile from the top. We looked like two gingerbread boys, made out of pizzas with a few shreds of bib overalls laying on it. The road looked like a bomb had gone off and we looked like we had either fallen out of the sky from a tornado or blew out of the ground from an earthquake!

I was already starting to hurt in places I didn't know existed. I looked around, expecting Justin to be dead. But, if he were dead, he was doing a good job of acting like he wasn't, because he was starting to get up. I managed to get up and tried standing for a while. It takes a lot of standing still after such an experience. Your balance has to come back, the world has to stop spinning, your vision has to come back, your brain has to start sorting things out again, and you have to start testing your arms and legs to see if they will work again. Then you have to see if anything needs medical attention. The last thing you want is somebody asking you questions, because you don't know any answers yet.

It really hurt and everything was still spinning. Everything seemed to be working, but nothing wanted to. It was all working against its will. We managed to convince ourselves we were all right, but neither one of us believed it. The definition of all right is relative. In the hard life of the Ozarks it means, "Will I live long enough to get revenge on my relatives?" Since both of us were still alive and able to leave the scene of the crime, then we were "all right."

To most folks in the real world, this would have been a bad experience. But for any hardcore hillbilly in the hard life of the Ozarks, it was just another day in paradise. Just business as usual. While we were mending, we began to make plans to build a better go cart! Which leads us to story number two!

#2 The Manure Spreader

One beautiful summer day, right after we had moved into a new house ($200 per month, 200 acres of pasture, swimming holes, and complete with outbuildings and barn), I went exploring. It wasn't a new house; it was just new to us. We didn't own it; we were renting it and the 200 acres of pasture that went with it. The house was actually very old but it was also very modern, for it had electricity and running water. It also still had the old well along with the hand operated pump that we were VERY accustomed to. There are many great stories that came out of that house. This is just one of them.

As I was saying, I had gone exploring the 200 acres that went with the house which included a giant-sized barn that was in great condition. There was also a smaller building, perhaps 15 ft. square, that had no floor, but the walls and roof were in excellent shape. The foundation was stone. It was obvious the missing floor was intentional, for there were no mortise joints or sleeper notches for a floor of any kind. This building construction made no sense to me, but I converted it into a tool shed and spent a lot of time in it, building and fixing many a mastermind project. There was a garage beside the house, but if I made "anything "out

STORIES

there, Dad would see it. That meant he would put a stop to my many inventions. This out-of-the-way shed was ideal.

I discovered there was an old horse-drawn manure spreader rotting away in the tall weeds in the pasture behind the house, which set my mind into high gear as to what I could possibly do with all the hardware from it. The best solution, of course, was to make me a go cart!

Without getting anyone's guidance or approval, I started my self-appointed masterminded go cart project. After removing the wheels and running gear hardware from the manure spreader, I hauled it all up to the barn for my next phase of self-destruction; I mean construction! The front wheels of a manure spreader are half the height of the rear wheels. These wheels were 100 percent, cast iron metal. They had small hubs and more than enough round metal spokes. The rims were about three inches wide with a smooth finish. Most manure spreaders had metal cleats on the wheels for traction, but these had none. Since the metal rims were wide, and the spokes connected in the center of the rim, it made a spinning, cutting edge as the wheels turned. All four wheels were made the same. The front wheels were about 2 ft tall. The rear wheels were about 4 ft tall. And so I began my master-minded project. This was going to be the beginning of how all go carts in the future would be made. I used railroad ties for timber, a logging chain for steering, and a metal tractor seat to keep me from falling off. I also used my feet for steering and holding me in place. I thought it a good idea to put stopping blocks on the front axle to keep it from pivoting so far as to pinch my legs off or getting locked in place from making too sharp of a turn.

In the end, I discovered it was wider than it was long. This worked out great, because if I started sliding sideways, it would be harder to tip over. The go cart was as wide as a normal car and its steel wheels fit right into the ruts of the road. This was also a great improvement. I found the large wheels would run over anything without getting jammed stopped. Jammed stopped meant everything comes to an instant stop except you. If you have ever seen a dog run full speed and come to the end of his rope, then you get the idea why jammed stopped on a go cart was not good, particularly if you had the steering rope wrapped around your wrist a few times. I will not elaborate on how I happen to have known this.

So with all these new and improved ideas, there was still one thing go carts didn't have.! BRAKES! We all wanted them but nobody had them, (except once, But THAT won't happen again!). It was always important to be ready to bail off those things when the impact was going to be worse than road rash.

This new improved go cart rolled so easy and fast it was scary. I mean scary. A tiny push would coast a loooooong ways. Also, it was rather heavy. A normal go cart made out of 2x4's and lawnmower wheels would self-destruct if you hit something. This was painful to the victims riding it but extremely entertaining to the onlookers, who somehow found it funny to watch you bounce off the road like a skipping rock in the pond. But this dinosaur version crashed right through gates, barbed wire fences, split rail fences, and closed doors. No self-incriminating explanation needed. Warning! Before you coast down a hill with no brakes, ALWAYS look ahead to see if there is a closed gate, ditch, tree, wrecked car neighbor's tractor, etc., waiting for you at the bottom. You can duck your head, grit your teeth, close your eyes, and say to yourself "This is really going to hurt," once. People who do not put hooks, wires, studs, nails, and other sharp objects in their face on

STORIES

purpose do not know what they are missing! They need a Missouri go cart to be really up to date.

Somehow, word got around about my go cart. Everybody knew, feared, and wanted it, except my dad, who happened to notice the manure spreader was missing a few parts. His very biased opinion completely overlooked my sister and suspected me! So one day when coming home from school, my hidden go cart was not hidden any more. It was sitting in the yard. My dad was standing on the porch and did not look like a happy camper. My sisters scattered in all directions. The dog didn't even show up with his normal barking and running around under your feet. My dad believed in the laying on of hands, but it had nothing to do with church!

I will skip all these unnecessary details that I'm sure nobody wants to read about. and get to the conclusion of that tiny little meeting with me and Dad. The go cart had to go or there was going to be another tiny little meeting with me and Dad. My dad wore a wide, black leather belt that he could whip out faster than you could say, "I didn't do it." I was given the instruction the go cart had to go. There was somebody at school who wanted it really bad and they were the only ones close enough to give it to, for I knew I would have to walk and pull it to take it anywhere.

The next morning was Saturday. That meant I had the whole day to deliver it. They lived several miles away. I could take it there by staying on the road but coming back I could cut through the woods. So early in the morning I started out with my go cart in tow. I had gone about halfway, when my cousins, Justin and Slim, came by in their car. They stopped and visited a while and then they decided to push the go cart with their car while I could stay on it and steer. They were driving this little, tiny car called a Triumph. It was much smaller than a Volkswagen and it was a convertible too! It was also as smooth as an onion.

So we sized it up. Justin pulled his car up behind the go cart, and we discovered it had about 6 inches of free space on each side. So I got on the go cart and they got in their Triumph and off we went.

If you know anything about hillbilly driving, you know there is only one way to do it. Full speed or nothing. I was going faster than I had ever gone on this go cart. That little car could fly! Then something happened! There was this terrible sound like a jet roars when it takes off. Justin stomped on the brakes but I couldn't stop. I made the mistake of looking back while flying forward.

The front fenders of Justin's car looked like a water buffalo. Apparently we had gotten off center and the wide metal rims were cutting into the fenders. Then the spokes hit the cut metal and rolled it up like a tuna can. This had happened to both sides! Meanwhile I had missed the road and went down into the ditch, somehow missing the mailboxes and the road sign. Then I came back up in the road, still going like 50 mph plus. An oncoming car was coming around the bend as I "got air" coming back up the bank and onto the road. The look on that guy's face was amazing. Then he passed Justin and his water buffalo car! He had swerved to miss me and then he swerved to miss Justin. That guy was driving crazy! He should get off the road!

I eventually coasted to a stop but it took a while. Then Justin showed up and wanted to make sure everybody was okay after my scenic ride through the brush. When we examined the new custom body work to his car, he wasn't impressed with it, but thought it looked really cool.

STORIES

    This is when it got really ugly. Slim said, "Let me sit on the hood of the car with my feet on the go cart. Then I can keep the two apart." Nobody thought about the car being as smooth as an onion except for the fenders that now stuck out about a foot on each side. So Slim gets on the hood and placed his feet firmly on the back of the go cart. Then Justin takes off like everybody in the Ozarks does. We're going fast and faster and fastest! But there is another turn in the road! Justin knew if he slowed down, I could not. That would leave Slim hanging out in space with nothing to keep him from falling under the car. So Justin does the only right thing he could do at the time. He instantly dynamites the brakes as hard as he could. That got me away from the car and safe from grinding Slim up in my rear wheels. It also stopped the car as soon as possible before Slim went under it. As soon as the car stopped pushing, I knew what was going to happen to Slim. The go cart was holding him up! When Justin hit the brakes, it launched Slim off the hood like an airplane off an aircraft carrier. Slim had laid back on the hood and was trying to get hold of something behind him. He had grabbed the windshield wipers and when he got launched off, he took the wipers with him. When I looked back, Slim was somehow suspended in the air in front of the car, leaning way backwards, taking these huge sliding steps on the pavement with his arms above his head, saying something. I had no idea what it was. Unfortunately, my turning around sent me on another adventure through the ditch, though the brush and small sapling trees, and again missing the mailboxes and barbed wire fence just a few feet to my right. I was able to come back up on the road again, and looked to see what had happened to Slim. Here he comes down the road doing this spinning-wheel/cannon ball/cartwheel thing. I ain't never seen that before! He had a wiper in each hand and was waving them like he was trying to fly. Picture a blurry, spinning ball of eyes, arms and legs, with two arms stuck out in each side, with a wiper blade in them, skipping like a rock on the pond, bouncing by as he passes you!.

I had come to a stop by then, and Justin had stopped way back up the road. When Slim came to a stop, we both though he was dead. He wasn't moving or groaning. This worried us a tiny bit. But after his world stopped spinning, he started moving. He did manage to stand up but couldn't walk in a straight line. He was hurting in places he didn't even have. His eyes were red and blurry. His clothes, or what was left of them, were in hanging shreds. His skin looked like pizza with an extra topping of gravel. His shoes were on his feet, but had no bottoms. Only his hair looked the same. Justin came racing up in the car, but Slim wouldn't talk for some strange reason. He still had the wiper blades in his hands, but probably didn't know it. He went limping and hobbling to the car. Finally, he said, "I'm going home." He fell into the car, and Justin took off back to town. I pulled my go cart out of the ditch and started pulling it down the road. A few more miles to go, and just another day in paradise. By the way, the go cart survived and handled beautifully.

#33 The Granny Story

This is another part of the story about Granny. I call her the last of the pioneer women. Her real name was Dora Agnus Wolfe Bryan.

Granny was a little short in stature. Her hair was white and silver and she always wore an apron. It is suspected that she had the entire Bible memorized. Ask her any question you wanted, and she would start quoting verses long before she opened her well-worn Bible to one of the quoted verses.

STORIES

She normally had several real-life illustrations to teach every verse she quoted. The outstanding and remarkable character about Granny was her amazing prayer life and faith. When Granny prayed, she touched God. Nobody knows how she did it, but she did it. It's one of those things that's hard to explain, but once you experienced it, you will never forget it. People came from everywhere to ask her to pray about something or to ask some deep and hard questions. I've never known her to be stumped on any of them.

When my dad's parents both died, Dad was on the street at 9 years old. Granny took him in and raised him up.

One day, in a conversation with someone, Dad and Buster overheard Granny say that she needed some flour. Both boys were about ten or eleven. So Dad and Buster left the house to get some, but didn't tell Granny. When they came back, they had a full sack of flour. Granny asked, "Where did you get that flour?" and was totally embarrassed when she found out. They had barrowed it, one cup at a time, from every home they could find, till the sack was full. The kids were out begging flour from strangers and kinfolk alike and she didn't know how she would ever return that flour. She laughed at the story as she told it, her eyes having that joyful sparkle when she recalled the event. She said that she couldn't spank 'em for it, but she sternly warned them never to do that again! Her words were, "There ain't no tellin' what everybody must have thought about their family sending their kids out to beg for flour."

Many years later, when my parents' marriage and life got broken up, I ended up on the street. I was thirteen. Granny took me in and did her best to raise me up. Like Dad, I didn't stay at Granny's place full time. My heart was carnal and my feet were longing to wander. Granny's godliness and spirit would always put me under conviction, and soon I was back on the street, under the bridges and alleyways, emptiness would drive me back to Granny's again. The cycle would repeat many times until one night the hound of heaven got on my trail and treed me for the last time. God started using the hardcore street life to break my hardcore spirit. It's amazing what God can use to bring us to the breaking point where he can use us. Granny was praying for me the whole time. There were several times that I should have been dead. For example, I was set up to be murdered and it was supposed to look like a hunting accident, But "somehow" I was delivered by some divine intervention and I miraculously escaped. I knew then that Granny was praying for me. There was no doubt that her prayers could find me in places where no feet could ever follow.

It was her family side, the Wolfe's, that raised the famous Missouri mules. They were a giant of a mule. To look at them you would think they were black as coal, but if you were close enough, you'd see that when they moved, the fold of hair was actually a deep blue that shone in the bright sun. Once we went out to see Granny's folks and we were looking at their mules. A big, tall guy picked me up and sat me on top of one of those mules. He was very tall, but he had to reach up to get me there. However, what struck me the most was when Dad went to the other side of the mule to center me, he barely stooped over and walked underneath the front flank. That was when I saw the blue shine of the hair and realized why they referred to them as blue mules when they looked so black.

Granny told me stories of her childhood that always fascinated me. I was always asking her about her past as "back then," or "when you were a kid." She was always happy to share her childhood memories with me and answer all my childhood questions.

She was born in May 25, 1888. She told me about traveling with her folks in a covered wagon. The girls would sleep under the wagon with their mom while her brothers and Dad would sleep "under the stars." This was done for protection and safety. Sometimes when they made camp for the night, they could see their last night's campsite. It was hard go'in for everyone. You had to leave late in the day to get the animals fed and ready. Then you had to stop early for the same reason, except at night you also had to get the firewood, water, and meals fixed for the family as well. Breakfast and noon meals were normally hardtack and leftovers, such as boiled potatoes. If you had a milk cow, milk was a real treat. Stopping for people wasn't done unless it was a serious situation. But stopping for the livestock was normal.

I wish I could have written down all her stories, but I was just a kid myself, and writing things down wasn't even in my vocabulary.

Granny was head of the clan in the Bryan family. That meant she was the family judge, and final say so in any matters brought to her, or any matters she thought she needed to get involved with. In her case she was also the family doctor, mediator, and preacher. She delivered the babies, buried the dead, and doctored them up in between. She was a very remarkable woman.

#34 Clans at War!

Granny was totally fearless. It didn't matter who you were, what you did, how bad you were, or how mad you got, nothing intimidated her. She didn't use any theological words, but her simple faith was stronger than all the darkness. Her southern wisdom and holy boldness always went straight to the heart. There was never any criticism of any kind. But the spirit of Christ poured forth is such a way that not even the atheist could deny her spirit but had to say, "that woman's got something to her that ain't nobody else got."

I saw her face down two opposing clans that were at war with each other (Brown's/Maples vs Longs). They killed each other, buried their own, held their own clan courts, and carried out their own punishments. it was the law of the land, and it was their land. There was nothing but hatred between them, but one thing they couldn't do was play doctor. When a real doctor was needed, they would send a couple of young kids to fetch Granny. These "kids," being under 10 years of age, in the darkest of night, could slip off their land, make their way to Granny's house and quietly knock on the screen door. They didn't look like they had ever seen a bathtub in their entire life. They had a wild look to them. They wouldn't enter any house or building whatsoever. But they would stand outside and ask Granny to come quick and bring your bag. (Her bag was a big, store-bought, almost briefcase-sized, calico carpet bag, used for everything medical or burying), and away she would go with these "kids" into the darkness, being led only by a lantern; the three silhouettes disappearing into the night. She usually came back before sunrise. She seldom talked about those trips or what she was needed for, but only spoke in kind and general terms concerning her journeys into the darkness.

I saw this happen several times. Granny somehow knew when they were coming and during the day she would say to me, "Go get my bag and put it by my chair." Then, just like clockwork, after darkness set in tight, there would be this quiet knocking on the screen door and a voice would say, "Granny could you come quick, and bring your bag?"

One particular day she had me get her bag as usual in the daytime and when darkness set in there came that quiet knock. As Granny was about to leave the house and go off into the night, she turned and ask me if I wanted to go along. I was very surprised of course but I said yes. That was a night I will never forget for the rest of my life.

We went together that night, the ancient wise sage and the young fool, following two half-wild kids by lantern into forbidden territory, under the cover of darkness. I clung to her apron like I was scared to death. There was a very good reason for that; I WAS! I must have been somewhere between 7-10 years old at the most. But I was about 110 years old when I got back. Granny made many more journeys into the night after that, but I never went a second time. I didn't ask and she didn't ask because she knew it was too much for me, even then.

We walked together down the lane by lantern until we came to the streetlights. At the end of the streetlights, we walked by moonlight and stars, following a dirt lane. I knew where we were up to that point. That lane took us to Moonshiner's Field.

It was called Moonshiner's Field because those warring clans both sold their moonshine there. Jars and jugs were set out in two groups. Each clan had their place to put their "sour mash." Anyone could take a jar or a jug of moonshine if they wanted to. But there was a place to put your dollars. I think it was $1 for a jar, $5 for a jug. They didn't care who came to buy, and they didn't care who you bought from. The pile was always watched by the sentries and if you tried leaving without paying, a bullet would stop you. Or at least that was the story we all heard, but I don't know of anyone who ever tried it, (at least not twice).

When we crossed Moonshiner's Field, I knew we were crossing the line where most people never came back from, even in the day. You could call the law, but they would not go beyond Moonshiner's Field. They said that it was private land and they had no jurisdiction there. But we all heard that too many law officers had gone back there and disappeared. Somehow nothing ever came of it back then. Now here were Granny and I being led under darkness across those very forbidden grounds. She had no fear at all, probably because I had enough for all of us.

When we came to the far edge of field, there was an opening into the timber. It wasn't very wide. You could see it in the day, but in the night you would never know it was there. As we entered the opening, a very loud, deep, raspy voice said, "Who goes there!" (It is possible to be about 7 years old and lose at least 10 years instantly.)

There was always a rumor that both clans had an armed sentry guarding the entrance to their land. I had heard that many times, but this was the first time I was ever close enough to actually witness it for real. He was clearly armed, and I had the impression he knew just how to use it.

Granny said, "It's me, Jed." (I really don't have any idea what his name was but I'm grabbing at one so whoever is reading this will make sense of it.)

He said to come on and as we passed him he stood up and lifted a big bucket, under which was a lantern sitting on the ground. The upside-down bucket had kept him in total darkness and at the same time kept him nice and warm because he was sitting on the bucket. When he lifted the bucket, we could see his face and his rifle. He used his lantern to light the lantern of the two "kids," and they used their lantern to lead us through the long winding trail that led to their main house.

Notice here, we approached the house on our left. The house was a shanty, with many an add-on, made up mostly of barn tin, tar paper, glassless windows with dark curtains hanging in them, and busted up screen doors. It was flat-roofed and extended in every direction except up. There was more than one stove pipe reaching up through the roof.

Outside it was dark, but when the big curtain that hung over the door was thrown back, it seemed like it flooded the whole yard with light. They had electricity, but no running water. I was surprised they had electricity. Some town folks still didn't have electricity, but this clan had plenty!

As we entered the house, just to the right, and next to the door were more rifles than I had ever seen in my whole life. They were all standing up, leaning in the corner. There were so many of them, perhaps a hundred or more, that they reached the door and down the other wall. They all shined like they were new or well taken care of. I knew some of them were muzzle loaders.

To the right of the first room was a solid wall of people and faces of every size, age, gender, and mentality. All the he-males wore bib overalls. Most wore black leather boots. Some had tee-shirts, some didn't, and all the she-males wore dresses of every color and size. Some had shoes and some didn't, but, NOT ONE OF THEM HAD EVER TAKEN A BATH! Their faces were streaked with sweat lines. They had mud necklaces and plastered hair and their clothes were filthy and mud-smeared. All of them had empty eyes and carried an atmosphere of emptiness. Some were weeping and the tears made even more streaks. (You can't tell me that God wasn't looking on at that scene, or that his heart wasn't breaking wide open!)

Granny made her way through the open path that was made just for her. At the end of that path stood a table. Without saying a word, she went straight to the table. All those people were there, but there was a single plate sitting on that table. The table was SPOTLESS and had a tablecloth too! The plate had some food on it and there was a glass of water. She sat right down and started eating! The head of their clan was in the room also and he sat down on the floor, but at the head of the table. Nothing was said while she ate. I knew that if she didn't eat that food, it meant she was rejecting them and they would be offended beyond measure.

After she ate her silent meal, she reached over into her doctor's bag and pulled out her Bible. I don't remember what book or verse she read, but whatever it was, it set the whole bunch to wailing and crying. I could tell by the way she was reading that she was getting mad. It wasn't long before she stood up and pointed her ancient finger at them and started telling them off! My thoughts were ...so this is how we die!

She knew every one of them by name and she pointed her finger in their face, and said, "I know you, (first name, middle name)! You've been (naming explicit actions in exact details) and you are going to hell for what you did! You thought nobody knew! But now everybody knows it! You're a (insert content: such as thief, liar, pervert, drunkard etc.) and God's word says that all (repeat content) are going to hell!" Then, she would step back, look at that person with eyes overflowing with love and tears, and move on to the next one. And down the line she would go! She didn't address everyone in the group, but only those whom she was led to confront. When I said Granny was fearless, I really meant it! She wore herself out. She sat down in the kitchen chair and took to breathing and wiping sweat. The head of clan, still sitting on the floor, pulled his knees up to his chest and started rocking back and forth on his haunches, wailing and crying like he was gonna die right there. All the while, tears were making mud streaks down his face. I thought we were as sure as dead. Granny turned around in her chair and faced the head of clan, pointed her finger at him and said, "(First Name), you're a liar. Just look at what your bunch is a doin'! He would cry out, "I'm sorry Granny. I'll change!" Granny said, "You're a-lyin' to me again! You said that last time, but you didn't change. Don't say that if you don't mean it (first name). You know all about it, and so do I. I also know you're setting the example by letting it go by. But your fate in hell will be much worse for your leading the way. Now look at them young'ens!" He looked up but I don't know if he saw anything. "Which one do you want to see in hell, (insert first name)? They love you, and follow you like little sheep. And you're leading them to hell." The wailing that busted out from the whole bunch at the same time was deafening! But Granny didn't stop to bother with any of their emotional outbursts. She was pouring it on. She finally began to settle down and sat in the chair again. After a few minutes of breathing and wiping sweat, without saying anything to anyone, she began to pray out loud. I couldn't hear what she was saying with all the wailing going on, but they obviously could hear very well. Whatever it was, it was powerful. In the reading over of this event, it sounds like Granny was yelling or mad; but she wasn't. I don't know how to relate the pure love that came from her heart to these people she loved so much. Even her accusations were spoken in brokenness. She loved them beyond anything she said or they did.

After a few minutes she was done and things quieted down. As she got up, she said, "We got business to take care of." The head of clan got off the floor and headed for a small door with a curtain hanging over it from the other side. Granny followed with her bag. I stayed by the chair where Granny had been sitting. No one spoke to me, and I didn't speak to no one. We all just stood there looking each other over real good. With not a sound in the room, it was awkward. Even from the back of the house where Granny had gone, there was no sound. After what seemed like many weeks had passed, Granny came back with the head of clan. They both looked very somber. What ever happened back there was serious stuff. It didn't look good.

There was some small talk between them and soon Granny said goodbye. The wall of people parted and we went to the door. The same two kids were waiting for us outside the door, but when they led us out, they went straight ahead! Now I knew we came in from the right, so why were we going straight out? Again we followed them through the dark night down the winding trail. We came to a sentry who was very much aware of our presence. He thanked Granny for coming and said, "We can't take you any further." Granny said, "I know, (first name)." The kids fell back behind us as we walked along in the open areas between the two warring clans. We didn't get very far when a voice just as raspy and just as deep as our first encounter said, "Who goes there?"

Granny: It's me (first name).

Voice: We've been a lookin' fer ya, Granny.

Now I trust the reader will understand me when I say the events of the second clan were almost identical in every way as the first clan. And when I say identical, I mean identical. Even some of the names were the same. And I suspect some of their sins were identical as well.

Same type of house, same corner of rifles, same dirty faces, same table and single plate. Same fearless and fiery preacher Granny. The same wailing and crying. Same medical bag. Same three weeks of standing by the chair.

But this time, when we departed, we went to the left. So I knew we were going in the direction of home. The kids led us to the last sentry, but they could go no further. Granny and I walked alone across Moonshiner's Field toward the lane that would lead us to the road that would take us home.

There were many injuries, gunshot wounds, stabbings, births and deaths back in the clans' territory. Granny was called up frequently when things got out of control but she only took me with her once. That was more than enough for me!

#35 Too Old

From as far back as I can remember, Granny was 88 years old; even in our vintage family photos, Granny was ancient. I asked her one day why she stayed at 88. She said she has had so many birthdays, she lost count, but she did remember one that was 88. So she decided to stay with one she knew.

I asked her what it was like being old and she said she wouldn't wish that on her worst enemy. Her folks were both gone, all her sisters and brothers were all gone and most of her kids were gone. Everything she knew as home or family is long gone. She said that being homesick for home is like missing another world.

Men aren't men anymore. She couldn't remember the last time she saw a real man, and she felt that women weren't women anymore. They didn't know how to be a lady or what that's even like. Kids are just monsters. She was sick of this world and everything in it. She felt that getting old was a curse, and she wouldn't wish it on anybody.

#36 Landing on the Moon

One summer night, Granny and I watched as the television showed astronauts landing on the moon. I asked her, "What do you think of that, Granny?" She said, "I don't believe it. I've seen the automobile come, electricity come, I've seen the phone come, I've seen a lot of things change in this old and wicked world. But I do not believe they landed on the moon. I think they are in Hollywood or on some island somewhere, but I don't believe they are on the moon. She never was convinced that they really had landed there.

There were many nights spent at Granny's house. She would read her Bible to me and help me to understand it. I sat on the floor and rubbed her feet as I listened to every word. I went to Granny with all my hard questions. She would say, "Well, let's see what God has to say about it," and start reaching for her Bible. As she reached, she would start quoting scripture and by the time she had her Bible open to the verse, she had already quoted it. Then we would talk about it at length. There was absolutely nothing that could not be asked, and she always had her answers straight from her Bible.

I've considered sitting at Granny's feet the place where I learned to pray. If I would be willing to ask, she would gladly answer. I didn't always understand her answers, nor did I always like them, but she was always faithful to answer me in a straight-forward way, with never any criticism or condemnation. What a wonderful way to learn to pray.

#37 Granny's Threshold

I've shared bits and pieces of my past with others and almost always I'm met with disbelief. I understand that Granny had a threshold. She had seen things in her world change. But when those changes became too great, she struggled with accepting them. I know my experiences are beyond what most people can understand, and I know they also struggle to accept them. I don't fault anyone for questioning my stories; I know they are not your usual nighttime stories. I've learned how Granny must have felt when she longed for a home where everything was "normal" again. Yet I cannot change the past or the people in it. I've been ridiculed and ostracized and called various names of interesting content. I have also been outright rejected and attacked by others.

The greatest skeptics have been the church people. Those were the very ones I thought would have understood and rejoiced with me. I thought they would have been encouraged by it only to find out that I was asking them to step into another world they just could not accept. It's just to "different" for them to accept. But <u>I have to leave them with the Lord and keep pressing for the kingdom.</u>

I've also found a lot of God's people who see beyond the here and now (perhaps they have read the New Testament!). They have understood the types of battles I have faced and have proven to be a tremendous encouragement. Praise God for His people! The body of Christ has many parts and thankfully we are not all the same. Each of us has our area of influence and our different ministries, and sometimes, like Paul and Barnabas, they may not always agree. But they continue to love and encourage one another.

I have a lot of wonderful memories about Granny. Her life was an amazing example of how the early Christians must have lived. Her walk with God, her faith, and her fearlessness were all so remarkable that they left an example for me to follow. I've met a lot of good and godly people, but, so far, I've never met another Granny. She is in heaven today and has been there for several years. But one day I will meet her again and she will know her prayers have been answered! The testimony will be the unchanging story of God's love reaching into the darkness of men's lives and drawing them into the light.

#38 Ginger the Monkey

Granny had such a soft heart for everybody and everything. If anyone were sick, they would go to Granny's. But it was also true that whenever anyone had a sick animal, they would drop it off at Granny's also. One day somebody showed up with a monkey that had a severe ear infection. They said it was a spider monkey, so named because of its long arms, legs and tail. When they brought it, one side of its head was covered in dried mucus. Its ear was packed with it. And, it had an attitude of: Do not touch me or I will bite you! It would show its teeth and make this screeching sound while charging at you and acting like it was gonna bite you. Everyone left it alone except Granny.

They brought the monkey to Granny and set it down in her lap. The monkey laid down on Granny's lap and hugged her, no teeth showing, no screeching, no running at you and stopping just before it got to where you used to be standing. Nothing like that. It just laid down on her lap, wrapped its long arms around her as far as they would go, and laid there quietly looking around.

It smelled awful. Granny petted it gently, avoiding the head. Finally she said, "Bring me my bag." She took out some peroxide and began to put drops on the ear and wait. After a while, she would use toilet paper to absorb the peroxide back up. She repeated the process for hours. The monkey would reach up and wrap its little hand around her finger. When it let go, Granny would continue. I saw the sparkle in her eyes and I knew she was having a ball. We were too scared to get close to the thing! After a very long while, the ear was cleaned up. Then she started the process on its little head. She had us fetch her some warm soapy water and a wash rag. The monkey never seemed to mind. Even when Granny got deep in its ear, the monkey would squeeze her finger, and Granny would stop. Finally, it fell asleep on Granny's lap. The person who had brought it also brought some bananas. They gave the monkey and the bananas to Granny and left.

Later that night, Granny put more peroxide in the monkey's ear; just a drop or two. When she turned its little head over so that the ear could drain, the STUFF that came out of that monkey's ear was BAD. It smelled up the whole house. She repeated the process several times and each time more junk would come out. The monkey was wide awake the whole time. Each day this was repeated until there was no more junk coming out. Granny got some ear drops out of her bag and I asked, "if that's people medicine, will it work on monkeys?" Granny said, "Yes." Then she put a few drops in the ear and left it. The monkey got better every day, but there were a few problems. Nobody could get close to Granny or that monkey would show its teeth and screech at you. Even if it was across the room, if you got close to

Granny, here came Ginger, screeching and running to the rescue. Granny thought that was the funniest thing to see. She laughed all over after having been "rescued" by Ginger.

A day or two later, Granny noticed the monkey hadn't gone to the bathroom since it got there. So Granny sent me for her bag. She would clap her hands once and that monkey was in her lap. It didn't matter where in the house it was, if Granny clapped her hands, that goofy monkey would come running. Usually it ran with its hands raised straight up, running upright like a person, and screeching. As soon as it came through the door, it would make this actual flying leap, and land right in Granny's lap. Us kids joked and said, "You called, master?"

She took some medicine out of her bag and put some on her finger before inserting it into the monkey's mouth. I was shocked! This was the day we saw Granny about to lose her finger! The monkey didn't like it one bit. It turned its head away and stuck out its tongue. Granny said "Ginnnnnnger!" The monkey looked down and then, after a short wait, started licking her finger for the rest of the medicine.

I don't know what the medicine was Granny gave it, but she should have done it outside. The monkey went outside a lot and climbed on everything and we could never get it to come down, no matter what we did. Banana bribes didn't work if you were outside. Granny was concerned as the monkey had hightailed it to the top of a tree and would not come down. Then she said, "I know." She went back inside, sat in her favorite rocker, and clapped her hands. That monkey leaped from the very top of the tree, landed in a roll, and came up running for the door, like it was nothing!

STORIES

Granny then said that she'd better put a diaper on it. So she got this rag, cut a hole in it for the tail, and, as far as I know, was the first to ever diaper a monkey. Ginger didn't seem to mind at all and it wasn't 5 minutes before there was this smell. It was BAD. What is that? Everyone looked at Ginger, Ginger looked at Granny, and Granny started laughing. She said, "Well, we didn't put that on her anytime too soon!" Now a diaper change was in progress. Ginger always wore diapers after that. Granny also found a little child's dress and put that on Ginger also. Several of us kids almost lost a lung laughing at how funny that looked. And again, Ginger didn't mind and it certainly didn't slow her down one bit!

When Ginger ran, she would jump from her feet from a sitting position, leaping forward a great distance. But instead of landing on its feet, it would land on its hands. Then it would launch forward again using its arms. Then land back on its feet, repeating the cycle. Feet, hands, feet, hands. Us boys discovered that even if we rode a bicycle on flat ground, we could not outrun Ginger!

There were always dogs running around the neighborhood at Granny's house. One day this big mangy dog shows up and sees Ginger. The dog was about the size of a full-grown German shepherd. It must not have liked Ginger because it came running full speed after her. Ginger ran for the house and we ran after the dog. The dog got away, and the monkey made it to the house in plenty of time, but we worried that one day. . .

Then one day it happened. That same dog kept coming back to get Ginger, hiding outside the door and waiting. Sure enough, one day we were all outside and didn't see the big mangy dog lying under the hedges. The monkey came out the door and was heading for its favorite tree, a small Chinese elm about 20ft tall that stood in the yard. When the dog lunged, Ginger saw it. The monkey jumped on the dog's back and started biting it furiously. It all happened in a split second. The dog rolled over to get rid of the monkey, so Ginger jumped off. Then the dog came back up and Ginger was back on the dog's back Incredibly fast, resuming the biting. This happened several times. Finally the very bloody dog takes off running and yelping, but it was too late to get away. That dog had chased Ginger several times before and now she was mad and it was time to teach the dog a lesson. They were both almost out of sight when Ginger finally jumped off. The dog kept running and yelping until we could not hear it anymore. Soon we saw Ginger running like the wind to get back home. Her doll dress was a-waving and the diaper was gone, but here she came! Needless to say, she got a hero's welcome! No dog EVER came around Granny's house again. Apparently, they had all been watching! I suppose bad news travels fast in dog circles!

Granny's house had every wall covered in shelves or hanging items on the wall. She had started collecting trinkets as a young girl. When people found out, the trinkets came in from every direction. Some sat on shelves, some hung on walls. The front room walls were entirely covered with hanging pictures and other items. There were many clocks. One day we were playing with Ginger. She had long since gotten used to us, and we all loved that little monkey. Ginger even started sharing Granny with us. It was not unusual to see someone coming through the house with a monkey on their head or giving a piggyback ride. It was a lot of fun. On this day we were playing with Ginger as usual. Something happened, I don't remember what, but it scared Ginger. We were in the front room and this spider monkey starts running in circles around the room. But she was doing it ON THE WALLS! She was moving like a fast wind. I think centrifugal force was keeping her up. She went faster and faster and higher and higher! Now she is circling the room, on the walls next to the ceiling, and not one thing got knocked off the walls or even touched! This monkey was amazing. Then, instantly, she stopped. She was at the ceiling in the corner of the room, somehow just wedged there with her back to the wall and her little arms and legs spread out and pressed against the wall. How could she do that? We were spellbound by it. But try as we might, she would not come down. Granny heard the commotion and knew something was wrong. All the time Ginger was tearing around the walls, she was screeching her, "I'm afraid" sound of screech. We had learned her different types of screeches. So Granny came into the room and wants to know what happened. We pointed to Ginger, still hanging in the air in the corner. Then Ginger got scared again and took off. She couldn't run into the other rooms like she usually does, so she circled the room, on the walls, and stopped up there! So, Granny clapped her hands, and Ginger leaped from her lofty height, landing in Granny's arms, looking at us and showing her teeth. Whatever we had done, Ginger did not like it. After a while she calmed down, but she would not play with any of us. We never did find out what we did that set her off.

Ginger was a big source of entertainment to everyone but she had started getting cranky and reclusive. Granny said that something was wrong. So arrangements were made to take Ginger to the vet. The day finally came to go, but no one was happy about it. We were all worried about Ginger. When they brought her back, we heard that the vet said she was nearing the end of her life and would eventually die. Ginger somehow knew all this. She did slow down a lot and was less interactive with everyone except Granny. Ginger spent most of her time resting in Granny's lap. One morning, Ginger was found cold and lifeless in her little baby bed next to Granny's. We all bawled and cried until we could not weep anymore. We all went in and said our goodbyes, and came out crushed. Somebody came and took Ginger away and buried her somewhere. I did not know where. Only Granny and the guy who took her away knew of the place.

Slowly the pain went away, but those happy memories never did. It was a surprise to everyone how attached we had become to a monkey. And yet the pain was very real.

We had placed our hearts on something that was almost human, full of character, very entertaining, and had a personality. But in the final conclusion, Ginger was a monkey placed into the role of a child. I think the lesson is very debatable, but there are certain areas where our affections should not go. Keeping things in God's perspective is always best. It's not wrong to like or appreciate the animal kingdom, but there is a line that should not be crossed. In these days of wickedness, you can go to prison for killing a pet, and yet walk away freely from murdering or giving away your child. Our days of innocence warned of misplaced priorities that one day would prevail all over America.

#39 James and Martha Saiders

James and Martha Saiders lived on a 40-acre farm just north of New Bloomfield, MO. He and his wife were from the old school of family values and personal integrity. You couldn't find a more righteous couple. They raised 21 kids altogether and I think I was number 22. Most of the kids they raised were not their own. Anybody in need was always a welcomed guest in their home. They had several kids that were theirs, (I think about 9) but they always had room for anyone else.

STORIES

They never lacked in happy faces around the table, or some of the best tasting home-cooked meals. Martha taught the girls how to cook and they did it very well. Of course, us boys were more than willing to eat up anything they cooked up. It was a working arrangement.

James raised kids with hard work and respect. Some of the happiest days of my youth were enjoying the privilege of staying with them.

James always did his farming using horses or by hand. Just before I arrived at their farm, James had gotten a small Farmall tractor to pull the horse drawn machinery and put the horse out to pasture. His boys were more than happy to let me ride and run the machinery while James pulled it along with the tractor. They had spent many a summer doing that very thing. Letting me do it was a happy day for them and me. I never got tired of it. And James loved doing things with the tractor. It was a win-win for all.

There were many chores to be done on a working farm, but everyone did their part and there was plenty of time for playing around; swimming, hunting, fishing, etc., etc... One of the chores was feeding the chickens. Since they raised their own corn, they also had to shuck it and shell it or chop it. I devised a method that worked very well for feeding the chickens. (Shucking corn is removing the outer leaves that wrap the corn. Shelling it is removing the corn kernels from the cob).

After I shucked it, I would take a machete and chop the corn, while still on the cob, into "checker-sized disks of about two or three rows of kernels. I did this very rapidly because it caused the corn to literally fly away as I chopped it, spreading corn everywhere. The chickens ate it right up and would peck at the cob disc for days. One day Martha said, "You'd better be careful, you get so close to your hand. Someday you're gonna cut your fingers right off!" I thought it was humorous the way she said it. But it wasn't long before I slammed a deep groove in my finger that went all the way to the bone! It really hurt, but I wasn't going to admit it. While she bandaged it up she gave me a good scolding for being so reckless, but I still chopped the corn the same way. However, I never got so close to my hand again!

James and Martha spent a lot of private time with me. We would sit on the porch swing that hung from a tree out in the yard. It was away from the house and allowed for some very private conversation. I told them my past; all of it. It broke their hearts and Martha would cry and shake her head, many times saying, "How could anybody…." They were very tender-hearted, and I was a hardened streetwise kid. They knew I was a fighter, but Martha said I was still tender inside but hurt has calloused over a hurting heart.

They knew I was as strong as an ox, but I tried never to show it. I deliberately kept that hidden because it always started trouble. I didn't look strong at all.

#40 Hauling Water

We didn't have running water on the farm, so we took a truck bed that was turned into a trailer, put four 55-gallon barrels in it, and pulled it with the tractor to the well that was a little distance away. It was an open, very deep, hand-dug well with a rock lining and rock rim about 3 ft. high around the top of it. A piece of plywood kept debris out of it. We would back the trailer up to the side of the well and stand with one foot on the trailer and the other on the side of the well. We kept a large bucket with a long rope tied to it at the well for filling up the barrels.

This was a chore Dug liked doing, so he usually did it. But one day James asked me to go fill up the barrels. As I was backing the trailer up to the side of the well, the trailer kept turning at the last minute. I wasn't very good at backing the trailer, and this was a good experience for me. Finally I was frustrated with it so I backed it up as close as I could and went behind the trailer, picking it up and moving it over to where it needed to be. No one was around, so I wasn't worried about being seen doing this. I didn't know that Dug had decided to secretly follow me to see how I did on my first water run. It must have made an impression on him because by the time I got back with the water, he had reported the whole matter to everyone.

When I got back, everyone was staring at me, but not saying anything. I wondered what was going on. Then James asked me how it went. I said that I wasn't very good at backing the trailer but managed to get it done. I did not say how I had done it. However, James said, "Dug saw you pick up the trailer and move it around. He came back telling everyone all about it, You didn't want people to know and I understand why, but here, I think you're safe." He was right. Nobody there wanted to pick fight with me before that, and nobody wanted to afterwards. I was safe again for a while.

#41 Frog Gigging at Frog Lake

Frog legs taste great if cooked right. At the back of James's property was a lake. Originally it was a strip mine, but a spring had burst through and filled it up. One end was very deep and scary, but the other end was very shallow for a good long way. The one end was so deep that nobody wanted to get in it and the shallow end had leaches, so we didn't want to swim in it either. But, besides the leaches, the shallow end had frogs, fish, and snakes in abundance. It was perfect for frog gigging. We did that a lot in the summer.

One night all the guys went frog gigging. We took the tractor and the hay wagon with us. Several of us rode on the hay wagon, while James drove the tractor. Just before we got to the lake, there was a wooded area that we had to pass through. Even though there was a tractor road through the woods, we couldn't take the tractor with us because of the hay wagon. It was just too wide. And once we broke out of the woods at the other end, there was no place to turn the wagon around. So we parked right at the edge of the wood, and started walking down the tractor road. The trees hung low over the road and would sometimes brush your hat off if you didn't watch out. We could see the moonlight at the other end of this wooded tunnel, so off we went.

We hadn't gone five steps when all of a sudden there was this hair-raising panther squall right over our heads! We had walked right under it not knowing it was there! Instantly all gigs went straight up! The flashlights came on and we were ready for a fight! The panther jumped from limb to limb in the thick wooded tunnel and the limbs would come swishing down from his weight. He stayed right in front of us so we never had to wonder where he was. His squalls had our hair standing straight up but the problem was that we couldn't see him. The woods were as black as coal and he was too! Plus, all the brush and limbs kept him well concealed. We knew to stay together, but not so close that we couldn't put up a fight. Any straggler was bait. So we made our way through the tunnel with this very large panther jumping around over our heads. One thing you have to say about country people; they've got guts!

STORIES

We continued our frog gigging journey but the weeds and grass in the open area around the lake were about waist high. We were all ready for this irate cat to come lunging out of the tall grass at any moment. I managed to stab James in the back of the leg with my frog gig before it was over. I can't tell you how terrible I felt over it, even though it was an accident. But that didn't help one bit.

When we had a gunny sack about half full of big frogs, we turned around and headed for the tunnel. We hadn't heard or seen anything of the panther after we got to the lake, so we thought he had moved on. But, was he waiting for us?

Sure enough, just before we entered the tunnel he cut loose with this big cat squall that left no question whether or not he was still there. And again, all gigs went up and all the flashlights came on. He was still in the trees jumping around, but he was much slower about it. I think he was looking for a straggler or a weak break in our line. But, needless to say, we stuck tighter than a cocoon the whole way back through. The panther didn't like it at all for he gave many an angry growl and long drawn-out squall. We weren't real impressed with him either. We made it through the tunnel the second time and was glad to be back at the tractor. But even in the open field we were not safe. That was one of the rare occasions we went frog gigging without a gun. You always take a gun with you when you go frog gigging, normally for snakes. Somehow we all thought somebody else had the gun but as it turned out, nobody did! We made it back home and enjoyed the frog legs that much more! Too bad they weren't panther legs!

#42 Escaped Prisoners

Every Friday there was a big auction at the auction house in the town of Fulton which was about 30 minutes away. It was James and Martha's favorite thing to do, going to the auction. So one night the adults went to the auction leaving us kids at home alone. Normally we sat around and watched T.V. while they were gone. That was movie night for us, with popcorn or some other treat. Friday night was the only time we watched T.V.

We would dogpile on the furniture, eat snacks, and take turns churning butter as we watched a movie. So here we were, watching TV, when a news bulletin came on relating the fact that several prisoners had escaped from the penitentiary. There was a dragnet going on and they were in the area of our farm! The news bulletin had said that they were armed and dangerous and to stay inside and call the police immediately if you see anything suspicious.

Now that had our attention! We had enough guns in the house to start a war. If anybody tried getting in, they would have to come through a wall of lead. So the movie came back on and we're all sitting around when I got the idea to shake things up. I left the room going towards the back of the house, but once in there I slipped out a window and went outside to the front door. The front door was made of a whole bunch of little windows. It was really a fancy screen door. There was a lacy curtain hanging on the inside. I started slowly moving the door handle while looking through the window. It was dark outside so no one could see me, but I could see them. Sure enough, they all saw it but didn't want to cause a panic. I saw them looking to one another and nodding towards the door, trying to act calm. They weren't grabbing the guns yet, so I thought I was safe.

I was still watching when suddenly, out of nowhere, this huge hand lays on my shoulder! I knew I was dead meat! No doubt about it! My guts sank like a rock! Then this very deep voice says, "What are you doing, Bob?" IT WAS JAMES! They had heard the bulletin and come straight home. I never heard them drive up, but they were surely there. I told James that I was scaring everybody, but my voice was still shaky and high pitched! All he said was, "Let's go inside." I really thought I was going to be in serious trouble, but actually, not much was said about it except how foolish it was. My respect for them was very high, so any rebuke I received went straight to my heart. I knew they were right. I never tried anything like that again. The next day we heard the prisoners were all captured so there was a big sense of relief. And yes, they were not far away when they were caught.

#43 The Football

Behind the house, across the fence and into the pasture, there were these giant metal towers that carried the "transmission line" for electrical power. These huge, behemoth towers were situated in such a way that the power lines dropped closest to the ground in the area behind the house. They were very high, but in our "kids" thinking, we thought it was cool to be so close to the wires.

As a pastime, Dug and I would go into the pasture and throw a football back and forth. One day we decided to see if we could reach the bottom cable of that power line. We had no idea that there were about 13 thousand volts flowing through that wire. We just wanted to reach it with a football, and we did! If we stood just below it and off to the side just a few steps, we could consistently get the football to go over it or hit it. If we hit it, then that was way cool! So, hitting the wire became the latest pastime. We spent a lot of time together in the field doing just that. We hit the wire about 1 throw out of 100, but that didn't matter to us. We just enjoyed doing it. Like all pastimes, that also tended to fade away as our interest moved on to other things.

Several years later it was brought to my attention how high ALL transmission lines were. I remembered how Dug and I used to throw a football over one. I was called several interesting names for telling that story which made me wonder if the lines were really that low, or were the wires behind our house just lower than most? I really didn't know. So, one day I returned to James's house and walked over to take a look at the wires. They were extremely high which raised some questions in my mind. I walked out into the pasture, picked up a rock, and made a valiant effort trying to reach the bottom wire but I only reached about a fourth of the way to the wire, hurting my arm in the attempt.

I sometimes wonder if people can do things outside of the norm simply because they have no idea they aren't supposed to be able to do that! I knew we had done it but I had no idea how we did it. I also knew I wasn't ever going to be able to do it again. Some things we may never know, so we just have to leave them behind and not get tangled up over it. We must keep going forward. People may not know what keeps us going, and sometimes it's none of their business, especially if they are full of criticism about it. They just don't need to know. We all have treasured memories and if others don't understand them, you may open yourself up to many hurtful accusations. I think it's because some people have never been there and asking them to step outside of their box is way too frightening for them, so they stay inside their box and throw stones at those on the outside. That may not be the wise thing to do, but I have found it be very common. So, keep pressing forward and bypass the sand traps. It isn't worth the battle, and you can't get them to look outside of their little world of safety.

#44 The Fight in the Corn Bin

Since we grew our own corn for food and feed, it was natural to harvest it and store it. We did all this by hand; about three acres worth. And when we were finished, we shoveled it into a corn bin. The bin was square, made of barn roof tin, and had a pitched roof and a single door opening to it. When the bin was full, we would sometimes climb into the bin, each of us toting a gallon-sized metal bucket. We would shell corn till our buckets were full and then us boys would throw the empty corn cobs at each other in fun play. One day things got a little out of hand when the corn cob throwing got a bit forceful, accompanied by a lot of challenging words. Since the pile of corn had a peaked center, we sat across from each other with the piled corn rising up between us. We could duck behind the peaked corn to avoid being hit by the flying cobs. So I started thinking (which usually got me in trouble). I had two empty cobs ready for flight but I also had a third cob that I had intentionally left about a fourth of the corn still on it. This gave it the ability to fly straight like an arrow and hit with a hard impact. So I threw the first empty cob with the intent of getting the victim to duck, which they did. Then I threw the loaded cob right after the first one, but with much more force! Sure enough, the victim ducked at the first one and raised back up just in time to "eat" the heavy loaded cob. Dead center! He came flying over the corn straight at me. I had awakened a sleeping bear! The fight was on! Needless to say, our gallon buckets went topsy-turvy and corn went everywhere.

After a while, when we both had cooled off, we made apologies to each other. Then the questions started coming. "How did you do that?" But there was a problem. If James found out about our fighting, we would be in big trouble. So we agreed to keep our mouths shut, and went to shelling corn fast and furious to make up for our lost time and lost corn. We climbed out of the corn bin like nothing had happened, and James never found out.

#45 The Bluff

There is a bluff that runs alongside of Rabbit City field and the creek. This bluff runs for a very long way. I never reached the far end of it, but the county road in front of our house is where the bluff started. If you left the fields and followed the creek, not far away was a dried waterfall that at one time came spilling over the bluff and into the creek. Now some waterfalls are seasonal, but this one I never found running in any season. There were signs that indicated it had been dry long before anyone came to the area. That raised many questions in my thinking. Where did the water come from? Why did it stop? The deep cuts in the rock wall of the bluff told me the waterfall had run for a very long time but the large trees that grew out of those ruts, told me the fall had been dry for a long time. Some of those ruts were deep but narrow. This gave me an idea of how to climb the bluff and follow that dry waterway. Where did it go? What secrets did it hide? So one day, I climbed one of those deep cut ruts by placing my feet on one side and walking with my hands on the other side of the deeply cut grooves. This turned out to be hard work. By the time I got to the top, I was in no condition to try to go back down. Once at the top of the rut, and almost to the top of the bluff, the thick layers of soil and rocks made it a challenge to keep going but there were some large tree roots further up. If I made it that far I was going to be on top of it, but at the last few feet, the rut widened and I was pressing against rock and sand and dirt. This made it very unsafe. I did make it to the top, but resolved to find another way up for this way was far too risky and too painful. I thought I was going to have rock indents in my hands forever! But, in reality, they eventually went away, as did the soreness. The dried and ancient creek bed was still there, but I could tell at one time it was much wider. I knew that in time it would all disappear. I followed the dried bed for some time. There were places where springs had at one time made their contributions to the waterway, but they too had dried up. Then things got very interesting indeed! The creek seemed to have been fed with the natural ground water runoff from the area on top of the bluff. No big mystery to that except, why did it stop running off? The waterfall was dry even when it rained. However, I discovered a much bigger mystery not 30 feet from the dry bed. As I traversed the areas on top of the bluff, I came to a place where there was large hole in the ground. It wasn't a sinkhole, but it was entirely out of place. A person could be standing right next to it and not see it, as was the case with me. What brought it to my attention was the path of a well-traveled trail. It was a very narrow trail that was very low, as if used by small game. This led me to wonder where all these critters were going. I noticed the path and followed it, only to discover it led me right back to the place I had just left. I had been standing right above the opening and did not know it. The little narrow trail that seemed to be a small animal trail took me right to the opening. The ground just in front of the opening slanted downward. It was solid rock and totally clean of any debris. It widened to about 3 ft. as it slanted downhill and led to a perfectly squared rock door opening. It was out of place for the rock to be void of debris from above or from the trail that was so well used. The opening was a little narrower than the slab and about 5ft high; everything about it was true squared. This was clearly a man-made opening or nature had me fooled. You could see the entryway was very short and the tunnel made a hard turn to the left. This appeared to me to be a natural barrier for forced entry. The entire scene looked as ancient as the dried waterfall. Even the moss that hung on the walls was dead and brittle to the touch. It seemed like no one had been through there in a very long time. But why was the rock slab so clear with so much dead moss hanging around it? Another mystery. I started to enter the opening when everything inside of me exploded in fear and caution. I backed away instantly and stood concealed in the ground brush that covered the area. I stood motionless for quite some time, watching and listening for anything inside or outside, but there was no indication as to why I had such a gut feeling of fear. While standing there I noticed there was no older growth anywhere around the opening. The waterfall had been dried up for many years and the trees growing at the top of it were sizable. But if this opening had anything to do with the water drying up, then the age of trees around it would have been the same. Also, if that much water had passed through it, there would have been erosion marks everywhere, but there were none. There was no visible connection between the dried creek bed and this unusual opening. After some time of riding shotgun on this place and seeing no sign of life, I crept very cautiously toward the opening. I could not feel any coolness coming out of the ground which made me think it had a dead end to it. I didn't see any tracks of any kind on the trail and wondered about the possibilities of what could be in there. But whatever it was I didn't want to find out. My gut feeling was still screaming at me to get out of there. I learned a long time ago never to ignore your gut feelings, so I left with no answers to the mystery. Though I returned to the top of the bluff many times afterwards, I avoided this dark and mysterious opening in the ground.

#46 The Blizzard

As sometimes happens during the start of the winter months, the weather has a way of playing games with the poor people who have to endure it. On this occasion winter came with a record-breaking blizzard all at once. It almost cost the lives of myself and James.

If you leave the homeplace by walking down the driveway, then turn right onto the graveled county road, continue down the hill about 300 yards to the wood-bottom bridge, cross the bridge, turn to the left and follow a path through the grass and volunteer saplings which is about 40 ft long to the creek, follow the creek downstream which empties out into a very large field that lies between the creek on the left, and a rising bluff on the right, traverse the field through the knee high grass which widens as you go, at the very far end, where the creek comes together at the base of the bluff, there stands what's left of an old three wired fence where they meet. This area is called Rabbit City due to the very prolific rabbits that always keep it well populated.

The creek most of the time was about waist deep in the shallow parts, and more than deep enough to dive in at other points. It ran between 30 ft to 100 ft wide, depending on where you were at, and the current was always fast. After a good rain, the creek turns a burnt orange color from the old alkali strip mine located upstream at the far end of James's property. This strip mine flooded when a large spring burst through the wall and turned the pit into a lake with machinery rusting away at the bottom of it.

It was approaching dinner time when I was sent out to get the meat for everyone's dinner. We boys took turns getting the meat for the family meals. The girls usually told us what they needed, and somebody would go get it. That request might be chickens out of the barnyard that volunteered to be the dinner, or at times squirrel was on the menu. This time it was rabbit. That meant Rabbit City was about to get a visitor. Since it was my turn to fetch the meat, that visitor was going to be me.

It was late in the fall and the air had a chilly bite to it. That's perfect for hunting. I took my 410 shotgun along with a big pocketful of shells. I chose a medium jacket because I assumed I would be returning very quickly. I had the usual rubber boots we all wore on the farm, no gloves, and a ballcap style hat. It only takes about 10 minutes to reach Rabbit City, add another 30 minutes of gathering rabbits, and another ten minutes to get back home. Yes, I'd be back in no time at all, or so I thought.

As I started down the hill toward the bridge, I encountered a very light sparkling of snow, almost an air frost. By the time I'd reached the bridge, it had become much worse and the air had become much colder. Visibility was still good, so I never anticipated the drama that was about to unfold. By the time I had entered Rabbit City, the ground was white. A fresh snow is prime time to hunt rabbits, so I thought this was going to be easy and fast. I was wrong. For some reason there were no rabbits to be seen anywhere. I knew if a hawk or other birds of prey flew over, the rabbits would disappear fast. I also knew they would return in a short while. But they never returned. As I walked father out into Rabbit City, the snow became very intense. It wasn't long until it became a full-blown white out. Visibility was down to about 20 ft at best. The wind had a strong push to it and walking became very difficult. The fresh snow packed to my feet like it was wet clay making every step a sideways slide. Every clump of grass was bent low with snow and had to be stepped over. My world became a small circle of white that was empty of any recognizable character. I thought about following my tracks back to the road, but there were no tracks because the onslaught of snow was covering them up as fast as I made them. I knew the creek was to my left when I had come in, and the wind was to my back. But now the wind was turning from everywhere. I turned toward the creek and discovered it was bridged over with snow anywhere there was even a hint of brush. The open places of the creek showed frigid, dark, and fast-moving, churning water which made walking anywhere near the creek extremely dangerous. One step into what was thought to be solid ground could send a victim falling into a freezing world of dark and fast-running water. I backed away from the creek and started making my way to what I thought to be toward the road. By now I was soaked around the shoulders and up to my knees. I hadn't started shaking yet, but I knew it wasn't very far away.

When I came to a place I recognized, it was the first time I had any bearing as to where I was since I had left the road at least half hour ago. I knew that I was just downstream from where a log had fallen across the creek and provided a shortcut towards home. So I carefully picked my way through the snow till I found the fallen log. It was covered in snow and I knew crossing it would be risky, but I was already in dire straits. It proved to be a bad decision, for as soon as I started onto the log, both my feet slipped out from underneath me, and down I went. I hit the log hard enough to knock the wind out of me, which dumped me into the freezing, churning waters. I remember going under and grabbing for something to stop my wild underwater ride downstream. I thought if I get to where the creek had bridged over, perhaps I be able to get out, but probably not. I did manage to grab something, that didn't move when I grabbed it. I think it was only a sapling, but it stopped my wild ride and, somehow, I was on the other side. I wasted no time in kicking and clawing my way up the bank to make my escape. Somehow I had managed to retain my shot gun. It wasn't until I was trying to climb out that I realized I still had it. I was glad to have made it out of the freezing creek on the right side, but now I had another problem far worse than before. I was soaking wet and freezing. The blizzard had limited my visibility down to about 20 ft and the wind was now howling. I had no idea how cold it was, but it was clearly a death sentence for me. I was now in an extremely large field, and far across it I knew was the road and the house. The snow was now anywhere from knee deep, to bare in places where the wind kept it blown away. I couldn't see very far, but by dead reckoning I set out in the right direction. However, after I had climbed out of the creek, my clothes immediately began to freeze. I lost feeling in my arms, hands, and legs and I had to cradle my gun in my arms because I couldn't hold it any longer. The wind blew me over very easily and I kept falling. I ended up crawling and pushing, dropping my gun. I knew I was going to die and had no fear of it. But the idea of giving up wasn't an option for me. Something inside said, "Fight back, don't give up, keep moving." Crawling in such extreme conditions seemed impossible but at times like these, being hardheaded was a virtue. I got to a place in the open field where there was no snow on the ground, but the wind was brutal. My limbs simply would not work.

STORIES

The snow began to pile up against me and for a time it seemed to block the wind. I wondered how long it would be before anyone found me. Who would it be? The thought made me mad at death and I struggled to at least move somehow.

Meanwhile, back at the house when the blizzard hit, several of the gang were outside. Some took refuge in the corn bin, others ran for the tractor shed and some made it back to the house. They said there was short moment when the wind died off, and all of them, like on cue, ran for the house. A head count was taken, and they found there was one short, me. So now the questions started; where was I, who saw me leave, where did I go? Did I say anything? When it was determined that I was sent to Rabbit City for that night's meat, they all knew I was too far away, in those conditions, to be safe. Someone knew I left with just a light jacket. There were some very somber faces in the house. They all knew what they did not want to know. I think even the little one knew. Martha ordered everyone to stay inside, not even to step outside the door. I don't think anyone wanted to go outside for anything, except James! James donned his heaviest coat and boots, grabbed a hat and said, "Don't come out for anything." And with that he disappeared out the door. After two, or maybe three steps and he could no longer be seen. Then all faces ran for the big window in the kitchen which faced the yard and driveway, but all they saw was white. Everything seemed to stand still for those in the house. Every sound outside brought hope of somebody's return, but all were false alarms. It was a weird and fearful silence that filled the house.

James knew the wind would blow him around, so he went to the tractor shed and started the old machinery going. Leaving the lane to the house, he turned downhill toward the bridge, all the time looking for an odd or out-of-place lump of snow. He had no foolish notions about what he was looking for. When he got to the bridge and found nothing, he turned around and retraced his journey. The wind was a howling monster and visibility was almost zero. He kept the tractor lights on in hopes they would be seen; but they were not. He was driving slowly and blindly, calling my name frequently, but the wind stole his voice away. He prayed, "Lord, let me at least find him." He searched the road several times to no avail, but James was just as hardheaded as the one he was trying to find. He kept going and praying.

It was on one of his return trips back up the hill, when suddenly the wind stopped as still as a picture. The wall of snow to his right parted like curtains in a front room window, and far out in the open field, James saw a white pile of snow, in a white background, with a strange shape, all alone on the bare ground. It was out of place, not moving, but there. James had found the lump he was looking for but there was a heavy weight in his heart. He turned the tractor toward the strange opening, leaving the lights on to help guide him back, leaped off the tractor, and fought his way through the bitter cold and drifted snow. He was extremely cold himself, as his coat and hat seemed to offer no protection, but he pressed on into the world of white.

I had no idea anyone was anywhere around. I never heard a sound. I knew I was as good as dead, but I would not die a coward. There was no fear, no bitterness, no blaming. I was dying and I accepted that while inwardly I was still not giving up. I was still a fighter. Then suddenly there was a voice. It was James's voice and he was calling my name. There are times when no human language can express the emotional waves that overflow it. And in this case that wave was hope. A different kind of victory. A different reason for determination. James kept calling my name when he got close, but he never slacked his pace. Suddenly he was there, kneeling over me, wiping the snow off my face. I tried to answer him, but there was no sound, and I didn't know why. He saw that life was still in me and it brought a wave of hope to him. He who brought hope has now received hope himself. He tried getting me up but my body wouldn't cooperate for either of us.

Then this 70-year-old man literally picked up this 14 year old and carried him across his shoulders. As he made his way toward the lights he started stumbling. By then my voice had returned but only in sound, for I couldn't pronounce anything. He stood me up beside him and with his arm mostly carrying me, we made our way toward the tractor. He clung to me and held me up lest he lose his precious load. The wind started back up, the curtain closed, and we were on our way, if you could call it that. By that time the snow was terribly deep and the wind had returned in full force.

Those in the house said they heard the tractor coming with the engine wrapped up tight. They knew something was wrong as nobody ever drove the tractor like that. Yes, something was wrong, but nothing made sense to those inside the house. James pulled into the tractor shed and out of the wind. As soon as Martha heard the sound, she grabbed her coat and scarf and went out the door. It was an amazing challenge for her small frame to reach the tractor shed. She came through the big door, shutting it behind her, but when she turned around, she said her heart almost stopped. James looked like death carrying a corpse. She said she didn't even see me when the tractor stopped to make the turn into the shed. She only saw James, and only vaguely.

In the tractor shed there was a watering trough for the animals that was about 8 ft long, maybe 30 inches high, and about two feet wide. We always kept it full but never was it heated in any way. James and Martha laid me down on the ground and began cutting away any clothes that weren't frozen to my body. They worked silently and quickly. They seemed to know what the other was thinking and what to do. I did not resist. My limbs still would not work and they said I was making odd noises. I thought I was talking, or at least trying to. They picked me up and lowered me into the watering trough. I somehow expected it to be cold, but to my amazement, it was extremely warm and wonderful. I asked how they had heated the water, but they didn't understand what I was saying. James said, "The water will get cold soon enough and then it will be time to get out." That water felt so warm and good, I didn't want to ever get out, but James was right, and sure enough when the water got cold, it got cold fast. By then I was more than happy to get out. Meanwhile Martha had returned to the house and retrieved some clothes and a blanket for me. The wind had died down to some extent, and the snow had let off. But the cold was biting hard. With me between them, they almost carried me into the house. The fire in the wood stove had been stoked up, and there were chairs next to it. They put me on one of the chairs, but I couldn't sit up on my own so one of the girls got a sheet and tied me upright in the chair. Meanwhile they kept giving James and me hot chocolate, as much as we could hold with many admonitions to drink more. I was glad to oblige. Just how good life was feeling at that moment would be impossible to say. Soon the questions began to come from all directions. We pieced together the events that had unfolded in the last 6 hours; events that were amazing and staggering. I think Martha summed it up very well when she said, "The Lord gave both of you back to us today." The repercussions I have suffered from the experience have lasted even until this very day. Cold means pain to me. If it's cold, it hurts. Not the cold like water or ice cream, but outside cold to me is brutal.

I don't remember what happened to the 410-gauge shot gun. But somehow, when the ordeal was over, we found it in the tractor shed. Neither of us remember how it got there. The last I saw it, it was in the field. James said he never saw it at all. Some things we will never know how or why.

#47 Big Wind

This experience took place on top of the well-known bluff. It was a beautiful summer day and I was on top of the bluff hunting squirrels because squirrels were on the menu that night. I went to the area where the mulberry trees were everywhere and that meant squirrels were everywhere eating the mulberries. When I approached the area, the squirrels had holed up and I noticed it was very quiet. That usually happens right after you get there because the squirrels hear you coming and run for cover. They wait about 10 minutes and come back out. I assumed something had passed through there before me, and the squirrels had disappeared. So I waited for their return and sat quietly and motionless. As I sat there, I noticed something else. Everything had become as silent and motionless as a photograph. No flies buzzing around, no butterflies, no birds, there were not even any bugs on the ground. If you've got mulberries anywhere, you've always got bugs and birds. I thought it was very unusual but did not have any idea where they went or why the left. As I sat there wondering what all this meant, the sky and light all around the area became as yellow as a dandelion. I had seen that happen in stormy weather, and I knew it sometimes happens when a tornado is about to hit. But this was clear weather, so what was all this yellow all about? I did not have long to wait to find out!

I heard a sound like a far away roar. Then instantly it became a deafening roar! At that very instant the wind, as strong as any tornado, hit like a bulldozer. Trees started falling over and blowing away. The leaves, sticks, rocks, sand and anything on the ground became like a sandblaster on my face. Limbs of all sizes were being ripped from the trees and went crashing away. I had dropped onto the ground to avoid most of it, but I knew if a tree came down across me it would be bad. It took only a moment to see that I could not stay there and be safe. The debris hitting my face and body was very painful and blinding. I had just started to move when the wind caught me and sent me rolling like a tumbleweed. I soon hit a small tree about as big around as a pop bottle. I clung to the tree, but the wind latterly held me up and I was waving like a flag on a pole. I never thought that I would die, but I knew this was a bad situation for sure. Then as suddenly as it started, it stopped. I fell to the ground and landed hard. I did not know what had just happened, or if it was coming back, so I stayed low on the ground and clung to the tree. It took some time but the bugs came back, the birds came through and the forest returned to normal. I felt it was over. I got up and took inventory of myself. Nothing was broken, but I had some bruises and scrapes. I thought I had come out pretty good considering the mysterious event that had just happened. I went looking for my shotgun and found it a ways off down wind. I had let go of it when I was pretending to be a tumbleweed. The squirrels stayed out of sight and I took that to mean I needed to do the same, so I left that area in a hurry. I wanted to get off the bluff as soon as I could. There were other places to fill the menu for tonight, and surely they would be a lot safer than the bluff. The bluff was a mysterious place, and it held a lot of secrets. If anything was going to happen that was really odd, it would always be on the bluff.

It would be many years later that I would learn about jet streams and downdrafts. I can only guess that was what happened on that day so long ago.

#48 The Outhouse and the Dirt Clod

Any farm that does not have running water has an outhouse and our place was no exception. Outhouses are normally located downhill and far away for good reasons. Downhill was to protect our ground water. And far away was to protect one's privacy and our noses. I guess they also created some very interesting stories. Mail order catalogues were very useful. You simply ripped out a page, crumbled it into a tight ball, and unfolded it for use. The wadding it up made it very soft and usable. If that was not enough, repeat.

Unfortunately, we boys discovered that if you took a dirt clod about the size of your fist and threw it arching high into the air, if it hit the door of the outhouse there was a loud unsuspected crashing sound. This proved to be very funny. But it also always made the door fly wide open and stay open, much to the dismay of its occupants. This was a very good thing to know, especially when cranky city people came around. However, one day it happened. Somebody threw a very large dirt clod at the outhouse and, unfortunately, the timing was bad because just before the dirt clod hit the door, the occupant came out. The dirt clod clobbered them dead square in the head, knocking them back inside. Fortunately they didn't fall back into the opening on the bench seat.

I wasn't the one who threw it, and I don't remember who did. But once the victim had come to life and been rightfully treated with all kinds of ice bags and homemade remedies and family apologies, there was a meeting in the front yard with all of us kids. Then there was a meeting with just us boys. Then there was a meeting with the one who threw it. But that meeting was behind the woodshed and none of us wanted to take part in that one! Then there was a meeting with the one who threw it and the one he had hit where apologies were made and many tears of sincere regret. The thrower felt terrible, and we felt terrible for him and the accidental target. But the victim felt far worse than any of us. There was never another dirt clod thrown at the outhouse.

#49 The Dug Story

Dug was just a year or so younger than I. At first we were like brothers. My past street life and his sheltered farm life put us worlds apart, but as friends we started out very close. However, the closeness that developed between myself and Dug's family eventually made him very jealous of me. He somehow felt threatened, particularly by his parents whom I spent hours with in the yard, sitting on the "porch swing" and benches, as they helped me reconcile my past and get a new handle on life.

Eventually the strife between Dug and I became so intense that it had to be dealt with. I deliberately took the back seat to everything in an attempt to help him, but nothing seemed to help. One day, it was Dug who settled it the hard way. We were all sitting out in the yard when Dug spoke up saying he wanted to wrestle with me. I knew this would turn into a fight, so I told Dug that I did not know how to wrestle. In truth, I had no idea how to wrestle, and I still do not. My world had nothing to do with wrestling. I had been living on the street and nobody wrestles on the street. Dug kept pushing me by saying that I was a coward. However, that had no effect on me whatsoever because I thought it was stupid. This made him even madder. He strutted in front of his sisters saying, "I'll go easy on Babies." I just sat there watching him make a fool of himself. I respected James so much that I would endure a great deal before offending James or his family. James and Martha were not impressed with Dug or his attitude and told him he'd best be shutting up. But Dug was determined to make a scene. He did not know my past. Finally, James said, "Bob, it looks to me like your gonna have to teach Dug a lesson." The smirk on James's face told me he was giving me permission. I got the impression James was looking forward to this and did not want to miss anything. As I was getting up and walking past Martha, she whispers, "Go easy on him." So I walked over to Dug who had walked away to get some fighting room. Dug turned around with his fist up in front of his face. I'll not say what happened then.

This episode completely changed the family. Dug left me alone for good; No more pushing, criticizing, mocking, etc., in front of everybody. The girls felt sorry for Dug and Danny lost all respect for me. The more the story was told, the greater the rift came between me and the kids, except for Herman. He thought it was long overdue for Dug to be put in his place. Everything was different after that. Even Cora, who was Dug's twin, felt like I was wrong to have hurt her brother. She seemed to forget that Dug was pushing for a fight for at least a month. But I kept backing up from it. I was backing up out of respect for James; it had nothing to do with Dug. I had no desire to hurt anybody, especially someone in James's family. But the event signaled the beginning of the end for my stay at James's.

#50 Leaving James's Farm

Time goes by so quickly, and soon I had the itch to get moving on down the road. I was a wanderer, a drifter. I did not stay anywhere very long. My time at James's was about one year and it was the happiest time that I had ever known. In some ways they had become my family. In other ways it reminded me of the deep hurt I was packing around. That was a constant inner struggle I faced every day.

I got to missing my family, but my family was all torn to bits and ugly pieces. There was no family to go back to. The emptiness it created in my heart was hurting and I longed for a life that could never be real again. It became my daily battle to run from my past. So, I drifted again. I was back on the streets, ended up in the navy, went to Vietnam and got married when I returned to the states. After I got out of the navy, I took my new bride to Missouri. I was about 14 or 15 while at James's, but my time there was so dear to me, I considered them as my family. They were closer to me than my family. James and Martha had taught me how to grow up the right way. James, Martha and I sat out in the porch swing, out in the yard, and had many a heart-to-heart talk. They had wisdom far beyond my years and their advice and insights were a lighthouse in my stormy world.

#51 Returning

Now at 21 years old and back in Missouri, I took my bride and went looking for James and Martha. As I drove up into the yard, (this is what everybody did back then), I saw James out in front of the chicken shed, shelling corn and feeding chickens. He chopped corn into big chunks. He looked at me as I entered the gate, but never said anything. (Strangers never go past the yard gate. It is considered a threatening action) So I went over, squatted down beside him, picked up the machete and an ear of corn, and started chopping corn like crazy into thin checkers, like I had never left. James's face lit up and he broke into a big smile! There was only one person who fed chickens like that! He said, "Well Bob! Where you been?" What a time we had together! Martha came home from town a few minutes later and we again had a wonderful reunion. They got to meet my bride, and I got to see them again. And my bride got to meet the people who took me off the street, taught me some values, and changed my life for the good. A debt I will forever owe.

#52 I Say Old Chap!

Somewhere in every past there is a hall of shame. I do not believe that hindsight is 20/20. When I look back on some of the things I did, I still do not know what I was thinking. Neither can I explain what world I was in when I masterminded some of those all-time high exploits. This experience is one of those hall-of-shame stories. Just how dumb can one person get and still breathe on their own? I do not know! I think I was in 6th grade at the time and, for who knows why, I was reading up on the English or British. It struck me just how proper everybody looked and acted. Everyone "over there" had properness and rightness flowing in their blood. Of this I was convinced. I wished I had lived "over there." I had no idea just where "over there" was, but wherever it was I wanted to be there. So after completely infatuating myself with all this supposed properness, it was very clear that there were no hillbillies living "over there." Time went by, and after filling my mind with just how wonderful these imaginary people were, along with their imaginary ways, I slowly developed one of my masterminded pieces of creative thinking. I could not take my family to "over there," BUT I could bring their thinking "OVER HERE"!

As the possibility of doing this raced through my mind, it became clear. I was going to start the "new wave of thinking" in the Ozarks! Yes, I was going to do this. I was going to be the historical figure everyone came to for advice on how to be proper. Now, if anyone knew the Ozark people, and how hardheaded they can be, then you knew this was not going to be easy. BUT! I had worked out a plan that would save the south. It was all very plain to me. All I had to do was get a derby hat because everyone over there wore a derby hat. Then I needed an umbrella. Umbrella's made people wearing a derby hat even more important! I did not know why, but all the pictures I saw showed them wearing a derby hat and packing an umbrella. Then, the last thing, was to make a speech full of amazing wisdom that would make everyone listen to me. Of course, it had to have lots of words the English used, or else nobody would notice the new me! I went to my room, I typed out on this very vintage typewriter, (it was about the size of a Mack truck, and took two people to pack it), my change-the-world speech! It started with, "I say old chap!" As an introduction, you ALWAYS tapped the person to whom you were speaking, on the shoulder with two quick and fast taps, using your umbrella. That meant "pay attention, I'm speaking to you."

After several trips to the county dump, and foraging through every box and bag and pile, I finally secured a derby hat and an umbrella. The hat was way too big and sunk down over my eyes and ears. I had to be careful to not move very much or it would come falling down over most of my head. The umbrella absolutely could not be opened because it was torn to shreds. And if it ever opened, you had a real time trying to get it to close again. Also, it was inverted, like somebody had gotten caught in a terrible wind that was way too strong for the umbrella. If it were opened by pushing a secret button on the handle, it would pop open very quickly and look like a giant cloth funnel with spider legs sticking out in every direction. Therefore, no matter what happened, I must remember not open the umbrella, especially if I happened to be tapping a person on the shoulder at the time.

So now the stage is all set. I had memorized my speech, practiced my umbrella tapping without hitting the button, and my hat was reshaped and cleaned up. Now for just the right time and history was going to be changed for the south. It was very evident to me that the most unacceptable display of the south was when I was getting a whipping from my dad. He could remove his wide leather belt faster than you could say "I didn't do it." He was a firm believer in the laying on of hands, but it had nothing to do with the church. The remembrance of him holding onto my arm, swinging that belt as I ran around him in circles trying to get away while my sisters would laugh at the sight, was clearly the best time to turn things around.

I don't remember the events that led up to me getting whipped from Dad. But my destiny was calling. He called me into the dining room/living room and I could tell he was mad about something. I had heard him talking to my sisters and my mom in there, and I knew it was not a good conversation. I could not hear everything, and I did not know it was about me. So when I got called in there, I was met with a bad situation. My dad started with "Did you..." and immediately I interrupted him. Interrupting your Redneck, hardcore, tough-as-nails dad, who is about to give you a whippin' is NEVER a good idea. Take my word for it. I yelled "STOP! Just a minute!" and ran as fast as I could upstairs. I grabbed my derby hat and umbrella and raced back down the stairs. I knew the English never ran. That was improper. So I stopped racing at the bottom of the stairs and I was still out of sight. Carefully placing my derby hat on my head and strolling in with this "air of authority," I placed my umbrella on the ground like I had seen Bob Hope do on stage with his golf club. Then I walked back to where my dad was still standing with this most unusual expression on his face. I walked right up to him, gave him two sharp taps on the shoulder, and started my speech! "I say old chap!" and MY MIND WENT BLANK! I could not remember any of my speech except how it started! My mind was racing. I didn't know what to do! So I started over, giving him another two sharp taps on the shoulder and saying, "I say old chap!" but it was to no avail. The speech was gone. I could tell by the fire in my dad's eyes, the heaviness in the room, and the hilarious laughter coming from my mom and sisters, this wasn't working out very well.

My dad then said to me, in a tone that would make the dogs run away, "I'll make you think, 'old chap.'" He grabbed me by the arm and started letting me have it. I started going in circles around him and jumping around at the same time. Unfortunately, the umbrella's secret button got pushed and it exploded into its usual inverted shape. In the process the lamp got knocked over, the house cat exploded out of the room, and then my hat fell down over my eyes and was bobbing around like an oversized hat on a small head in an earthquake. Things were not working out too well. So I started my speech again, saying, "I say old chap! I say old chap, I say old chap!" But it was no use. I simply could not resurrect that speech.

I saw between the times when my hat was up and the umbrella was down, my mom and sisters sitting on the floor, holding their sides, tears running down their faces, and saying, "I say old chap!"

Dad wore me out real good. I took my derby hat and worthless umbrella and threw them both back into the dump, just where they belonged! Soon things would die down in the house and then somebody would say very loudly, "I say old chap!" Then another round of expensive entertainment would follow, along with all their antics of repeating the hat and umbrella scenario.

I was disappointed to say the least. As far as I was concerned, the classless south could rot into the ground.

Many years went by and for a long time, "I say old chap!" was still the popular topic. It might be at a family reunion, or a BBQ, or just anytime. And somebody would speak up and say, "Tell us again old chap! What happened now?"

#53 Lee Lee and the Outhouse

Living outside Guthrie, MO was like a dream world to me. Those were, no doubt, some of the best times I ever had! Guthrie was in the New Bloomfield area and that whole area is full of wonderful memories.

It was at the Guthrie house where my favorite aunt Anna lived. Aunt Anna and Uncle Ben lived in a very old farmhouse out past 7 Hills Road. Behind their house was a large back porch, and behind that porch was a very small house. Someone had closed in the back porch with a roof and walls that made a really nice breezeway to the small house in the back. It was in that small house where Aunt Anna's mother lived; Granny. This was that Granny's house where my dad took me and dropped me off when Granny took me in to pull me from my world of torment. Granny walked with God like nobody I've ever met or heard of, even until this day.

Here is one of those experiences unique to Aunt Anna's house.

Since Aunt Anna's house had no running water, it naturally had an outhouse. Baths were the typical Ozark bath on the back porch. The kitchen sink didn't have a hand pump, but it did have a drain where water went out the wall to the ground outside. That sounds funny now, but at that time it was the common way everybody did it, even in town.

The outhouse was well over the hill for very good reasons. Sometimes it was because you didn't want it close to your well, or you wanted it downhill from your water supply, such as a spring. You never wanted it up hill from the stock pond or up wind from the house. The list could go on and on for all the things you had to take into consideration when placing the outhouse. Their construction was not as simple as people think. There was certain way to do it and for very good reasons.

This outhouse was a bit too far from the house, but it had to be that way. When that happens, you use the honey bucket system. That meant you used it during the night, but in the morning it had to be emptied at the outhouse in the proper fashion. If the outhouse was built correctly, the whole shelf of the seating area was a big lid that lifted up. This was to accommodate many things; the honey bucket being one of them. Honey buckets were always a wintertime experience. In the summer you simply went the distance.

A honey bucket was normally a store-bought oversized wooden chair that had groves underneath to accommodate the top of the honey bucket. They came with a lid on the seat. The instructions went something like this: "It is up the user to move the "chair" to an appropriate spot for proper utilization to accommodate the acceptable application of this humble but modern device." These instructions were normally printed and pasted on the underside of the lid by the manufacturer. I noticed there were never any instructions on "who or how" it was to be emptied!

Our "proper spot" in the winter was in the breezeway between the two houses. I often wonder if the statement "colder than a cast iron commode" came from the Ozarks.

Uncle Ben was a well-known, extremely good cook at the infamous truck stop in Kingdom City, MO. Back then it was the only truck stop in the whole area. It was surrounded by a giant gravel parking lot. Many hair-raising stories came from that infamous truck stop.

In the wintertime, Uncle Ben would not get home until just after dark, and wintertime was honey bucket time. There was a rule at our house that every night a different child had to empty the honey bucket. Uncle Ben was tired of "comin' home ever' night and finding it full to the brim cause lazy kids don't do nuthin.'" That's actually how he said it.

On this almost fatal night, there was a big argument about whose turn it was. There were 6 kids, or thereabouts. Company didn't count. So this terribly cold night there was a good snow on the ground with a layer of ice on top of the snow. The cold had a strong bite to it and the worse it was outside, the more important it became to make sure it wasn't your turn for the humble chore.

So after a lot of hillbilly style discussion, (which involved a lot of finger pointing, slander, a kick and a bite or two mixed with lots of volume by everybody at the same time, and promises made with one hand raised (to prove you were telling the truth) and the other hand behind your back with your fingers crossed, (crossed fingers meant whatever you said didn't count)because you knew you were not telling the truth), Aunt Anna decided EVERYONE would do it. Incidentally, there was never any mercy to anyone who was caught crossing their fingers and raising their hands at the same time. So you had to be careful about who was standing behind you during these very mature hillbilly family discussions! Being caught might also involve a little blackmail by the one who caught you.

After Aunt Anna made the decision, we calculated the steps, divided it by the number of victims carrying the bucket, and took great pains to not go too many steps over. Each kid would take the so-called "humble bucket" just two steps with everyone counting the steps and watching to make sure they were full steps. Then VERY ceremoniously hand the full-to-the-brim bucket to the next victim. And when we got to the last victim, the first person started over again. And so forth. The ground was cold, slippery and steep, so everyone had to be careful!

By and by the "humble bucket" made it to the outhouse. And as it turned out, "Lee Lee" had it last, and she was MAD! So to prove how mad she was, she opened the outhouse door and without ever stepping inside, just slung the honey bucket and its contents full force through the door, slammed the door and started to turn around.

Everyone was shocked! Lee Lee had her nose pointed upward and was very proud of herself for this display of self-righteousness.

Suddenly the outhouse door EXPLODED into many pieces with the greater part of it flying/sliding down the hill and there was this terrific growl/cuss/scream from something coming out of the outhouse door with its arms reaching forward like it was going to get somebody! It had (I don't know what) long stringy things that looked like seaweed hanging from it and a really foul odor (a mild description). It was walking like a monster coming out of a graveyard! It's as miracle we didn't all of us faint dead away instantly!

Then things turned really bad! Debbie Sue screamed out in this horrible voice, "RUN LEE LEE! IT'S BEHIND YOU!" Lee Lee knew it was behind her! She did the only reasonable thing she could do at the time. She clobbered the monster on the side of its head with the honey bucket, knocking "Monster" back into the outhouse! Now monster was REALLY MAD! She tried to run, but that didn't work too well on the ice. She ended up on the ground trying to run like a dog. All of a sudden, Monster comes out of the outhouse again, and, amazingly, Monster had a voice that sounded remarkably like Uncle Ben! I won't repeat the verbiage but the message was somewhat clear, WE WERE ALL DEAD MEAT! Horrified, we watched the unusual performance of Monster and Doggie making their way back up the steep, icy hill. Not everything that happens in the Ozarks is normal. Very few things were normal. This un-normal was our normal, and that was very abnormal.

Unknown to us, Uncle Ben had come home, knew the pot would be full, and didn't even bother to come inside first. SOOOOO guess where he was! Sitting in the outhouse of course! Nobody knew he was there! He later told us that the door opened up, and when he looked up to say something, the unthinkable happened. He stepped outside to breathe and see, when something clobbered him, knocking him back inside the outhouse.

When he came out the second time, he was visibly upset. That's the mild version of it.

Aunt Anna heard the wild commotion outside and came running with the shot gun. It was very true that we had problems in that area with wolves and wild dogs that would kill everything they came across. I suppose she expected something along those lines, but she came out the door gun first and scared. I don't know how she managed to <u>not</u> shoot this monster, but somehow she recognized the voice of Monster as Uncle Ben. So, while we expecting to be delivered by way of shot gun, she was standing there partly in shock and confusion, not shooting anything! Meanwhile there was a tremendous stampede of kids coming up the hill with all of us screaming bloody murder, "It's got Lee Lee! It's got Lee Lee!

I'm not sure exactly what they were all saying, and I really don't remember what I was saying, but I'm sure I was saying something like, "the scientific reasoning behind self-control in extreme circumstance"! I realize there could be **a slight** possibility of me saying something less than that, but I'm sure it was nothing like "HELP! THE MONSTER'S GONNA EAT ME! Or "I'll be good, I'll be good!" but I could be wrong! Like I said, I really don't remember exactly what I said.

After what seemed like hours of sliding up the icy hill and miles of ice-covered ground, we made it to the house again. And before it was over, we were dragging out the bathtub, building a really big fire, melting snow and heating water cause SOMEBODY had to take at least three full-blown baths, in HOT water, in the dead of winter. And the last one had to be in bleach water! I'll leave it up to the reader about "who" needed the baths, but it WASN'T me! We all got a good "lickin' over the ordeal, but we survived it. Then we got to repeat the whole process to clean up the outhouse.

Uncle Ben hung a new door the next day and we all noticed there was this HUGE inside lock on the new door! No more monsters showing up, and no more unthinkable surprises!

#54 KXEN With 1000 Watts to Serve You

Many years ago as a young kid, I think I was in 1st or 2nd grade at that time, on Friday nights when my dad got off from work, we would load the truck and drive to Jefferson City MO. We lived in Cahokia IL, and it was about a two hour drive or more. There was a special restaurant we sometimes would stop at; a white farmhouse set about 2 ft from the road. The road made a sharp curve to go around that little house, but it did not miss it by far! I remember thinking, if you stuck your head out that window, you would probably lose it! The owners had turned it into a café and people came from miles around to eat there. There was a field behind the house where the big 18 wheelers would park and sometimes spend the night, and many cars were in-between the trucks. It was a very popular and well-known place. I also remember the first time my parents let me order what I wanted. I wanted a hamburger, French fries, and a coke and they let me have it! Funny how some things get stuck in your head and never leave! It made me feel sooooo important! (Yep, I was an official big boy after that! Just ask me!)

Many years later, I told my Uncle Herman about that memory. He knew the place immediately because Uncle Herman had been a truck driver for many years. He even told me the name of the place, but I failed to write it down. He said drivers talked about that café all the way to Texas and back. And yes, it was 2 ft from the shoulder of the road!

One of the things we did on those week-end trips was listen to the radio. I remember the truck dash was metal and had a round curve to it. It was green. The radio was rounded to match the dash. It was sort of tall and narrow with a chrome frame around the little window. The number were lit up and there were big round buttons to push to go directly to whatever station you wanted. There were a few knobs for tuning, and one for volume. I do not remember what the third one did.

So, on each trip we listened to the radio. There was Paul Harvey news and then a country music station would come on, and finally there was a station called KXEN. They would always sign on and off with, "This is KXEN with 1000 watts to serve you." it was a gospel radio station. The two older folks who did the talking, singing, preaching, warning and praying, were Fred and Zelma May Cox. They were out of Sarcoxie MO. (don't trust my spelling on that!) I seldom understood what they were saying because the words they used were unknown to me. But I remember there was something very special about them, something that drew me and made me hungry for something, but I did not know what it was. My dad would always be driving and Mom sat by the door. My sister and I sat side by side in the middle. I was next to Dad and right in front of the radio. The station would play these odd songs that I had never heard before. I heard the words very clearly, but they did not make sense. Sometimes my folks would start to cry while listening to those songs. My sister and I would sometimes place our ears on the speaker, trying to understand what they were saying even though we heard them very clearly. Then this guy would give what I thought was a speech which moved everyone in the truck to silence, and sometimes more tears from Dad or Mom. I never knew what it was about these people, but we were all drawn to them, like some kind of hand was pulling us. My sister and I knew not to talk during KXEN. We could argue and fight and punch when it was music time, but NEVER during Paul Harvey or KXEN. We were too engrossed in that spell we all were under during KXEN. Finally, the guy would start talking differently. (Dad said they were praying.) Then they would sign off the air with, "This is KXEN with 1000 watts to serve you."

Dad always turned the radio off after KXEN was over and would keep on driving in silence. Eventually, the conversation would start up again on "just about anything." and we were back to normal. If Mom did not bring a bag of sandwiches or goodies, we would be stopping at our favorite place not far up the road!

About 20 years went by. Time was turning the pages very quickly. I was all grown up, married, and had three kids. I was far from God and could not find him. My life was a shipwreck.

One morning, unknown to me, God had an appointment with me, but first he had to get my undivided attention! I was working maintenance in a factory in Jefferson City MO doing third shift on a Friday night. It was winter. There was about 6 inches of slushy snow and water on the ground. When my shift ended it was early Saturday morning and I headed to my car, (a green, '78 Dodge Dart) but it didn't want to start. Normally it started right up. I finally did get it to start, but as I got out of the car to close the hood, my feet slipped and I went down hard on my back, clobbering the door with my elbow as I made my wonderful descent. I got up and SLAMMED the door. I had slush running down the inside of my clothes from my collar to my shoes. However, after I had slammed the hood, I soon discovered that in clobbering the door with my elbow, I had hit the lock button on the door! The trunk was full of tools, but I could not get into it. So I tried to re-enter the factory, but it was locked also. I began knocking normally, but as that brought nobody out, I tried a LITTLE harder. Thankfully somebody down the hall on the factory floor heard me and decided to go and see what the noise was all about!

Once inside, I got a coat hanger and a pair of pliers, went back outside, and gained entry into the car. I started to back up and leave when I discovered I had a flat tire on the rear passenger side. So, I got out, making sure the door was not locked, opened the trunk and removed the tire, only to find the spare was flat and had a hole in it. With the flat tire under my arm, I started walking towards town. There was a gas station about half a mile down the road. I got there right after they had opened and they fixed my flat tire. But when I went to pay, I discovered my wife had removed the money from my billfold and had not told me. After leaving my driver's license with them, I returned to the car, replaced the tire and left. I was approaching town when the car started sputtering. I looked at the gas gauge and it was empty, so I coasted into a gas station and right to the pumps. It was then that I remembered my wife had cleaned me out. I could not restart the car to move it and I knew I could not leave my driver's license because the station that did my tire still had it.

I went inside, looking like I had worked all night, crawled around a greasy, oily motor in the morning, tried to beat a door off the hinges with my fist, rolled around in the slush and packed a tire for one mile. I had reached a point of anger that should have killed me, and wandered into this station wanting free gas with a promise to return. Guess what was not going to happen! I was there for a long while trying to barter with something. Finally I sold the guy my watch for gas money. It was an expensive watch I had bought while in the navy. I had paid over $100 dollars for it in 1975 and sold it for 10 dollars in gas to get home. It was almost noon by now.

During all this time, each trial pushed me to a new level of hatred and anger. I don't know why my heart or brain didn't explode. It was off the chart. It had to be God's mercy. It was not my time to go. But wait till I get home! We had this argument before of, don't take money from my wallet without telling me!

Back on the highway and headed home, I was so angry it was close to murder. I turned on the radio to try and find something to help me and heard some familiar voices. Where had I heard those voices before? In addition, they were singing such beautiful music, and their Spirits were full of peace. They sang several songs followed by a short devotional.

A still small voice began to speak to me. Through it, I saw how terrible I was on the inside and how much hurt I was dishing out to my family. How lost and miserable I really was. And how I could not find God. My despair must have reached heaven and God heard. I was crying so hard that I could hardly drive. The elderly voice prayed and the station signed off. "THIS IS KXEN WITH 1000 WATTS TO SERVE YOU." I knew then where I had heard that voice. This time I understood completely.

I left the road, screeching tires to the shoulder. I could no longer see the road because my tears were blinding and overflowing. I fell over in the seat and wept my way back to God. When I couldn't find him, he found me! God changed my heart and turned my burning hatred and anger into brokenness. He took them all away and He filled me with His peace, praise Him forever!

I eventually started home again. This time a new creature. God works in mysterious ways.

I tried to find that radio station but discovered it had gone out of business many years before. I do not know about their farewell broadcast, but I know they had one broadcast from heavens shore, looking for that lost kid who could not understand!

Music

#55 Music

Music has always played an important role in my personal life. As a young man, singing was a favorite pastime. The culture offered Hillbilly Hoedowns every weekend, and often during the week on a nightly basis. Front porch hoedowns were as common as fleas on a cat's belly.

#56 Music Lesson #1

There were things about music that stood out to me; things I don't think others noticed. I couldn't put my finger on it at first, or give a rightful explanation for it, but they were there. Then one day I saw the explanation on a cartoon. There it was, the very thing I had been seeing, but could not explain.

The cartoon showed Indians dancing around a fire. The drummers were drumming faster and faster and the chants were getting faster and faster. The fire was burning higher and higher. Then the scene changed. It showed only the shadows of the dancers and the shadows became monsters of all sorts. These monsters had entered the dancers, and they did outstanding things!

So there it was in plain cartoon sight! That something I was seeing but could not explain. It all made a very clear picture to me. I had seen the dance floors full, heard the music, and saw a change that I could not identify. Something was different. The people were different. But what?

#57 Music Lesson #2

Years later, my parents started going to the taverns on Friday nights and they took me along for different reasons. It all started when my dad gave me some money to put in the jukebox but the songs I selected were not random. I deliberately picked the songs that would build upon each other, with each song being a little faster and louder. I called it "stacking." The pace, the message, and the volume accelerated, and sure enough, the dancers responded accordingly! It got wild. The juke box was doing more than the band. When the people are wound up, they get thirsty, so the drinks flowed, and the money flowed with it.

Somehow, the bartender noticed what I was doing. He even went over and selected some songs himself, but his selections failed to have the desired effect. So he came over to our table, gave me a free soda and a hand full of dimes, and told me to get things going. So I did.

I became a welcome sight to the taverns we visited because it meant money for the bar. So one night I had a different plan. The question was just how far could this go? How tight could I wind things up? What would happen?

This particular night I put my plan to work. I just kept it up, getting things faster and faster. Songs became louder and louder and the lyrics became more and more graphic. The dancers responded as always, but as I kept it up things began to get ugly. Fights broke out, and then more fights. So many that the bar tender was spending all his time breaking up fights. In the middle of all this, somehow, he realized that I was behind it. He ran over to our table, slammed down a fist full of dimes, and yelled, "I don't know you did, but stop it right now!" He was truly mad! I grabbed some dimes, ran for the jukebox, and hit the cancel button repeatedly. Soon it was playing songs that were a lot milder and more easy listening. Good songs. Almost instantly everything returned to normal. The first record brought everything back to center line. It was safe now. Fewer and fewer dancers were on the floor and the atmosphere was completely changed. The bartender returned to our table with another free soda and said, "I don't know what you did, but please don't ever do it again!"

#58 Music Lesson #3

Years later, I was involved in church and I assumed the same rules of music applied there. Those rules do apply, but I found them to be completely against God. You can stir people up and get them emotionally involved with the music. I've seen song leaders use this ploy to get a good offering. I've also seen it used to try and stir up the people to get a response to the message. But this was all fake emotionalism. When the song leader repeats the song over and over until he wears out the song and the people, I know it is all fake, and so is the song leader.

This knowledge almost destroyed my complete faith in God. I thought, there is no real church here, it's a sing-along and a sing-it-up for the money and to get the numbers up at the altar, so the speaker could have bragging rights for his accomplishments. This got him more revivals. The blow to my faith was staggering.

Then we went to another church, looking for reality but I found the same thing. And that blow was even worse. By now I was mad! I knew God was real, so what was all this fakery about? Is there any such thing as a real church?

God was surely watching these events unfold. One day we were compelled to go to this so-called holiness camp meeting. I knew nothing about it, but God was working in ways that I had no idea about. When we walked in, I knew something was different that put me on edge. But what? When the congregation started singing, I immediately noticed there was a different spirit in that place. A spirit I had met before. It was surely God's presence that I felt, and I knew it was Him. I looked around expecting to see Him! The song leader was picking songs that would not "stack up" the people and the atmosphere there was a beautiful presence of peace. I knew that it was God!

Then it happened! Somebody started running around the front of the tabernacle, yelling his head off, but I could not understand what he was saying. Then this other fellow jumped up, a much younger man, and he started chasing the older guy and he is yelling his head off also. I was shocked beyond measure! In my thinking, these two were fighting and he was being chased! But the most shocking thing was that NOBODY was breaking it up! How could this be? One minute I am enraptured in God's presence, the next minute in a bar room fight. Talk about sudden confusion! Well, needless to say, that did not set to well with me! I was madder than a whipped pig!

Now, by chance, I happened to be sitting on the end of the pew, right next to the aisle. I thought to myself, if that old man runs this way, and the younger fellow follows him, when he gets to me, there is no doubt that I can knock him into the middle of next week! When he gains consciousness again, he will probably be in the hospital or nursing home! I will not need a second chance. If no one is going to break this up, I WILL!

MUSIC

I sat there and prayed for the old guy to come up my aisle! And he did! Here he came, running like he had a nest of hornets on him. And sure enough, here came the younger guy right behind him! This is where #1 church jerk meets #1 ex-street fighter, and he is about to go down! But God had other plans. One pew away the younger guy did this about face and ran the other way! Did he see me cocked and ready to put him away? I did not know, but I watched him just the same! These two guys are still running around the tabernacle in opposite directions. When they meet in the rear of the building and pass each other like everything was okay, maybe they were not fighting after all? Maybe I was not supposed to break his jaw and neck in church? Maybe the something different in this place was that running around and yelling your head off in church is okay? I had never seen that before, so I had no answers.

Meanwhile the singing was still going on, but my attitude was not very favorable to singing! I was still in fighting mode. I really wanted to clobber somebody, but soon the spirit filled music brought me back to normal, which I needed.

Meanwhile the spirit was still showing me the real difference between what I had seen and known before, compared to what I was seeing now. And what a wonderful difference it was, including the restored peace in my heart, right after that near disaster!

Yes, there was a very different spirit to this kind of singing and the desire to worship and praise God was natural and overflowing. The music was not anything like I thought it would be like, but it was real and powerful. I saw the difference of spirit led music for the first time, and now, I'm addicted to it!

#59 Music Lesson #4

The Mechanical Church

Some time ago I went to a church rally. At that time God was blessing certain churches in that denomination. To go to a service was to expect to see God's glory manifested. We went with that expectation. It was a full house and you had to get there early to get a seat inside the door.

As the service began and the singing started, I was expecting God's visitation, but it didn't happen. Instead I witnessed a disgusting sight that made me mad. I think other people were expecting God's visit also and when God didn't come as they expected, they began their own sacrifices like King Saul did when Samuel didn't show up in Saul's expected time. Saul started his own sacrifice services.

People had seen what happened when the Glory comes down, so when it didn't come, they began re-enacting it on their own. The spirit of the service became very heavy. The presence of God in the music was not there and, instead, there was a spirit of mockery.

One elderly man, sitting on the very end of the pew toward the center aisle, decided he wanted to make a show. Instead of standing up and moving into the aisle, he decided to climb over the pew in front of him. Remember, he was sitting on the very end of the pew in the first place! But he couldn't do it without physical help. Others came and assisted moving the people out of the pew in front of him, so he could climb over! After they had moved, they helped him to climb over, then helped him climb back down to the floor, where he

MUSIC

started running around, pretending to be blessed. But the heaviness in the whole thing was disgusting.

Meanwhile, another very elderly man decided he wanted to run back and forth on top of the altar in front of everybody. However, he could not do it on his own. Others came to help him so he would not fall and hurt himself. So here they were, leading him by the hand, holding him up as he wobbles along the top of the altar. He was trying to get excited but he didn't have the breath. He was a sad spectacle trying to imitate the Glory.

Meanwhile, the song leader decided they needed to sing the same song over and over and over. He had everyone stand first and then he wore out the people and the song. You cannot say it hindered the spirit because there was no spirit to hinder, except the spirit of mockery. They were all offering their own sacrifices, trying to fill in for God.

Meanwhile certain ones decided they needed to get blessed. A few thought they needed to roam the aisles and Praise the Lord. But it did not work out that way. They were competing for sound against each other, so it was more like a yelling match. It was embarrassing to others in the whole church.

Some visitors had come to this Zone Rally and I saw the total shock on their faces. They looked down or at each other and just shook their heads. Some just stared off at the wall. It seemed they were embarrassed to get up in front of everyone to leave, so they stuck it out. Perhaps they had ridden with someone and could not leave. I do not really know.

A general leader, who sitting on the platform, saw this total chaos and decided it needed to be shut down. He was right! He went to the pulpit where the song leader was still repeating the same stanzas in the same song and stopped the song leader, and the song leader sat down. (Thank you, Lord)! He also sat the people down. This however did not stop the commotion by those who still thought they could force God to come by pretending he was there.

The leader started saying how good it was to be there, and, isn't God wonderful? and we all certainly enjoy the presence of the Lord, and so forth along those lines. He went on for quite a while. Meanwhile they took the old guy off the altar and helped him back to his wife who was still sitting on the pew. The fellow that left his place by climbing over the pews returned to his seat without having to climb over the pew in front of him to get back in. The praisers, who were still trying to outdo each other, sat down almost instantly. The speaker kept up his "wonderful" address, but he did mention the two old guys and their "freedom of worship." Both sat panting in their pews and wiping sweat with their handkerchiefs.

Now I hope the reader understands where I am coming from because while all this was happening I was sitting right next to a line of several light switches that controlled the lighting to the whole sanctuary. I was disgusted with the whole thing and I fought the biggest battle not to take my arm and shut the whole thing down in one sweep. Nobody wants to run and yell if nobody can see them doing it. It would be hard to tramp up and down God's altar in the dark and it's very hard to read the hymnal if the lights go out. Pew climbing is not a good idea in the dark either, because you may step on someone. A song leader might even shut up, possibly, hopefully.

My wife saw me and somehow knew what I was thinking. (amazing). The look she gave me saved us both. I thought about it later and I think she was right. My actions would have only added to the circus.

MUSIC

The speaker took us right into prayer time and this helped a lot and things progressed sanely from there, right up to the message. However, God's presence never did come in that service. The message was so flat and boring, it was painful. At the close of that service there was a mass exodus. You could have gotten run over in the parking lot because people were leaving so fast.

I have seen a lot of the world in music and in life. I have seen it in the world, in the bars, in the homes, and in the churches. I've seen a worship service on board a naval destroyer, all sung by sinners, and seen them weep openly in the presence of God that came upon that mess deck. (dining room). But by far, the most pitiful sight is a fake church service. Trying to force God to come, when He is not there, is mocking Him. No stacking of the music, or turning the hymns into a chant, or fleshly outbreaks of pretended holiness can bring Him. Neither can people who are offering their own sacrifices.

I went away from that service with a heavy heart. There aren't enough words to describe the importance of using Spirit-filled saints to lead in a church service. Praise God for Spirit-filled people who can be used of God and invite His presence with purity and sincerity.

Unusual Experiences

#60 An Unusual Experience

As a child I had a great deal of strange experiences that were unexplainable. Some still are. When falling asleep, I'd see, as it were, a kaleidoscope of color that were very beautiful and very entertaining. I really enjoyed the time between awake and asleep. During this transition, I would sometimes hear people talking. At times I would see them also. I never had any explanation for these experiences, but I remember on one particular occasion I saw my mom and my aunts sitting around the table in Mom's house. I heard their conversation very clearly. This made me think of my mom, whom I missed a lot, so I called her the next day. It was during that conversation she repeated a statement that had been made the night before while her sisters were visiting. So I asked if Aunt Harriot was sitting next to Aunt Joyce, and then Aunt Shirley, and then Tina, and then herself. Was there a large air pot on the table? And did the conversation go like this....... and so and so on. She was speechless. She finally asked, "How did you know that?" So I told her of my seeing them and hearing them as they talked. They were 2300 miles away at the time of that experience. She felt it was weird, even spooky. We got off the phone and I wondered if all the other experiences were just as real. I had never considered them to be real, but rather just a part of falling asleep. But after that day I knew there was something to those experiences, though I cannot explain them.

#61 The Fjords of Hell

This experience was a nightmare, or a scream-mare. Dreams can seem so real. They come packed with all the emotions and thoughts and feelings. I don't put every dream in print to be remembered because I know how fickle and shallow they are. But some dreams haunt you for days and some have a special something about them that says to pay attention to this. This dream is one of them. I saw in my dream a great ocean liner being filled with people. It was tied to the dock, the sun was shining, everyone was happy and excited, and streams of people were filing onto it. Soon it set out for the open sea. I was a passenger on that vessel. I began to notice there seemed to be fewer and fewer people around. Where was everybody going? I didn't know and I couldn't find out. Everything was making sense and fitting together, the people that I did see were happy and everything seemed to just fine, except the people were getting fewer and fewer. I searched for them and found no sign of them or of any foul play. But something was wrong, and it was terribly wrong. After a while I approached one of the passengers and shared with him my wonderment. He too had noticed it and was getting nervous. A few minutes later he was gone. Soon I was the only one on that vessel. The doors to the crews' quarters were all locked as was the door to the pilot house. I looked through the portals, but there was no one to be seen. Who was driving and running the ship? I went to the engineering compartment and it too was locked. I ran topside to the after deck, but I was all alone. On the horizon I saw dark clouds hanging close to the water that I knew brought terror to the old sailors, and I was about to find out why. We sailed into the blackness of the clouds and it was like sailing into the pitch darkness of the blackest of night. I could hear groans and screams and hideous laughter. The air smelled of a great heat. Soon the blackness began to lift and I saw we were sailing in a very narrow passageway and we were going very slowly. The walls on each side of the vessel were so close you could reach out and touch them. There were heinous creatures chained to the walls on little shelves that were reaching out to grab someone or something. The water was starting to glow with a bright orange hue and it continued getting very hot and dark. It was then I saw a family that I knew. I ran to them. They were doing the same thing I was, staying in the center of the vessel so as to not be reached by the heinous creatures on the sides. They too were terrified. Some of them were missing, so I asked the dad what had happened to the missing ones. If he could tell me, it would solve a riddle and possibly be the answer I was looking for. But he was scared half out of his mind. He couldn't talk, and his horrid appearance made it frightful to look at him. There he stood with only a few of his kids huddled with him on the deck. The glow was getting brighter but the darkness was coming back. I knew even while in the dream that I was in the fjords that enter hell. At that point, I awoke.

62 The Vision of Hell

Years ago I had asked God to show me hell, thinking it would somehow motivate me in my Christian walk. He didn't show me hell, he showed me heaven on three different occasions. He showed me he throne room, the river of peace and then the library. But one night, without any warning, he showed me hell for three seconds. I will never ask God to show me hell again. That was a very stupid request on my part. Be careful what you ask for, you just might get it. I will continually set my heart for heaven.

I saw a cast iron chair with holes in it and sitting in this chair was a creature of great size. It was horrifying to look upon. It had a huge alligator-type muzzle with fang-like teeth and its eyes were very large in proportion to its head. It was covered with scales and it seemed to be in a continuous fit of raging anger. It held in its lap a soul of some unknown person. The size of the creature was such that the soul of the man it held in its lap was like unto an infant in size. This horrible creature would tear and twist and bite and chew and claw and break and stretch and rip apart the soul it had in its clutches.

Meanwhile, out of the holes in the chair, leaped flames, great and hot. Out of these holes also came forth serpents of many sizes and many forms. The creature was a demon of torture. The soul made a gargled, high pitched sound of tormented pain as these serpents, like the flames, attacked the victim that was being tormented by the creature. Behind the chair stood a short dead snag of a tree. This tree looked like a hanging tree, but this tree would change into a heinous creature of such dreadful despair, or into things of sin that the soul had engaged in.

In all my years in dark sin, never had I seen such intensity of rage and cruelty. The screams of this soul sounded high pitched like unto an animal. It was like a wild cat that's being torn to pieces by dogs. The more pain and suffering inflicted upon its victim, the greater the cruelty and the greater the rage of the wretched creature who was doing the tormenting. It was a cycle that would never end.

As I stood and marveled at this sickening sight, the creature stopped in its brutal and cruel attack upon the soul it was tormenting. It froze motionless for a brief moment. I knew it was recognizing my presence, for I had been watching it. Then suddenly and instantly I found myself at the feet of this demon of pain. I was on my back with the creature's long hairy feet across my chest. My back was pressed against glowing coals and flames of fire. I screamed NOOOOO and it came out gargled, screech-like and filled with unrestrained fear! I writhed and twisted to make some escape, but there was no escape. The feeling of hopelessness was as a mountain of great weight upon me as I knew I was going to be next. The animalistic screams continued from my burning throat, and the hopelessness of it all was more than any words could ever tell. Then the loud screams from hell woke me. Behold, it was a vision. I had been in hell! I immediately asked God how long I was in hell. His answer was three seconds.

My Visits to Heaven

So far I've been to heaven three times. I have seen:

1. The throne room of God

2. The River of peace

3. God's library

4. One drop of Heaven

On a separate occasion I had asked God for one drop of heaven, and He gave it. I will never forget that experience.

63 My First Visit to Heaven: God's Throne Room

I had never been to heaven before but have heard of others who have been, and I had supposed you had to die to get there. On this occasion I had no idea I was about to enter God's domain. But I did. This is my testimony of that experience.

I was working in the logging industry back in the early '80's. Our routine was to arrive at the base camp where the log trucks started, in Cosmopolis, around 5:30 am. This was called the "show up." I usually arrived early and got on the crew bus that would take us the 45 minute to an hour ride to the logging site, known as "the landing" or "the tower." While waiting for the remainder of the crew to show up, I would spend the time in prayer, as I did this day also. I was sitting in the back of the crew bus with my arms folded on the back of the seat in front of me with my head on my arms as I prayed. My life was about to change, but I didn't know it.

I was suddenly in God's throne room, the control room of eternity! God was on his throne! His visage was like unto a great and shining light, with an even brighter light radiating around him. He was sitting on a great throne that was also made of light. All around him, from behind and from horizon to horizon, was this beautiful multi-colored light that I would liken unto a rainbow. I was kneeling before him and I was alone. I looked up and saw him there! I began to praise him and thank him! My entire being was flooded with peace and happiness and praise. All thought and memory of this earth was gone. All I could think of was his majestic glory and worshipping him! This continued for what seemed like a few minutes but then I realized I was back on the crew bus and somebody was shaking me saying it was time to get off. Over one hour had passed, but it seemed like just a few minutes. I don't know why God invited me there, except I knew he searched the highways and the byways to bring in the poor, the lost and the lame. Somehow I was privileged to be invited. I have never forgotten that experience and refer to it often. It still brings a blessedness with it.

#64 The River of Peace

While pastoring, we were going through a very difficult time. I made the comment to someone, "I wish God would give me a tour of heaven, it would sure help us." Well, God heard that request. A few weeks later I was scheduled to attend a foremen's meeting in a distant city for the company I worked for. Since it was out of town, I took my wife with me. We were driving down the highway together, talking as we usually do, when I suddenly stopped talking. That was something different so my wife looked at me to see what was wrong. She said, "You were all lit up like you were glowing, and weeping." She knew God was talking to me, but she didn't know what it was about, or what to do. One moment I am driving down the road, the next moment I'm in heaven standing next to Jesus, and he is saying, "You asked for a tour!" We were standing on a very high knoll of a grassy hill, looking down into a grassy valley below us. There was before us (though it was several miles away) a shining silver stream that meandered its way along the bottom of that valley. From our height it looked like a silver thread, but I knew it was a river. I could see that on the other side of this valley, the lay of the land rose up again to somewhere close to the same height as we were. As we stood there, Jesus said, "This is the river of peace." As I looked at it, the silver thread began widening and the river began to rise. It rose higher and higher until it filled the valley and was overflowing the mountain tops on which we stood. There was never a torrent or a pressing flow. It was nothing like a flash flood of any kind. It was a gentle rising that went hundreds of feet above our heads. I was laughing with a holy laughter and a joy that I could in no wise contain. The glory and the peace of that river was washing through me! I felt somewhat awkward, as I continued to act like a child with no restraints to my expressions of joy and gladness. Then I was driving down the road again, just as I was before, except that I felt like I might explode with the happiness inside me. My wife's first words to me were, "What did he say?" So I told her, wondering how she knew God had said anything to me. I later asked her, "How was my driving?" She said, "You were driving like you always do!" I could take that two ways. I asked her if she was afraid when she saw me over there glowing and driving like I always do. She said, "No, there was a peace that filled the van, and I was not afraid, for I knew God was talking to you." Praise God for his marvelous ways!

#65 God's Library

　　The following account is a vision God gave me some years back. I don't remember the circumstances surrounding the vision, but I have never forgotten the vision.

　　I found myself at the top of a winding stairwell. The steps and walls were made of large, magnificent stone blocks. There was light everywhere, but I never saw the source of it. This stairwell and the hallway and everything else in the vision was made of the same stonework. The stone steps went down for only a short way and at the bottom of the steps there was a short landing, perhaps 10 ft. across, in a half-round shape. In front of me there was a massive, wooden, double door, made of two half-doors which met in the center with double handles. The door was arched or rounded at the top. I saw no hinges. There was an angel with me that guided me there. The doors opened of their own accord and we went through them together and entered a hallway. As we started down this long hallway, I noticed there were rooms on either side of the way. Each room had arched open doorways, with bars running up and down from the floor to the top of the doorway. It reminded me of a jail except there was no door to enter these rooms. Each room had something in the center of it to look at. They were simple everyday things, but I knew not the meaning of any of them, and later I could not even recall what they were except for one room which had a large, deep blue blanket covering whatever was on display there. I asked the angel what it was, but he replied we were not to look upon it or know it for now, so we passed on. At the end of this hallway, directly in front of us, was another room like unto the rest. But I recall it had, what I supposed to be, a baptistry. It was a white stone box about 3 ft. by 6 ft.

with a white stone cross at the head of it. It wasn't until later that I realized it wasn't a baptistry at all, but an empty crypt. This explained the lid that laid against it. To the left of this empty crypt, in the adjoining room, was a water fountain with water running over a rock and into a small pool. I did not know the significance of it either, but it was beautiful to see. Now just before this last room, and to the right, was another open doorway with the same archway as before. I could see inside there was a library, with long rows of bookshelves that reached to the ceiling. I also noticed the lowness of the ceiling; I could just about touch it. There were small tables scattered along the wide isles, between the shelves. There were angels everywhere, some rushing along the aisles, some writing in the books, other were sitting at a table and looked to be editing the books. I again asked the angel, "What are all these books?" He said, "Look and see." So I walked over to the shelves and saw that every book was identical in shape and of a dark brown color. Some were thicker than others. I also saw that each book had a different name on the spine of the book. I dared not touch them, for I clearly understood what they were. The names were not in alphabetical order; they were in order by genealogy. These were the book of records for every man's soul, and I knew that inside were recorded the deeds, the acts, the sins, the motives, the thoughts and much more, of every man, whether living or dead. Each had a book with their name on it. At the judgment, these books would be brought forth and every man would be judged according to their works, and they would judged against God's book, the Holy Bible.

Rev 20:12 *And I saw the dead, small and great, stand before God; and the books were opened: and another book was opened, which is the book of life: and the dead were judged out of those things which were written in the books, according to their works.*

I have often wondered since this vision, why didn't I look into MY book? What would I have found?

#66 One Drop of Heaven

This unusual experience took place off the coast of Vietnam, onboard the USS England DLG-22. We were doing ship-to-shore bombardment. We would go far out to sea during the daylight. Then, after dark, we would come in close to land and spend the night firing artillery fire somewhere inland. It was during this time that this experience occurred. The tension amongst the crew was so tight that fights broke out daily. The lack of sleep, the all night boom, boom, boom of artillery fire, shook the ship at every shot. The stifling conditions of spending all night at battle stations, along with the immense heat from which there was no escape and the fear that hung over us like a shadow, put everyone's nerves on keen edge. If you dropped a cup on the mess decks during a meal, it would send several men into reactionary violence. There were always apologies afterwards from both sides, and I believe they were sincere, but the stress we all carried was really indescribable.

Just before daylight we had returned to the open sea where we would get prepared for our next round. Almost everyone slept, except for those who had to stand watch. I had gotten off watch in the boiler room as upper levelmen and was totally exhausted (and fried) and knew I needed sleep. But as my custom was, I went to the place of prayer before I retired. On this occasion, I went to the after steering compartment. I hadn't prayed very long when I asked God for one drop of heaven. He wouldn't miss a small drop, but I was sure it would be a great help to me and my soul. I was sitting on a metal folding chair as I prayed and making my request. I was still praying when it all started. It was like being hit with a giant wave of happiness and joy. I began to shout and laugh and stomp my feet and clap my hands and wave my arms and shout, praise God! Tears of great joy were flowing unrestrained down my face and I felt as though I would explode with such unrestrained glory! I didn't know this kind of experience existed anywhere and I really didn't know how God would answer such a strange request. I don't know how long this went on; wave after wave of unearthly glory.

I was so immensely strengthened and refreshed by this experience that the glow of it lasted for days. My experience with one drop of heaven.

#67 Walking With Jesus for One Week

While I was pastoring the Burlington Iowa Church, the tree company I worked for had some work to be done in the quad cities where our church college, BMI (Bible Missionary Institute) was located. So instead of staying with the rest of the crew collectively in a motel room, I asked if I could stay at BMI. They said I could stay there for that week; praise God for answered prayer! I "checked in" at the school and went to work from there. At the end of the workday, when I returned to my room, I felt the presence of Jesus there very strongly. It was so nice and encouraging after being with the worldly crew of tree service people. The same guts it takes to do that sort of work, is the same guts that puts you in everybody's face. So the days can be very challenging. The presence of Jesus was indeed refreshing. However, I was in for a much greater blessing! Jesus came in person! He was there to meet me every day in my room. We sat and talked and visited as you would anyone else that would come to visit you. It was really quite an experience. He was a perfect gentleman in every way, and I must admit, he taught me what a perfect gentleman really is. He also created in me a tremendous desire to be like him in spirit and in wisdom and in understanding. One evening as Jesus and I visited, I asked if we could go and visit my daughter who was attending that very college. Of course, Jesus said he would go with me. So we went. We walked together across the campus to the library/study hall, where students went to study. Jesus and I walked up the steps and we went right in. I noticed as we went that people were looking at me as they would any visitor on the campus. I wondered what they were thinking. What did they see? We found my daughter in the study hall. She was sitting at a table, her back to the window, at the end of the table. I sat down across from her and Jesus stood at the end of the table between us. I said to her, "Jesus is here and we wanted to talk to you." Her answer was something to the effect that, "Yes, Jesus is there, he's always there, and I pray every day." I said, "Jesus is standing right there!" pointing to him standing there. "He's looking at you! Can't you see him?" She looked at where I was pointing as though it was across the room. She could not see him! That amazed me. "He's standing right here!" pointing to the floor where He stood. She looked amused, but obviously could not see him. I seemed to her as one that mocked. So Jesus and I left and went back to the room. Those visits lasted the entire week that I stayed at that college.

VOLUME II: MORE STORIES

Ships at Sea

- Upon the sea of life there are many ships that sail.
- Some are big and sturdy, some are small and frail.
- But among the ships and vessels, be they many or so few,
- One thing they hold in common, they stand for me and you.
- The sailboat is so pretty, but it's driven by the fads
- The battleship is mighty, but fighting is always sad.
- The motorboat seems humble, it carries two or three,
- But despite the winds or current, it goes where it wants to be.
- There are pleasure boats and drifters, speed boats seem so free
- They all teach us a lesson, of what we ought to be
- The tugboats look so rusty, and seem to be so slow,
- But without their gentle tugging, the big ships could not go
- There are many ships that teach us of fear or peace or strife
- But none are so dreaded as the shipwrecks of our lives'
- It really does not matter, if our ship be rich or poor,
- When we sink beneath the waves, our journey is no more.
- Upon the charts before us, we chose to set our course
- If we take a faulty compass the shipwreck will be ours

- The lighthouse will guide us, in the darkest of the night
- But wearing colored glasses, we will fail to see the light
- The fame we had on departure, or the bands that played so loud,
- The waving of our friends, or the cheering of the crowd,
- Will be of no avail to us when the storms break at sea.
- It will test our deepest character. Of what we ought to be
- And if we make it some glad day, into heavens harbor fair
- We then will know the final truth, of just what took us there!
- It wasn't the type of start we had, or the type of boat we be.
- It will be how close to Christ we walked. The master of the sea.

Time Warp Road

They say truth is stranger than fiction and I have certainly found that to be the case. This experience is one of the strangest and most controversial of all. I struggled if I should even include it with the rest of these experiences, but since the other experiences are already off the chart of most people today, one more experience of extreme reality of another time and another dimension won't change anything.

Since I have come out in the open with these stories, several have approached me and told me that they have had very similar experiences, but they have been afraid to speak up. So I know I'm not alone in some of these experiences. "Time Warp Road," strangely enough, is one experience that I hear the most about. Others have had the same experience in this phenomenon but in different locations, sometimes over 2000 miles away. I find it surprising just how many others have had these experiences.

I have titled this experience as such because it's the only explanation there is. I know of no other explanation. This was not a dream or a vision; it was an experience that was just as real as I am. But I have no explanation. I don't think there is one.

Here is a clip of my opinion as to how things like this took place. Worlds and times were clashing. Powers of both seen and unseen worlds were at war. The spiritual was being pushed aside for facts. People were abandoning the old ways of superstition and seances, while the spiritual was pushing back for dominance. Yes, many worlds were clashing and the area we call Missouri was the battle ground. Everyone had stories about their experiences, just as I did, but few would talk about it openly, and fewer yet would dare to face the ridicule of writing about it.

It was a typical summer Ozark afternoon. Things were laid back, I was bored, and so I did what I did the most. I got into my old junky 1951 Chevrolet and started driving the country roads. I did not know where many of those roads went, so I enjoyed driving them to see where they went and to see what there was to see on them. The Ozarks are absolutely beautiful all year round and I enjoyed them. I drove for several hours before night set in, and that's a good time to go home. I had passed Spring Valley Baptist church on blacktop "H." Then I turned right onto "BB." I knew this road very well and I knew it would take me to Eugene. Little did I know what was about to happen. As I rounded the second corner of the "S" curve, to the left I saw a gravel road shooting directly off to the left that fell off steeply. I was surprised to see it. I thought to myself, I didn't know that road was there. How could I have missed it? It was so obvious. But I had never seen it before. This was a section of road that I traveled every day, but that road was not there before. I backed up the car and turned down that road. I wanted to know where it went.

It was a very narrow road with white gravel. I thought I had turned into somebody's driveway, but no, it was a road. It went downhill all the way to the creek. To the right of the little narrow road, and just before the creek, there were several little well maintained shanties. All were silent and dark. There was a very SMALL creek with an even SMALLER bridge crossing it. I wondered if the little wooden bridge would hold the weight of the car, but I reasoned that if it had been there this long and held up, it would hold up one more time. So I drove across it. Directly in front of me, (for the little lane made an almost 90 degree turn to the left after the bridge.) was the front porch of a little white house which was worn but looking very well maintained. There was a kerosene lamp burning in the window. The lamp made me look for telephone poles, lest I hit one. Everything was so close and tight, but there were no poles that I could see. The road went hard by the porch at the end of the house and I was careful not to hit it, it was so close. As my headlights swept across the yard and the adjoining barnyard, I noticed the antique machinery that was everywhere; all types of horse-drawn farm equipment in beautiful shape. Even the hay tines were bright and shiny as though they had just been used that day. The road made another sharp turn to the right, passing between the house proper and the barn. I was so close to the house wall, just outside of my passenger window, it was like driving through a drive through burger joint, only it was on the passenger side. There was a window there and I felt bad about wakening these good people up at this time of the night. If they had opened the window, I could have shaken

MORE STORIES

their hand, it was that close. By then I was convinced I was literally driving through their yard and it had nothing to do with a road, and I just wanted out of there!

Fortunately for me it was a road and just in front of me it opened up very wide and it led uphill. I still didn't know where I was, but I wanted out of there. I drove as quietly by the house as I could and left as quietly as I could, hoping I didn't arouse some angry farmer by driving through his yard in the middle of the night.

The uphill road was pure rock. There was some gravel on it, but the roadbed was solid bare rock. It was very steep and the last thing I wanted was to start spinning out on loose gravel on the rock. I made it up the hill and as soon as it became a real road again I stepped on it. I'm outta there! After some time, I came to an intersection that was completely strange to me so I went by dead reckoning and turned right. I found myself back on "BB." That didn't make sense either, but I was glad to be somewhere I knew in the middle of the night. Soon I was home!

The next day I was at my dad and stepmom's house on "H" and I told them of the strange road I'd found along with all the details of it. Mom asked, "Where were you at?" So I told her again. She was completely confused as that road hadn't been there for many, many years. The area was an old coal mining community and she had been there as young girl visiting her dad. Miners had slept in those shanties and walked home on weekends. In the small house lived the owner of the mine, who also farmed the land. There was never any electricity down there. That place had closed down over 65 years ago and the road was abandoned, no one living there since. The buildings were all torn down when the land sold, but somehow I had described it in exact detail as she remembered it as a child. Her dad had worked that mine and rented one of those shanties, so she remembered it very well! But it's been gone for many, many years.

We were all confused as what had happened, but there was no doubt it happened. I cannot explain it. Neither can I explain why it happened. The very next day, I returned to the place and found there was no road there. How can someone visit a place that no longer exists, and describe in complete detail a place that vanished long before he was ever born? What would have happened if I had met someone? What would they have said? What would I have said? What would have happened if I left something there? Or if they had given me something?

No one But God can answer any of these kinds of questions. And only God can explain how and why it happened. I suspect there are people who have had strange things happen in their lives that they cannot explain. Perhaps they struggle over their event, or perhaps it left some kind of scar. Perhaps they have nightmares or fears or perhaps it has left them wounded in some invisible way. I'm one of the lucky ones because I was able to escape unharmed. But this I can say with confidence; no matter how deep the scars or the fears or the wounds, it doesn't matter if people understand, because I can tell you they won't. They will mock you and make fun of you because they have never experienced it themselves. They don't have the ability or the depth to understand. But there are those who do. Jesus is one of them that clearly understands. He is also the only one who can bring peace and healing to a troubled and wounded heart. Yes, He understands. If we are willing to take our cares and burdens to Him, He will gladly receive us and give us the peace we are looking for. Try Him and see!

MORE STORIES

You Sleep Here

Some time ago I took a trip to Missouri. I landed in Saint Louis where someone picked me up. Since her home was about 150 miles away, we naturally arrived there quite late. As we were unloading the car, I asked where I would be sleeping. I knew that tomorrow we would be loading up again and pushing on to my dad and mom's house, yet even further away. She said she had just the place all picked out and ready. (Boy did she ever!) She led me through the house to a VERY narrow door that led up a very narrow and steep stairwell to the attic. After reaching the top of the stairs, it was clear she had gotten into witchcraft. There, in front of me, was a bed under a cow skull and a pentagram. On the dresser next to the bed there were many candles and voodoo dolls with pins in them. She pointed to a heavily locked and reinforced door across the room and informed me about the "Spirits of dead men that come out of that door at night." She said they have tried to stop them, but it hasn't worked yet. (I don't think she was trying to stop ANYTHING.) She also told me of the murder that took place in that attic, and about the blood that keeps coming back, and the screams that seem to come from nowhere, and by the way, **you sleep here**, pointing to the bed!

NOW she had my attention! I knew this area of the Ozarks was infested with superstition. I knew how Satan had used that blindness to his fullest advantage to deceive and control and further blind, for I had grown up in that country and knew it all too well.

I had witnessed to everyone in the family tree about salvation and sanctification. I had made it very clear God is greater than sin, love is stronger than hate, and light is stronger than darkness. She knew everything that I had said, but still she had gotten into witchcraft.

So she said, "Good night" and turned around and walked away. I stood there listening to see if she locked the door at the bottom of the stairs, but I don't believe she did. She obviously thought I would never make it that far!

I must have an invisible message on my forehead that everyone can see, but me! It says "Victim!" or something to that effect.

So here we are, way out in the middle of nowhere, very late at night, dead tired (no pun intended) and I'm being thrown into this mount Carmel "show down." If God be God, then serve him, but, if Satan is bigger than your God, then "You're on the menu tonight"!

I watched her leave and wondered, "How did I get myself into this mess?" If I disappear tonight, she will say I never got off the plane. If I don't disappear, I'll wish I HADN'T gotten off the plane!

I looked around and examined the artifacts in the room. There was no mistake about it. I ran everything through my mind and wondered what I had missed. There should have been indicators, glaringly obvious, long before I had gotten this far, but there wasn't. Either I had missed some very important clues or this had been hidden VERY well. I'm taking the later excuse.

So I knelt down beside the bed I was to sleep on and prayed that God would show himself VERY strong in this "show down, and that right early!" And that God would somehow turn all this around for His glory.

It was never presented as a show down, but that's what I took it to be, and I wasn't going to turn and run (even though I wanted to!). God had never failed me yet and there were things many times more challenging than this. So the battle lines were drawn and night was closing in. But the SON comes up in the morning!

I pleaded the blood, put the battle into God's hands and went to bed. That wasn't presumption, it was faith! Plus, what else was there to do? And God did the work! I slept all night without as much as a stir. When I woke up in the morning, it was as though nothing had happened! If God hadn't helped, I could have been in BIG trouble! I could have been woken up in the night, surrounded by people with hoods on, with evil intentions, or demons having a heyday, or worse! (Believe me, there are worse.) But it was a very restful night FOR ME! I went downstairs and was shocked at what I saw!

My hostess was sitting up on the couch, (she hadn't slept at all) with her knees drawn up to her chest, and she looked terrible, awful! So I said, "What happened?" She said that the "Spirits" came out of that room last night, made a beeline down the stairs, "worked her over all night" (whatever that meant) and threatened her with, "Don't you EVER send us a CHRISTIAN!" I don't know what else transpired that night, or the mechanics of it, but I DO know what happened upstairs; ABSOLUTLY NOTHING! God was victor again. He protects his own, even the trembling ones that are scared half out of their mind! God is truly in control!

If we really knew what we are up against as Christians, we'd be shaken very badly. But God, in his grace and wisdom, may keep us "in the dark" for our best interest and to accomplish His purpose. Sometimes not knowing is our safest place and God knows it. He just keeps carrying us along and strengthens us as we go. Meanwhile, He pours His grace out in great abundance! By the way, you can sleep there!

Visiting with Aunt Bess

It was customary in the south for those you respected to be called by family names such as aunt or uncle. Very elderly people were called "Mom" or "Dad" out of respect, though in reality, they were not related in any way. Even so with Aunt Bess. I think she was my mom's, mom's, sister. Or Grandma Smith's sister. But to all who knew her, she was Aunt Bess!

Aunt Bess' home was a picture right out of the Ozark frontier. It had the typical four rooms. Most walls were unfinished on the inside, made of clapboard style construction and painted white. It had a full front porch with slanted roof, small glass windows, a crooked stove pipe, a steep, wooden shingled roof, no running water, no electricity, no insulation and kerosene lanterns for inside lighting.

The house sat on the side of a steep hill called the goat hill. It was the first house on the left as you started down the hill from the main road. The left side of the house sat directly on the ground. The right side of the house was supported by large flat rocks stacked up to support the house at two corners and a porch corner. An adult could easily walk right under her house on the downhill side.

The floor from underneath looked like it was a log house with the huge sleepers and puncheon floor. I got the impression it was previously a log house that had burned down, and a frame house was built on the existing floor. Whatever had happened was many years before my time. This place had been there forever. I had no idea what the dimension of her house was, but

MORE STORIES

looking back, I'd guess it to be about 20 ft. wide by 30 ft. long, single story with high pitched roof.

The uphill side of her house that sat on the ground, had the typical washboards, washtubs, hand wringers and bathtubs hanging on the outside wall. Usually there was big pile of firewood stacked along the house.

In the summer, the front porch was the favorite place to "visitate." The porch, being raised a foot or more off the ground, always provided much seating.

The front rooms of these very popular style homes always doubled as a sitting room and bedroom. If you visited these homes in the winter, adults normally sat at the table in the kitchen. However, the kids always sat in the front room, on the bed or on the floor, anyplace but the kitchen. The kitchen was for adults and for serious conversations.

The wood stoves were almost always in this front room. There were never any "built-in" things, such as closets or cabinets. All inside doorways were hanging blankets, always hanging low from the top of the door to allow heat to get into the room, but never low enough to violate privacy, and high enough off the floor to not drag. The front room normally held a few three-legged chairs, a single rocking chair, and a Lincoln closet, (a standing closet, usually with one door and a few drawers inside for personal things). Wherever the closet was located designated that room to be the bedroom. There was a feather bed framed with four slats and held up with a rope grid, a few pictures, a kerosene lantern hanging on the wall opposite of the wood stove, sometimes a mirror or a shelf for really important things such as a book, and a washing table with a large bowl and a water pitcher sitting on it. As you entered the room from the front porch, there was a doorway to the immediate right, leading to the kitchen. (You never put a blanket over a kitchen doorway. It was bad luck and impractical.) Next to the kitchen door was a stove. On the other side of the stove would be a firewood box. Then the rear wall of the room. Next to the wood box, and located in this corner, was another doorway, blanket included, that led to the bedroom. To the left of this door would be the feather bed. The bed was situated in the corner of the rear wall and the outside wall to the left. Next to the bed would be a little table stand, usually with a water pitcher in a bowl, sitting on it for washing up and a nail in the wall for the towel and wash rag. Behind this table was a window that usually opened by hinges at the top, with a stick laying on the sill to prop it open. Then to the left of that was the Lincoln closet. To the left of the closet, and in the corner, would be a rocking chair. Making that turn, and coming back to the front door, there would be a window with a three-legged chair in front of it and between the chair and the door you'd find several coat pegs on the wall, with a shelf on the wall above it. Most all of the front doors, looking at them from the outside, were hinged on the right. The door swinging inside and against the wall, was too short to block the doorway into the kitchen.

    The wooden doors were always made with thick planking and crisscrossed for strength. Some were pegged and some were nailed. Most ended up with both. They almost always had long steel strap hinges, top, middle and bottom. It was not uncommon to see the old worn out and broken leather hinges still tacked to the wall. Early on, none of them had doorknobs. All had handles for pulling. None had what we would call modern day locks. At night, if you wanted to lock the door, there was the long oak board that crossed the door on the inside, which set into notches for that purpose. It was common to see a door that had the slider type locks which consisted of a small board that slid, right or left, to latch or open the door. Sliders had a peg that went through the door so it could be opened from either side.

None of the entry doors had windows in them. And I don't ever remember seeing a second door in any of these type cabins, unless it was added much later.

Entering the front door and turning to the right took you into the kitchen. To your right, (facing the front porch wall) there was shelving from the ceiling to the floor loaded with foods of all sorts; canned, hanging, and dried, or in little wicker baskets rounded over or in boxer ("tins") of all colors and sizes.

In front of you facing the outside wall were shelves, loaded with food also, and reaching all the way to the floor. Underneath these shelves were large crock pots, sealed with lard, and covered with a fine cloth made from flour sacks and tied.

There was a small kitchen table with folding out "wings." On the table was the normal tableware that consisted of a jar or cup with spoons sticking out of it (handles always downward), salt, pepper, sugar bowl, and butter dish. The window beside the table would give much light and warmth. Coffee cups all sat upside down on the shelf above the window. They were upside down for practical reasons; it kept dirt, ash, bugs etc. out of the cups. The shelves were covered with newspaper. To the left of the table was the water bucket that sat on a little table made just for it that came out of the wall. A dipper hung from the side of the water bucket. It was all white with red trim. You would dip your water out of the pail with the dipper, drink what you wanted, throw the rest of the water that was left out the window, and hang the dipper back on the pail or the nail. Your choice.

Next to the water bucket was the kitchen sink. It was a large cast iron type, mounted on legs. It had a high back, no holes for faucets, a drain board, and it was deep. The drain came out of the sink, turned toward the wall where it went through, and stuck out the wall a foot or so on the outside and stopped. All water went on the ground outside of the house. The sink had a curtain around the front three sides. Stacked under the sink in wicker boxes were various cleaning products and hand tools. The shelf above the sink held all kinds of stuff for doing dishes; soap, dishrags, scrubbers, scrappers, and such, including pegs for drying towels and dishrags.

Now comes the rear wall facing the rear of the house. Centered on this wall was a large wood cook stove. It's stove pipe went straight up and through the roof. Hanging on the wall and setting neatly on shelves, all around this stove, were all sizes and shapes of pans, utensils, pots, bowls, etc. To the right of the stove was a tinder box. These arrangements took up the whole wall. There was a table sitting in the area in front of the wood stove that was strong and movable. On the left of this wall, and right at the corner was a doorway leading to the back room. That was a storage room, bedroom, sewing room and washroom all in one. It always had a blanket covering the door. The kitchen had three or four places where lanterns hung or were mounted to the wall.

The last wall of the kitchen, (that separated the front room from the kitchen) was entirely made of shelves. From the ceiling to the floor, food, boxes, "tins" etc. filled these shelves. There were large metal bins that held dry goods such as potatoes, onions, or whatever. Aunt Bess dried garden foods by tying or lacing them together and hanging them from the kitchen ceiling. There they would slowly dry and be stored out of the way.

The main bedroom was located straight behind the front room. I seldom went through it, for it was considered private area. You weren't supposed to ever go in there. The few times I did, I went clear through to the room behind the kitchen. All I remember about the main bedroom was that it had a feather bed, a closet, a dresser with a big mirror on it, and a washstand in front of the window. Going into someone's bedroom was considered very disrespectful and put you in a bad light. I don't remember much more about that room.

Aunt Bess had a garden out back. Almost everything she ate came out of that garden. Home-canned goods were everywhere! On the floor of her kitchen, next to the wall, were large metal bins full of flour, salt, corn meal, lard, etc. These she bought from the mill in an area of town they called Dutch Mill.

Aunt Bess had been married many, many years ago. Her husband had died back around the time of the depression. I think his last name was "Branson." I'm not aware that she had any children as there were pictures of her husband around her house but there were no pictures of kids or family anywhere.

She smoked a corn cob pipe and occasionally chewed "good money chewing tobacco" that she called "tobakay." She would sit in her rocker and spit dead center into the spittoon every time. She kept a 22-caliber rifle next to her bed or by her rocker but I never saw her shoot it. However, I heard she could shoot horseflies out of the air with it. She said she opened the kitchen window in the winter and shot rabbits down by the creek. I was totally convinced!

She kept a large Bible by her rocker and it was obvious she knew every word of it because she was always talking about "The Lord." When someone came to her house and used cussing, she would stop them right there and say, "Young man, you don't use that kind of talk around here!" If anything negative about somebody was said, she would again stop them and say, "We don't talk like that around here!" If she had to stop you on two violations, she would say, " I think you'd best be a-leavin'!"

She was in her 90's, but health wise was about 40. She could hear very well, see very well, and she was extremely observant. She saw right through people.

I loved going to Aunt Bess's. I'd walk around her house, asking all kinds of questions. She was happy for company and was glad to explain things to me. My favorite question was, "What was it like when you were a kid?" She'd say, "Let's go out on the porch and sit for a while." Once there, she could hold you spellbound for hours! I loved it!

She was a very remarkable woman; a breed that has long since passed from the scene. This world is much worse for its lack of these people. Little did I realize as a kid the treasure I was visiting with!

MORE STORIES

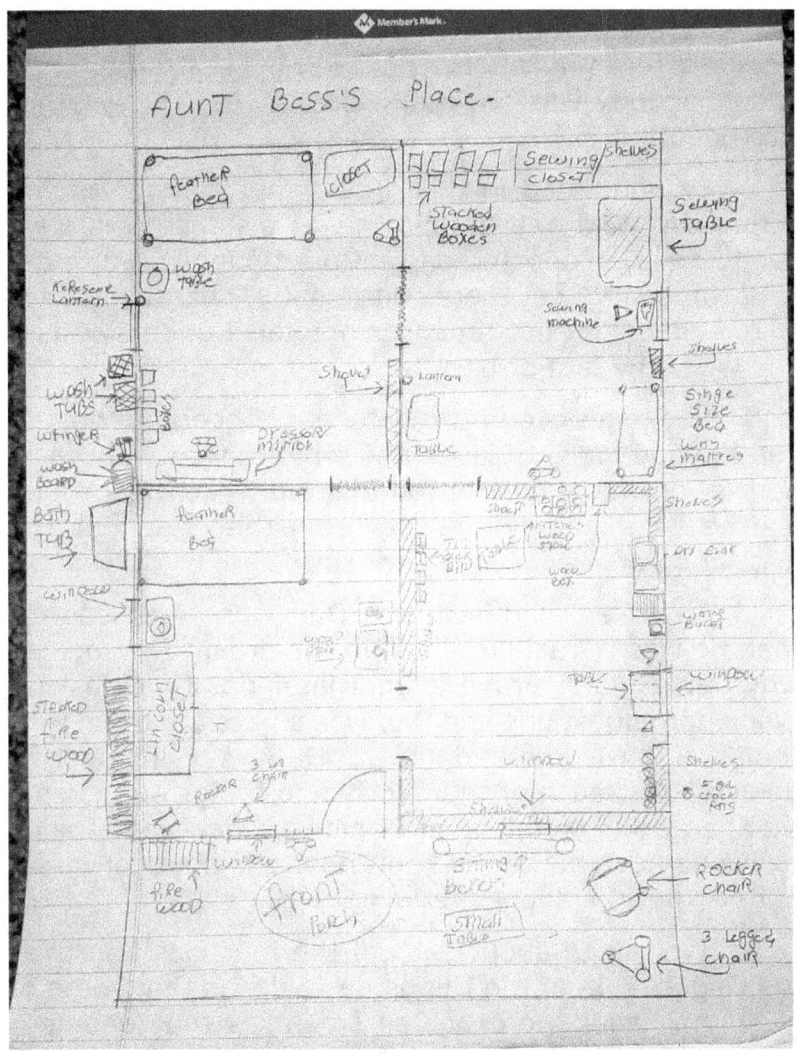

A Dream? With Dad

In this dream, Dad and I were walking through a grassy field. (Dad had passed away several years before this.) It seemed we were following a path of some kind. There were other people scattered about, some were standing alone, some were visiting others, some were also walking in the same direction as us, but from a different location. They were all scattered round about, nobody was physically close to us. The weather was beautiful.

I understood in this dream that we were going across this field to a gate in the far distance where we had to be at an appointed time. Our timing was of great importance. We got there a little early, but stayed back a little space, for our time was not yet. I understood no one would be late or early.

Looking beyond the gate was a beautiful orchid, and beyond were trellises and white paved walkways. Further on was a mist or fog that hid what was beyond it. The gate had no fencing on either side but the distinction of change was very clear.

I noticed in this dream Dad was much shorter than he was in real life. Even in the dream I suspected why but couldn't prove it until later on. I was asking many hard questions and Dad was answering them with remarkable wisdom and insight. He was giving specific details about each of them including things and events that had transpired long after his passing away. Things he would have no way of knowing in the physical world, but he knew all about them very well.

We talked about each of the four kids and their marriages. One of the things he said was that some of their marriages were not as stable as they seemed; some were on the verge of breaking up. And some would never make it to the gate before us. Their health was not good and their nerves were worn out. The specific details he gave were very up-to-date in the lives of each of them. Again, he knew all about them very well. Sometimes the things he said were answers to questions that I had not asked yet. He seemed to know what I was thinking.

MORE STORIES

We talked about my troubled past and the daily struggles I faced as a result of that past. He spoke in clear details. He spoke of my spiritual wellbeing and the daily oppression I was in, and had been in for some time. He said I was far more oppressed than I realized, but I had gotten used to it. He also said that when God lifts it, I will be amazed at the difference.

One of the things he said was that the mold I was formed in was God's mold, it was not the devil's mold. God made that mold and he made it just for me. The troubles and difficulties I faced as a child was God training me for what's ahead.

He answered, without being asked, why I had such a terrible time in the holiness movement. It seems God was watching all of it. God was not impressed and except they repent, they too would not make the gate. However, God used that time to redirect my priorities and get me established to walk alone. There would be no "religious crutches" and helps in the valley ahead. If I could not survive the religious world, just as Jesus had to survive it, then how could I ever make it through the valley?

We talked about Granny and the role she played in both of our lives. We talked about her prayers, her example, her sacrifices, her faith, and her rewards that she is currently enjoying. We both rejoiced greatly at her remembrance. It was a most precious time.

There is a valley through which I must pass. That valley is going to max and tax me to the uttermost. All the difficulties I have faced was my training for what's ahead. But it was very important that I understand that I must pass through that valley alone. No one will be with me. I will be totally alone. I understood he meant earthly friends and families.

Throughout this conversation, Dad repeatedly made reference to my having to go it alone, and how my remembering that was very important. There was some talk about this valley, but he couldn't say much about it. It was clear that he wasn't supposed to reveal anything about it except in preparing me to go through it.

After some time, we both knew the "appointment" was NOW. Dad walked away through the gate and as he went he was fading away out of sight. Then he turned and looked at me as he was fading away. The look he gave spoke volumes. I must go it alone; will I make it? And his shortness was representing my wife and her shortness. My aloneness was understood.

I pondered this dream for some time. About 2:00 AM, I got out of bed and went to the front room and stayed there until the dawn was breaking outside. I got down on my knees and went to prayer. There I talked with God, and God met me there. I reached out to God for relief from the oppression and strength for what's ahead. I tried to go to bed, but I could not sleep. I was sitting on the edge of the bed, remembering, looking back and weeping. I wept tears of sadness over things Dad had said about the kids. I did eventually lie down and I went to sleep.

That morning, I felt such a tremendous relief, as if a great and heavy weight had been lifted from my shoulders. The joy and peace were overflowing. The oppression was gone. Then I saw what Dad had seen and knew what he meant. I shared with my wife my experience and we both agreed that God had used my dad because he was the only one that I could have received this type of thing from. I think God could have used Himself in some way or some other, but He chose my dad, and I'm glad he did. We both (my wife and I) agreed I needed to write this down so I don't forget it or get it mixed up.

Sunday night at church there was a singing group from a church college. I had a very hard time understanding their words due to the sound system, but God came and reminded me about the dream and the relief he gave me and the peace that was filling my heart. He witnessed to me again and blessed my soul greatly.

Having Company!

Having Company used to be a highlight of Ozark living. When you live so far out in the sticks, and sunlight had to be pumped to you, you knew you were almost home.

The first sign of company had nothing to do with the mail, because you didn't get any mail. You had to go to the post office in town and ask for your name in general delivery to see if you had any mail. They usually saw you coming and had it ready before you walked in, and you were not surprised when they told you who else had mail waiting for them. If you saw them, you were to let them know!

Knowing that company was coming had nothing to do with the phone. You might not have a phone. Most of us did, and it was a crank phone mounted to the wall. It was the old party line type, meaning that while you were talking, everyone was eavesdropping and having a party at your news.

The first sign of company usually came from the dust cloud far off in the distance, rising high. That was your first short notice. If the dust cloud passed your lane, then they weren't coming to your place.

Every eye would watch to see if the dust cloud started getting lower and lower as it neared your lane. That was the sure-fire thing you had company coming and everyone would go into action with lots of excitement and lots of shouting, "We got company coming!" The kids would go running for the gate, so by the time your company got to the gate, there would be a pile of kids swinging on it and waiting for them. Everyone would be shouting and waving with great excitement. There were always a few to run to the house to announce who it was. Your guest would drive slowly through the gate as to not run over any excited, running, yelling, going hog wild little kids who were having a real good time at your appearance.

Once through the gate, the car would proceed slowly to the house. Meanwhile the gate got closed and all those gate riders would jump off and start chasing the car to the house, running behind it and yelling their lungs out, "They're here! They're here!" waving frantically. Meanwhile the kids in the car were hanging out the windows by then and yelling their greeting in return, waving back just as excited as everyone else.

Running too close behind the car was very self-correcting. One quick stop to dodge a small little fellow who couldn't keep his feet straight, was all the teaching you needed for running too close. But you didn't want to get too far behind or you'd look like a walking dirt clod by the time you got to the house. Then you couldn't visit at all; you had to go get washed up first.

Of course in the house there was a lot of activity as well. The mom, grandma, and older sister all had to change aprons, wipe the baby's face, and tell the little ones that were still inside to go wash their face and hands and change their shirt. Dad's job at the first sign of the little runners who came to announce who it was, was going to the hen house to start wringing the chicken's neck, and then to run it to the house and add it to the meal. Grandpa was to get his fiddle, banjo, guitar, or whatever he had, and start tuning it up. Adding water to the gravy, making more tea, dragging out the extra chairs, setting more places, all of this was done in record time!

By the time the company got out of the car, everyone would be outside, hugging and shaking hands, holding babies, and listening to the challenges of their journey to get there. Of course all the kids would still be yelling and telling their latest exploits. There was always the usual chore of putting the dogs in the barn for acting like excited dogs. Sometimes even the animals would sense the excitement and come to the fence to see what was going on.

When things settled down a bit they would all be welcomed inside to "sit a while" while supper was "gettin' ready." This sent all the kids to the back porch, where the water tub was sitting, to wash up, while the adult guests would wash up in the house. They even have a clean drying towel in the house. As for us kids, shirt sleeves and jeans worked just fine. After the meal, all the ladies and girls would join in for a major kitchen clean-up crew. It seemed like everyone was involved somehow, bringing in extra wood for both stoves, filling up the water bucket, feeding table scraps to the dogs, taking the trash out to the burn barrel or putting the rest of the animals up for the night. Of course, the taking of the chairs out to the front porch meant we were almost ready for the evening fun. For the adults it meant having the old-fashioned sing and play "ho-down." But for the younger kids, it meant all kinds of games in the yard. Hide and go seek was always popular along with Red Rover. Tag was a good game to start out with, but it usually wore out pretty fast.

Running around with a belly full of fried chicken and potatoes had a way of slowing things down.

Somewhere after the singing came the story telling. Many family adventures, and fears, were passed on by word of mouth at that time. Scary stories always separated the men from the mice. Once the story got scary enough, it was probably just a coincidence the guys ended up in the house, with all the lights on. Of course the kids were left outside to fend for themselves at whatever woods monster, sea creature or barn loft boogie man was lurking around.

Eventually things would wind down, beds were made, kids re-arranged, and couches that had beds folded up inside of them would be brought out. The kids got washed up and sent to bed. The adults gathered back on the porch or at the kitchen table to discuss all the things kids weren't supposed to hear. If the news was really bad as to what they had to say, the adults ended up outside out in the yard. There was always a round of chairs, and normally a porch swing hanging from a tree, out there somewhere. If adults were going to cry, they didn't want to be seen by everyone. They always shared their griefs out in the yard, away from little ears who didn't need to hear such things. Those "<u>out in the yard</u>" moments usually lasted well into the night, sometimes long after the bobwhites and the whippoorwills went to bed.

Morning was always a slow but exciting time. Folks were up early and chores were done with many hands helping. The girls and moms would cook up a breakfast that would make your nose pull you out of bed. Your mouth would start watering long before your eyes saw what was causing it. There isn't an alarm clock made that can equal the smell of breakfast in the kitchen!

The morning chores would go fast and getting cleaned up was in order. The very cold water in the wash tub, waiting on the back porch, didn't even slow us down when plates were being filled up on the table.

Days were filled with swimming, exploring, fort building and gossip. (Did I say that out loud?) Toward lunch or dinner, somebody would be responsible for shooting the meat for the meal. We always knew where to go for whatever meat was requested. The girls in the house would put in their requests for what was needed, and we boys took turns at filling the need. Sometimes we all went to get it. Hunting was as natural as eating. Fresh game was always on the menu.

Frog legs was not a normal dinner meat, so frog gigging was something the guys did just for the joy of doing it. Frog legs are a favorite, good times only, adventure. It meant a special meal long after supper. We'd get and gut the frogs while the girls got everything ready for the cook up. It was a tradition of good times, more than just feeding everybody.

By and by the company had to leave. It didn't matter how long they stayed, it always went by too fast. And no matter how hard the times were, we never seemed to notice that when company came. Even when certain kids had knockdown, drag out fight, there were always tears shed in saying good-by. There was no running behind the car or swinging on the gate. The excited greetings had turned to saddened faces. But memories had been made that would last a lifetime. And many life-changing decisions were made, because company came.

One day God is going to have company. He will sound a trumpet and come with a shout. There will be much shouting as his children pass through the gates. I also think there will be a lot of running to greet loved ones and waving hello. I think heaven will ring with laughter and shouts of victory and praise. It's not hard to imagine the loved ones who have gone before us, standing along the road to greet us upon our arrival. What a grand reunion that will be. I know there will be a great feast prepared for his own. I wonder if Heaven will have fried chicken and iced tea? I don't know. The Bible says, "of his kingdom there will be no end." No one on the porch swinging alone and bawling because company was leaving, no quietly loading up the car to depart, no tears in heaven. What a day that will be!

I want to hear the voice of my dad and mother once again. I want to see Granny's smile and hear her laughter. I want to hear them say, "I'm so glad you made it. Tell us, what was your journey here like?" I want to see them again, feel their embrace, and hear them laugh once again. I want to see that old familiar twinkle in their eye once more and hear them say, "Won't you come on in and sit a while; the supper is almost ready!"

I want to sing our Saviour praises, and see little children play in the grass. I wonder what would be said when we look across the yard and see that circle of chairs and the old porch swing under the tree are all gone. "What happened to them?" we may ask. The answer will probably be, "Son, up here we don't need them anymore. No more painful realities to face. No more sad news to protect the children from. No more weeping or sorrow of heart. We can hug each other and say, "Welcome Home... Forever."

Church Helper!

At one point in time, I was compelled to go house calling for the church. The pastor had spoken about our need to be a witness for Jesus and refusing to do so was

MORE STORIES

a type of denying Christ. He said we were keeping our lights hidden.

So, one Saturday I decided to go and knock on doors, as instructed. The pastor had said to always leave a calling card so your visit would be remembered. I didn't have any calling cards, but the pastor had a stack of them on the table as you came into the church, so I loaded up on them and went calling. This was a country church, and houses were far apart. But I went.

After knocking on several doors, I came to a house that had a big cattle gate across the driveway. It also had a big sign that said no trespassing; this means you. There were several bullet holes in the sign.

I reasoned this was the devil's way of keeping these people out of heaven, and I reasoned they really did need the truth. So I climbed over the locked gate and went up the driveway. Next to the door were some very large dog houses with big chains on the ground. I reasoned since I was doing God's business, I would be safe.

Fortunately, the dogs were in the house. I went to the door and knocked on it rather loudly. Nobody came to the door, but I clearly heard people moving around inside, so I determined not to be ignored. I knocked even louder and longer. But still no answer. So, I decided to bang on the door for Jesus! I pounded on this aluminum and glass screen door when the door broke off its top hinge. Imagine that! Then the dogs started barking. Now I know the sounds I was hearing were the dogs, not the people. At this point there was nothing I could do but leave. Remembering that the pastor admonished to leave a card, I propped the door back in place and wedged his card in it where it could be easily seen. I left thinking I had done a good deed.

That was on a Saturday. The next morning at church, first things first. Here comes the pastor! He was doing everything he could to be calm and collected but it was clear something was really bothering him.

It seems he had gotten this phone call from somebody who was screaming mad and who wanted to beat him up for some unknown reason. Something about trespassing, a gate and a door. And for some strange reason my name seemed to come to his attention. And he was just wondering if I happened to know anything about it? Of course, I did! I told him all about it! He was not impressed with me at all. He asked me to return all of his cards back to the table, and if I ever decided to go calling again, I could go with him. We would go together and he would keep me well within his sight.

He thanked me for my willingness to help, and my sincere desire to be a witness, but there are certain ways to do it and certain ways to not do it. He was very kind the whole time and did very well at manifesting a good spirit even though he was very troubled about something.

In my desire to be a witness for Jesus, I came up with some very interesting approaches. Most were not good, and some were a total self-destruct. Here is another that didn't work so well.

Along the highway coming into town, there was a trailer court. It was a typical hillbilly, Redneck, partying, fighting, everybody related, trailer court.

I decided that would be a good place to knock on doors and hand out tracts. So I went there and attempted just that. But is seemed nobody was ever home, or perhaps they just wouldn't answer the door. After a couple of attempts to reach the people in this place, I decided it was time to try another tactic. I

MORE STORIES

decided to start my door knocking around 10 o'clock at night.

I'd go up to the door and bang on it furiously, yelling, "Anybody in there?" Almost immediately somebody would come to the door and throw it wide open asking, "What's wrong?" And I would reply, "Without God you're dropping into hell and will burn worse than a house fire!" Then I'd shove this salvation tract in their hand and leave right away. I did this at several homes before I began to sense an uneasiness. It was very clear and urgent that I needed to leave right away! I left right then and drove back to town.

I wasn't very wise, and in many ways I was very foolish. I cannot say if there were ever any results spiritually with those whom I had encountered. But I am glad to say, that when the Spirit said, "Do this," I always did it right then. Looking back, I think God was watching over me in more ways than I realized.

How not to witness at a drive in.

One summer night I decided to go to the drive-in picture show. There were a whole bunch of us that went together. On certain nights they offered a flat rate per car, no matter how many were in it. We filled up the car and the trunk with people. I think there were about 15 of us all together. Of course, you cannot stay in the car very long when there are that many people. All you have to do is get past the entry booth, and then everybody scatters in all directions once you get inside. If you are not there when it's time to leave, then that's your fault. Find your own way home.

I had gotten inside and was looking for a place to sit and watch the show. This usually meant sitting on the playground equipment way up in the front. There was a big crowd already up there doing just that, so I decided to head for the concession stand.

I soon realized the people in the back row of the drive-in didn't go there to see the show. They were busy doing other things. So I decided it was time to intervene for Jesus. I started at the far end of the back row and went calling, walking right up to the car and watching through the window while knocking on the door. Knocking on the window wasn't loud enough to get their attention but knocking very loudly on the door always worked! Needless to say, they responded very quickly after that. I began by asking, "Do you think God would approve of you actions right now? That's called sin; are you going to marry this girl?" and other such intimidating questions. I always asked in a very loud voice.

It worked amazingly well. The car would start up with the engine roaring and they would peel out of there, throwing gravel as they went. Then I would proceed to the next car. Sometimes, the next car would already be making a fast exit before I got there. I emptied about half the row of cars (which put me right at the concession stand) when I remembered I had some money and could go buy a soda! So I paused in my "ministry for Jesus and reaching the lost" and went into the concession building.

When I came out a little while later, there was this guy all dressed up, (turned out to be the manager of the drive-in) storming around the empty back row looking very angry. He was obviously looking for something or someone. I asked him if he was okay and he exploded in a flash! He yelled, "HAVE YOU SEEN ANYBODY AROUND HERE RUNNING PEOPLE OFF?" I honestly hadn't seen anyone doing that! He said he was going to find them and things would be different! I watched him storm off and afterwards I wondered who it could have been? I was back there, but I hadn't seen anyone else.

I went back to the playground equipment and ran into somebody I knew. They were about to leave, so I rode back with them and they dropped me off at Granny's house.

I think sometimes God uses stupid people, who are as ignorant as the gingerbread man, to accomplish his will. Good intentions and unrealistic zeal has hurt the cause of Christ in many ways. A lot of maturity and wisdom are needed and that will go a long way.

I'm not saying emptying out the back row of the drive-in didn't need to be done, but I am confident not one of them was interested in going to church because of it. My bible thumping mindset hadn't convinced anyone!

All Things

Rom 8:32 *He that spared not his own Son, but delivered him up for us all, how shall he not with him also freely give us all things?*

Several years ago, we were in need of a coffee maker. It was about the time of my wife's birthday and also camp meeting time. So, on the way to camp meeting, we stopped at a popular shopping center. We both went in and I asked her what she wanted for her birthday. Sure enough, she wanted a coffee maker. She picked one out that she really liked and I helped her to realize the price of this new-fangled coffee maker was far out of our range. But I assured her I would try to find something similar, hopefully about half the price. While she went on about her shopping, I immediately went back to the very one she had picked out and rushed to the checkout counter. I didn't want her to see what I had gotten. After I had it safely hidden away, I returned inside the store and acted like everything was okay. A smaller and cheaper one would work for us. I could tell she was a little disappointed, but it was going to be okay. If we couldn't afford it, then we did what we had to do.

A few days later on her birthday, I gave her the "wrapped up in a bag" surprise! The look of surprise on her face and the joy in her eyes is a special memory that I still cherish today. My beautiful and much beloved wife had received a special gift of love from the one she loved! It was worth every penny!

Sometimes Gods children have expectations and sincere needs that they petition the father for. Somehow those requests come under direct attack from doubts, or circumstances. It's not hard to see the facts behind the circumstances and start to agree with them, thus questioning the father's ability to hear our prayers or to answer them.

When does our humble willingness to accept "whatever," due to circumstances, override our faith in our heavenly father's ability to care for us? It's like giving someone a wonderful gift, and they reply with this, I don't care "whatever" attitude. It would hurt both of us!

Now, suppose we stop and consider the father's promise. Then we must also ask, "Is God bigger than the circumstance or those dark doubts? In being humble and workable with God, we are never asked to lower our faith in Him. We should never be cocky, pushy, arrogant, assuming, or any such thing. That's not faith, it's sin.

As we make our request known unto God, we should always be thankful and hopeful, and yet trusting in his wisdom for He knows what's best. If God chooses to answer by another means, we should continue to keep our expectation at the high mark! Truly God can meet our needs, with many or with few. But our vision is upon God, and our vision should not be undermined by the methods He chooses to answer those prayers! Keeping our eyes on God, and not on His methods, will build our faith!

If we ask for a coffee pot, and He sends a cup, thank Him for the cup and don't let go of it! It's His way of saying, there's more to come!

Married to a Foreigner

On November 5, 1976, at 7:00 PM, I married my sweetheart! We lived in the pacific northwest at that time. She had nothing to do with Missouri. She had no family there and had not ever been there. The tiny bits and pieces about my past didn't make sense to her at first. When we moved to Missouri a few years later, my family filled her in, and then she understood. She has been my sweetheart ever since. However, there was waiting for me in Missouri an expected, yet unexpected surprise.

After my honorable discharge from the USN, my sweetheart and I moved to Missouri. We both wanted to see my family, and I wanted my family to meet my bride!

And that's when the clan war started!

It was customary in clans that each member marries someone in their clan. Anyone outside of the clan was considered a foreigner. Since I showed up with a foreigner, there was a big stir among the clan, lines were drawn, and plans were made to get rid of this foreigner and save Robert from destroying ancient hillbilly accepted customs, thereby preventing anyone else from following his terrible example.

It was simple at first. There was the normal harassment of making fun of anything my wife did, which ostracized us from the clan. With many reminders of how they loved me, and how much they cared for me, they made it a point to totally ignore my wife.

When "driving wedges" didn't work to separate us, plan "B" went into action. Plan B was to break into our house and not take anything, but let me know they were in control, they were watching, and the next time it could get ugly. When that didn't work, they started breaking into the house at night while I was at work, (I worked swing shift in town) and my wife was at home. Again the message was to get rid of the foreigner or things will get ugly; you can't stop us.

I didn't want to hurt anyone, but it was clearly time to start retaliations. One night my wife saw the intruder and she gave me a description of him. I already had in mind just who would be doing their dirty work but couldn't prove it. Now I knew.

The next day I called on this man, who was my cousin. We had grown up together and were very close. He also knew about my days of living on the street as he was also living on the street at that time. I was known as a fighter and I had a reputation of being fearless and brutal. And now I was mad.

He came to the door when I went over to his house, took one look at me and knew I was mad, and asked why I had come. (Duh!) I had found the "intruder" I was looking for. I knew he had family inside, so it was no surprise that he did not want me in the house, so he stepped outside onto the porch.

Instead of jumping into what he knew he had coming, I laid it out in simple terms. "I know it's you. You're my cousin. I love you as a cousin. We have been tight down through the years. I've always backed you up. When we were both on the street, I still backed you up. You know it's true. I didn't come over here to start anything, I came over to stop something. If it were anyone else, you would not be standing here right now. I love you like a brother, and time has proven it. If somebody was breaking into your place, or breaking in at night and scaring your wife half to death, you'd kill 'em flat out. And if you couldn't, you would call me and I'd gladly back you up again. You've got to protect your family, I've got to protect mine. If you come back, then I'll be coming back. But I'm tellin' you right now, we should not be having to stand here and talk like this. We've been too close to be having this kind of talk. You're forcing my hand and I'm asking you to consider what I'm sayin' to you 'cause I mean every word of it. And you know I don't blow smoke."

He apologized, and I think he really meant it because he never came back and that type of harassment stopped.

By now the clan was getting frustrated with me even more because:

1. I wasn't going along with their long-standing clan customs.

2. Their family harassments had failed.

3. I just ran their "hit man" off.

4. The whole clan was watching. If they failed, my example would destroy their "say-so" in other people's lives and they felt their kids future was at stake. (It was actually their kids freedom the clan was afraid of.)

Now the attacks took on a new twist. One of the clan leaders decided to handle this matter his own way. They knew I worked swing shift in town and they also knew I lived 13 miles out of town. A plan was made.

One day, my uncle showed up at my house with his single daughter who was just a few years younger than me. She was dressed like she was trying to say something without actually saying it. We called it "advertising." So, I'm standing in the front room with my wife beside me and he informs me that the clan wants me to divorce this foreigner (pointing to my wife) and marry a good girl, like "*name*" here. You can see she would make you a good wife, and she can cook, work, and whatever.

The look on my wife's face was total shock! It was clear she didn't have a sense of humor in this, so she saw nothing funny about this what-so-ever!

When I saw my uncle come in with his daughter following him, dressed like that, it was very obvious what was about to go down. Remember I grew up in this clan! I thanked him for trying to do what he thought was right but told him I was happily married and planned to stay that way. Of course he objected and presented the many virtues of his daughter. I agreed with him that one day she will make somebody a good wife, just as he had said, but I had no intentions of marrying her myself. I then told him I had to leave and go to work in town.

They left, but I knew they were not done playing that card yet. Sure enough, a few days later, right at the time I leave for work, here comes my uncle again, with his daughter. He told me her car broke down and wondered if I could give her a ride to work since we both worked so close together in town! That didn't work either, and I reminded him that his car was running just fine, and it would not be very ethical for us two to be riding together alone, going anywhere. It just wasn't right. He tried to argue with me, but I insisted I had to leave, and promptly did so. I noticed they followed me out the lane to the highway but at the highway they turned in the opposite direction from town!

I suspected their next move would be to get somebody to say, "Robert and I did something, but I want to confess MY part, and ask everyone's forgiveness," but in reality they would be making clear accusations while pretending to be the victim. Of course the whole clan would agree with them, and probably come to my house after I left for work, to "confess" to my wife our awful deeds, complete with tears and hillbilly wailing.

The motivation for the entire thing was to break us up. Not that they actually cared who I married, but their own kids were watching my example. If those kids followed that example, the clan would lose all control over those kids. The bottom line was a power struggle for who was in charge. Either the clan, with its superstitions and traditions, would govern the kids' lives, or every kid out there could make their own decisions in life, telling the clan where just where they stood. The pressures were tremendous at home and at work, and within the family that associated with me. It would be hard to express what that was really like. My beautiful wife faced many hardships because of it. She was so trusting and naive to the clan's dirty work.

As time went on, the weeks turned to months. I was beginning to fail in my walk with God, as well as in my own integrity. I even fell back into drinking alcohol again. By then, everything was falling apart. My wife and I stood our ground together in the presence of everyone, but behind the scenes there were serious issues involved.

Truly God Works in a Mysterious Way!

While living with my mom's parents in New Bloomfield, MO, another experience unfolded as I went exploring the "woods" around their country farm. I discovered a certain field behind their house and up the hill about ½ mile as the crow flies. It was a big field and hilly. But this field had very strange rocks spread all over it, of all sizes, but they all looked alike. I know Missouri has rocks everywhere, but there was something about these rocks that was different somehow. I had noticed this as soon as I broke out of the timber and brush, when I first found the field. Looking at them, I discovered they were fossils from the bottom of an ocean! It was like looking at a sponge with its holes and seams, but the imprints on these were tiny fish, plants, and lots of "vertebrae" as I called them. They were everywhere! I found this very interesting and put several into my pocket. A few days later at school, (5th grade) I told someone about the fossils I had at home. For whatever reason, they said there was no such thing and I was lying. This really surprised me a lot. Why would they say such things? Of course I tried to explain to them about the fossils, but they didn't want to hear it. That should have been the end of it, but they were not done yet. They went to the teacher and told him I was telling a big fat lie about fossils. So the teacher, who wanted harmony in his class, asked me about the fossils. When I told him all about it, he suggested that I bring some in the next day as he would like to see them. I went back to the field and collected a coffee can full of them and took them to school the very next day. This seemed to make a big impression on the teacher and the kids, so I gave the teacher the can of fossils to keep as I could get more. That made some of the kids mad, so this little war started in the class. I was the big fat liar and the rocks weren't mine and there was no field of fossils. Pointing to the can and fossils the teacher had laid out on the windowsill, so all could look at them, made no difference. Not all kids joined in on this slander, but those who did not stayed away from me because they didn't want to be attacked also. Somehow the teacher found out about it and he didn't like what was going on. To counteract, he addressed the class of the reality of the find and talked about fossils for a short while, but this only sent the war underground. It was extremely frustrating to say the least. Someone said that maybe I should bring everyone a can of fossils so they would shut up, but I said no, they were treating me like this because they were jealous. There was nothing I could ever do to change their foolishness as you can't bribe nonsense into silence, and there is no good in trying to buy friends. That was not received very well either.

My parents and grandparents taught me some very good insights into this problem. The problem was not the fossils, it was a people problem and I couldn't fix people problems. Needless to say, that event separated me from the rest of the class. I was the loner. I learned a very important lesson on the price of friendship, what true friends were really like, and to set ones priorities according to what's right, not on what's accepted. It started as a lesson on fossils but it ended up a lesson on who we really are and what we should be.

The New Bloomfield Discovery

It was a common sight in Missouri to find a cluster of trees completely overgrown with different vines, such as ivy, possum grapes, gooseberry, honeysuckle and blackberry vines. When this happened it killed the trees. They would not dry out, but instead they rotted while standing in place. Then the area would become a no-man's land because it wasn't safe beneath or around them. The area would become a mountainous pile of vines, leaves, branches, and normally several bees' nests. There would also be a vast infestation of insects, spiders, bugs, and snakes of all kinds.

On the lane going to my grandma and grandpa Smith's house, there stood, hard by the road, this giant sized "no-man's land." Each time anyone came or left they would drive right past that giant display of mother nature claiming its land.

For reasons I do not know, we had moved in with Grandma and Grampa Smith that summer and we stayed there for a long time. Every day, my mom and her mom would take bags into the woods and gather "greens" so we had something to eat. Grampa's health was very bad and he could not work. Dad went to town every day and tried to find work. Sometimes he came home with a little money from a job he found, and sometimes he didn't find anything.

Being the adventurous boy that I was, I decided to cut a tunnel into that giant pile of vines and branches. It was my idea this would be a good place to make a "fort" so when company came that I wanted to stay away from, I would have a hiding place, and still be close enough to the house to hear and see what was going on. I knew nobody in their right mind would come anywhere near this pile. So, starting in a place hidden from the road and the house, I started crawling and cutting a small tunnel into the forbidden area. I must admit it was tough work. Every bug, snake and vine was determined to keep me out but I was just as determined to cut my way in! Armed with a machete and a handsaw, the tunnel started taking shape. I had gone for a long way when I ran into a concrete wall! And attached to that wall was very thick and wide planking! The obvious question that flooded my brain was, "What is this?" So I cut and sawed my way along the foundation to this mysterious wall, turned a corner and eventually came to two very large sliding doors. Inset into one of the doors was a "man door." Again, cutting away the impossible vines and brush, I was able to get the door open. The first thing I noticed was the massiveness of the planking used to build this "whatever-it- is" building.

The door had obviously not been opened for several generations. It complained loudly when it was forced to open up. Once inside, I froze in place! The planking used to construct the building was spaced slightly apart that allowed air and light to flood the building. My entrance had raised a cloud of extremely fine dust that rose high into the air. I got the creeps immediately, as though I had entered some kind of tomb. This was a gigantic barn filled with saddles, tools, wooden barrels of all sizes, crated boxes, and long ropes all rolled up and tied that hung rotting along the walls. It was a barn, a blacksmith shop and a livery stable! It looked as if whoever ran it just stepped out and closed the door, never to return.

Here it had stood down through the years, untouched by anyone. Outside, Mother Nature had done her work, but inside there was a time machine that never left. It would be hard to decode the feeling of that moment; the awe of the mystery, the silence, the atmosphere of a tomb violated, the wonder and amazement of all the things so neatly stacked and arranged and untouched. I was still frozen in my tracks! It seemed almost wrong to go any further but the excitement on my insides was building. The hayloft above was empty, like it would have been in the summer or late fall. There were hide-boards everywhere along the wall that had been used to stretch hides to dry. Each one had a few scrapes of hardened hide, like it was in the fall of the year. I wondered if winter had struck early and hard with not enough time to get the hay in, but the animals had gotten their early winter fur, still in their prime with no scars to blemish them. The ashes in the forge were low and fine.

Someone had put some long hours at this forge just before they left. Or had they indeed left? What else was I going to discover this unusual day? The place was full and well stocked so it made me wonder if they were getting ready for the winter. But where were they? Who were they? Why did they leave so suddenly? If they had moved, they would not have left everything behind.

My self-guided tour through this time capsule of mysteries produced more riddles then answers. I searched every nook and cranny and looked into every room and shutter. I soaked it all in like a sponge. My sense of adventure still running high, I wanted to get up into the hayloft, sometimes called a haymow. There were ladders or steps to get up there, but I did the usual thing that all boys did; I climbed the wall just like a rat! Up the wall I went! All three stories of it! The haymow was as empty as it could be. There wasn't enough of anything up there for even a mouse to make a nest of.

But now I had a problem. My side of the barn was empty and barren but on the other side of the haymow was more rooms and boxes that needed my curiosity to investigated them. I would have to climb back down the wall and then climb back up the wall on the other side. The great gap between the two sides was very far, but I discovered a plank along the wall. So I started spidering my way across the wall, hanging on to the boards with one hand, while dragging that plank along behind me with the other hand! Fools rush in where angels fear to tread and I made it to the other side. I don't remember why I couldn't climb back down the wall on the other side, but for some reason I couldn't, so I made a bridge/ walkway to get back across. When it was time to cross back over, I positioned the plank and started walking across the gap; three stories straight up! But, as I went across the plank, it bowed in the center, making it shorter. The plank made a loud popping sound when it slipped off the decking of the loft and caught on the large beam that supported the flooring. The little ledge that stuck out was about ½ inch wide! I had not yet reached the center, so I knew I had more bowing ahead of me and I knew I was not going to make it. By this time I was getting scared. I was shaking, my feet were shaking, the board was shaking, and I couldn't walk backwards on the plank! So I suddenly became VERY religious! I had never prayed before, ever! But I was sure praying now! "Oh God! I'll be good. I'll be good! I'll be good! Please get me out of here! PLEASE!" I repeated that several times getting louder each time.

There was nothing I could do at that point except go forward and fall three stories and die. It's time to die! I inched my way across that shaking plank to the other side and just as I stepped off the plank, it fell all three stories and shattered into several pieces! To say I was shaken would be a terrible understatement! FROM NOW ON, IF IM GOING TO DO ANYTHING STUPID, I'M GOING TO BE VERY CAREFUL ABOUT IT!

Before I knew it, dusk was setting in outside. I knew I had to get out of there before it got too dark to see my way out through the tunnel. I closed the complaining door behind me and had plenty of time to get back to the house.

A mystery indeed! Here we were, living just a few hundred yards from a giant barn, blacksmith and livery stable, and no one knew it! Every person here went within a stone's toss away from it and did not have a clue it was there all the time.

I waited till that night when my dad came home and told him my secret. He was skeptical at first, but soon knew I wasn't just messing with him. The very next morning we both went to see this mystery place.

He was as excited and shocked as I was at first. We both went all over the barn as he told me about so many things that we found there. Eventually we both went back to the house and told everyone what I had found. Several kids set out to run there, but Dad called them all back saying, "You got no business going in there by yourself; you could get hurt so fast. Stay out of the barn for now."

They say bad news travels on horseback and good news travels on foot. But every person in the county knew about the find before sunset that day. I think this was probably the only time good news rode on a horse. Of course, our phone had a party line. Most folks, when they heard the phone ring, picked up the receiver and eavesdropped on everybody else's business. News like this got around faster than you could stop it. Every day we would find that people came up from the road and stole things out of the barn. It was less than a week until the barn was as empty as a flour bin. We all were so saddened by it, but there was nothing we could do.

The Hidden Tomb

There is a tomb on top of a bluff far away from anything. We found it by accident one summer while our family was hunting mushrooms. Driving on the blacktop road far out in the flat valley, you could see the mountainous bluff very well. There was a road that turned and went up the low draw very near to the bluff, and as you followed the road, it led you directly to the top of the bluff. This was a very large area of timber and brush that went on for miles.

We had gone to the top of the bluff and were walking through the woods looking for mushrooms. If you stood on the very top of the bluff and looked out to the east, it seemed like you were standing on top of the world. Looking down the face of the bluff was not possible because the ground became dangerously steep with very loose gravel. There were a few graves back away from the bluff area all of which appeared to have been there for several generations. I usually stayed close to Dad whenever we went anywhere in the woods and my sisters always stayed close to Mom. Mom did well in the woods but the girls were as awkward and clumsy. They were sometimes funny to watch, but sometimes they were very frustrating. I don't remember if we found any mushrooms up there, but we found something else that was truly amazing. Dad was walking towards the bluff. He wasn't looking for mushrooms, but he was walking like he was going somewhere. We went as far as we dared to go, but Dad was determined to go farther. We went through some very dense brush and pressed through to the other side. It had appeared that the brush was growing right on the very edge of the bluff, but once we got past the several bushes, we discovered there was a narrow path that turned and seemed to go along the face of the bare rock bluff! How could that be? Dad had noticed this brush was out of place for that area. Then he saw what appeared to be an indented path winding its way through the graveyard and going straight to this "out of place" brush. The sunken path was barely noticeable as it wasn't a deep impression at all but looked more like a slightly used small game trail. But why would small animals be going to the face of the bluff? I never even noticed it until Dad pointed it out.

    We cautiously went down this narrow path heading directly to the face of the bluff. Imagine our surprise to find the face of the bluff had been cut back about 50 ft. and there was a large grassy area from the face of the bluff to the edge of the drop off. This new cut-back face of the bluff had an enormous doorway that had been cemented and sealed off. There was a window on each side of this sealed off doorway, but the window to the right had been busted out which exposed the inside of a singular tomb. Meanwhile Mom and the girls had grown tired of waiting for us back at the cemetery and had followed the same path we had taken, so they showed up at the hidden tomb with us.

Dad said, "You guys stay here" as he used his lighter to see by, climbed into this exposed tomb and disappeared out of sight. He was gone long enough for us to start getting concerned, but soon showed up again looking extremely somber. When he climbed out of the tomb, I went up to the window and tried to look in. Dad said, "Robert. Don't go in there." The fact that he used my name told me it was important. All I could see was that the end of that tomb was open with nothing but darkness beyond. I felt very strange and immediately backed away from the tomb.

Dad said grave robbers had broken into the tomb by gaining access through the window. The window was not a real window, it was only there as part of the tomb's appearance. He told us that once they had gotten inside, they broke open every tomb and pulled the coffins out, breaking them open and searching for any valuables. Then they had dumped the bodies out, still searching the coffins. He said that the tomb went a long way back under the ground and there were hundreds of skeletons and busted up coffins. Seeing it through the flickering flame didn't help matters at all. I'm glad he protected me from such a gruesome sight.

We left the area immediately and hiked back to our car and left. We were rather solemn after that.

Looking up at the bluff from down below, you could not see the hidden tomb at all. It was set far enough back to be hidden from sight. Looking down from the top, you could not see the tomb due to the steepness and loose gravel at the top. The slight indentation of the path was the only outside indication that there was something strange going on in that place. Whoever had planted the brush was deliberately trying to conceal the entrance to the hidden path. They had done a good job, but unfortunately, the wrong people had found it and done their wicked deeds.

Dad said the Indians were very good at building such hiding places in plain sight. He suspected the Indians had started the endeavor, but somewhere along the way white man took over and made the tomb as we saw it that day.

Many years went by. I had a wife and family of small kids and we were living in Missouri. It was mushroom season once again, so I said, "Let's go for a drive." As it turned out, we ended up in the area of the Mocain Road, and that was where the bluff was. So I decided to take my family to the top of the bluff and show them the old cemetery. I had no intention of taking my wife and small kids anywhere near the path. As we neared the top of the bluff area, we saw there was a very high chain-link fence built across the road and into the woods in both directions and there was a security guard and shack sitting on the road just inside the chain-link gate. This security guard comes out and starts yelling at us to stop! The guy was not very observant because we had already stopped. He came to my driver's door window and started demanding to know who I am, why was I there, etc., etc. in a very caustic, demanding manner. I'm not telling this ranting clown anything!

The guy was so caustic and demanding that he was making me angry very quickly. I told him we were out driving around and came up here. But he started getting accusatory. Getting into somebody's face that you don't know, and yelling at them, is very foolish. This guy seems to have mastered it. Just when I was about to get out of the car and take this conversation to a different level for his threats to me and my family, he suddenly backed way off from my door and changed his attitude greatly.

Looking back, I think he was scared to death sitting around a graveyard and open tomb all by himself, way out in the middle of nowhere. He had no back up and no way to communicate if he did need help. Our sudden appearance must have really startled him. I backed up and left him standing there before I did something just as foolish. If he had presented himself with even a small amount of professionalism or even decency, I gladly would have shared with him what little I knew and encouraged him as best as I could. But he set a tone that completely destroyed his influence.

We learned a lesson that day. "Kindness is wiser in its weakness than headiness is with its inflated glory."

The Slave House

While staying with my mom's parents was a very good time for me, there were still more discoveries to be made. One such experience concerned the slave house. This event changes something inside of me, something that was angry. I wanted to do something radical. But inwardly I didn't know what to do with those feelings until much later.

While listening to my parents and grandparents talk, I heard something about the old slave house. I knew about slavery from things we had learned in school and I didn't like it. But they were talking about something that was right there, right now. What could it possibly be? Then one bright and beautiful day, I asked my dad about this slave house. He asked if I wanted to go and see it. Of course I did, and we set off walking up the hill in the direction of the fossil field. But before we got to the top of the hill, we took a detour to the right, through the woods, and came to a barbed wire fence. After crossing over the fence we started out across a partial clearing that had a lot of regrowth in it. We passed a small, little family cemetery surrounded by a cast iron fence. Continuing on downhill in a westerly direction once again, we came to a long, narrow, low-roofed building. It had no windows, and only one door which had an odd lock bar on the outside and a big hasp for locking. This was the first time I had ever seen a door with a lock bar on the outside.

When Dad opened the door we noticed that most of the solid wood siding was spaced apart and there was plenty of daylight and air inside. All along both sides of this long narrow building were wide shelves, from the floor to the ceiling. Dad said they were not shelves; they were bunks where the slaves slept. The floor was dirt. There were several poles in the center of this building that supported the roof. I'm guessing the poles were 15-20 ft. apart, but the middle pole was very large and sturdy. It had chains with cuffs on them, all around it and there were lots of marks, gouges and scratches on this pole. It was also very black from the bottom almost to the top.

Dad said this was the punishment pole. He guessed the blackness of the pole was from dried blood from years gone by. Dad dug around the bottom of the pole with his pocket knife, making scratches in the ground like he was looking for something. He struck something hard and pried it up. It looked odd and evil. He said it was a pair of thumb cuffs. By that time, something was turning sick inside of me. I hated that slave house and all it represented and wanted to run out of there right then. But I knew better. I stayed with

Dad as he looked around, and eventually we left. I never returned to the slave house. I returned to the cemetery a few times after that day and took some notes, but I avoided the slave house all together.

Something happened inside of me that day, something that has never changed or gone away. To look into the face of slavery and its horrors is to look into the face of torture and hell. The books said that there were slaves, but never defined what that meant. A first hand glimpse into its darkness reveals the true story. It's a story I will never forget.

Visiting the Vogels

This next story rather embarrassing and, unfortunately, it happened to me. Looking back, it is funny now. But it was not funny at the time.

It began after school, when our school bus was full of kids and we were all enduring the long ride home. This bus route was far out in the country, so going home took a while. A classmate whose bus stop was next to mine, was sitting near me and we were talking. It was a Friday, and he invited me to come out to his house on the following day, which was Saturday. I agreed to come over and visit with him the next day. He said he would be home all day, so it was settled

The following morning, Slim and I set out for Doug's house. It was very normal for anyone walking to avoid the roads. Going cross country was the norm. it was always shorter and faster to walk the wooded trails than to follow the lengthy roads. There were many trails and pathways that led everywhere. You just had to know where you were going. Almost all the foot paths followed a creek or always led to water if it was anywhere around. Meeting someone on the trail was very rare.

MORE STORIES

So Slim and I set out bright and early to go to Doug's house. We came out of the woods exactly across the road from where Doug's house was located. We crossed to the house and saw the mailbox with his family's name on it. But we discovered no one was home.

Knowing Doug had said he would be home all day led us to believe he hadn't gone far and would soon return, so we just hung around his place for a while. The dogs growled and barked at us but stayed away. Slim and I were standing on the porch waiting when we discovered the door was not locked. So, we stuck our heads in and yelled for someone. No reply came. We went inside and looked around and we made the wonderful discovery that their icebox was full of food! What a coincidence. All this food and nobody around! Not wanting to be rude and turn down good food, we decided to help ourselves. Slim started frying up the eggs and draining the milk bottles. He ate a dozen eggs by himself. Then started on all the sandwich supplies that were calling his name.

I made a dive for the store-bought cereal. It was going down really well, until it suddenly was gone. So, I started helping Slim on the homemade dagwood style sandwiches. The next thing we knew, the sandwich stuff was all gone, the milk jugs were all empty, and the store-bought bread was gone too. Then we decided it was time to help ourselves to the gallon of tea that was also calling our names. Of course we sampled several things along the way, such as the leftovers from dinner.

When we were done, there was a big pile of dishes in the sink, lots and lots of room in the ice box, and the tables were covered with food wrappings, empty containers, crumbs, spills and napkins.

We made our retreat back outside to the porch and hung around for a while, picking our teeth and soaking up the rest of the tea. Of course we had to throw a rock every once and a while at the pesky dogs who would not leave us alone. Finally, we decided nobody was going to come back any time soon, so we crossed the gravel road and disappeared back into the woods. We followed the path back home and were quite content.

The following Monday morning, I was back on the school bus and on my way back to school. Of course Doug and I were visiting again. He asked why I didn't come over Saturday. I told him we did, but nobody was home so we waited around for a while, then went back home. Doug was puzzled, for he had been home all day.

I described the house and mailbox to him. He said that was his mailbox, but not his house. The lane by the mailbox would have taken me to his house, but the house I was at was their neighbor's place. We went on visiting as always. I never thought to mention that somebody was with me, or that we had wiped out their neighbor's groceries for the upcoming week. Somehow it just didn't seem relevant at the time. We agreed I should come back later and try it again. I thought that would be a wonderful idea!

You Can't Fly Out of Hell

Several years ago while still a young man, I got totally immersed in flying and aviation. It became my passion straight from the heart. I read and studied everything I could get my hands on about flying. I even designed my own airplane. But when I started getting things together to build it, my uncle told my dad about it, and my dad shut it down. I still remember my uncle telling me, "There are a lot of people smarter than you building airplanes, and if what you're trying to do is worthwhile, somebody would have already done it." Years later as an adult, I was standing in the front yard playing with my kids when I heard this sound coming from above. I looked up and see the exact airplane I was trying to build. Today they call them ultralights. My dad and my uncle's skepticism shut down a new leap into the advancement of recreational flying.

Eventually I joined a flying club called the EAA, Experimental Aircraft Association. Their whole purpose was to encourage people to fly. They would teach you to fly in exchange for your help in building whatever project plane they were building. It is an amazing organization the world over.

One day I was my way to an EAA meeting, and the Lord spoke to me very clearly. He said, "I want you to get out of aviation." I questioned that with hard scrutiny. I reasoned the impression I had received was not the Lord. My wife was driving me to the meeting to drop me off but then I felt God's presence and he repeated the statement. I surely didn't understand it, but I wanted to always be obedient to God. This was a sacrifice of great proportions. Surely that was not God's voice because I had spent most of my life (at that time) in aviation. After the second admonition, I knew it was God. The witness of his spirit was clear.

We were approaching the exit we needed to go to the meeting, so I told my wife that we needed to turn around and go back home. She said, "Go back home? Why?" So I told her why. We turned around and went the 10 miles back home. It was silent in the car. My whole life just went down the drain because God wanted me to get out of my lifelong passion. Silently I was asking, why Lord? There was no answer from God, but clearly it was his instruction for me. When he did answer, he said he had a calling for my life and aviation was not it. He wanted me to be an evangelist, a preacher. I knew nothing about being either one of those. So I said, "Lord, I'll do what you want me to do. My life is yours but I don't know anything about this stuff. You're going to have to help me and show me how."

Time flew by quickly. The Lord had led us to move back to Missouri again. I was working for a tree trimming company that trimmed trees for the power company. While doing this line of work, one of our routes that we followed led us to a small airport. It was a private airfield. The owner came out to see what this big tree trimming truck was that had pulled into his lane. I discovered that he was a pilot, a mechanic, and a designer and builder of aircraft! We had a wonderful time visiting. He gave me a tour of his place and I fell in love with everything he was doing. I began to stop in at his place every day after work and we both completely enjoyed our time together. He was surprised to find out that I knew so much about it. The thought of God calling me out of aviation never crossed my mind. I was totally enjoying aircraft again!

This went on for a couple of weeks. Then one Saturday morning we heard about a plane crash behind the boy scout camp outside of town. Everyone had been killed and they were still investigating the site. Monday after work, on the way home, I stopped in at Bill Ferguson's airport again. His truck was there, but he was nowhere in the shop. His plane was there, so he wasn't out flying, but where was he? I went to the house and knocked on the door. His wife came out and asked, "Can I help you?" I replied, "I'm looking for Bill, but he's not in the shop." She broke into sobs and could only point to the driveway.

I apologized for coming at a bad time and excused myself. I started walking down the driveway, wondering what that was all about. I still didn't see bill anywhere, but somehow walking down the driveway I was supposed to find Bill. Then I saw this pile of fresh dirt next to the road which I hadn't noticed coming in. Standing by the mound of dirt was a temporary marker like they use in graveyards. I walked around to see what it said. It said "Bill Ferguson."

Suddenly it all came together. The plane crash was Bill. He had said his brother was having trouble with his plane's carburetor freezing up, and he was flying down to have bill look at it. It all made sense. My heart literally broke as I stood there. I couldn't stop the sadness that was flooding over me. The Lord asked me while I stood there, "Did you ever witness to Bill?" I had to answer that I had not, and even more sadness came over me. Then God spoke again saying, "Didn't I call you out of aviation?" I cringed at the answer, "Yes Lord, you did." There was silence. I felt ashamed of myself. All that time, the event that had called me out of aviation had never even entered my mind. The very thing I should have been doing, such as witnessing to Bill, I had not done. I felt even more ashamed and sad. Then the Lord spoke again saying, "You can't fly out of hell." I clearly understood God was saying that "I" couldn't fly out of hell.

I left the gravesite. No, I fled the gravesite. I couldn't get back to my truck fast enough. I was terribly sad and very ashamed. I confessed my failures to God and sought his forgiveness and His peace returned to my heart like a great refreshing wave. I was still very sad for Bill's family and their loss.

Gold Country Lessons

The Herman Nelson Story

Herman was a prospector from the old school. He grew up in Alaska in the prospector circles. It seems he worked with the best and the worst of them, so he learned very early and very well the do's and don'ts of a prospector's life. It became a part of him. From the far remote corners of the back country, to his hometown, Herman was known and respected. When he said there was "color" there, you'd better open a bank account. His advice was priceless, but he never charged for any of it. If he said there probably wasn't any color there, you'd best forget it, no matter what the collage- trained geologist said. Don't bother.

It was a great privilege to know this living relic from the past. Truly his kind is gone for good, and we are the lesser for it. I'll try to recount some of his stories. I won't do them justice in repeating them like Herman could, but I'll make a feeble attempt. So please bear with me.

The Ghost Town Bear

Bush pilots can only fly so far until they run out of gas. So in order to extend their trips, they will fly several hundred pounds of gas cans out to an area where they know their gas will be getting low. Then they will land and drop off all the gas cans. This way they can stockpile the gas. It's called a gas stop. On the return trip they stop there again to refuel to make it back to civilization. They repeated this process, making a daisy chain out of gas stops, to get where they wanted to go.

GOLD COUNTRY LESSONS

On this particular trip, Herman and his pilot had to stop and fuel up at one of their gas stops. This particular gas stop was on the edge of an ancient ghost town, a relic from the gold rush days of long ago. After they had landed and fueled up, they decided to follow the trail into the old ghost town and have a look around. They both thought it odd that the trail was so well traveled, knowing there was no one around for several hundred miles. Neither one of them thought to grab the rifle out of the plane. They just started hiking into the town on the trail that began less than a hundred feet from where they had landed.

When they approached the town, they noticed that all the windows had been pushed out, the doors had all been smashed in or out, and debris was littering the ground everywhere. The pilot said the old ghost town wasn't that way when he had started dropping of gas cans not long ago. They wondered who had come out there and caused such havoc. They weren't long in finding out!

There were several buildings on both sides of the street in this old town and at the far end was a very large water tower. The top of the water tower had long since rotted and fallen down through the legs and braces of the tower. While they were standing there looking at it, a king size grizzly came busting out of one of the buildings charging at them and there was nowhere to go but up that rickety and rotted water tower! Needless to say they went very quickly! They had gotten as high as they dared to go, but the grizzly wanted them back down! It walked around circling the base of the tower, pushing here and there against the legs and braces of the tower, growling and tearing at things in its rage. They decided they weren't nearly high enough, so they climbed even higher while the braces were falling down around them!

The bear kept this up for a very long time and they began to wonder how all this was going to turn out. They didn't like the obvious answer.

Soon the bear tried another approach. It would walk away into the dense brush seeming to have left. But after a few minutes, it would come charging out of the brush from someplace else in full speed. They both knew this couldn't go on forever, pieces of the water tower were still falling down and they were getting weaker as the hours slowly crept away. Then they started timing the bears disappearance. It was getting a little longer each time he left. So they decided the sooner they got off the rotted tower, the better chances they had for getting away.

So the time came for them to make their "do or die" escape. They both climbed down as quietly as possible and ran for their lives. No figure of speech here! Running as fast and quietly as they could., they had almost reached the trail when they heard the grizzly roaring and charging from somewhere behind them.

Just as they entered the trail, Herman saw an ancient lunch bucket on the ground. He grabbed it and kept running. When they broke out of the trail and were back in the open, Herman threw the lunch bucket down and kept running. He told me later he knew bears were extremely curious, and they had an eye for baskets and boxes. Sure enough, the bear came out of the trail and headed straight for them, but when it got to the lunch bucket, it stopped and started tearing at it and knocking it around.

They both reached the plane, started it up, and got it moving in record time. But the bear had started coming at them again. Now the bush pilot was trying to get up speed to take off, but it was rolling towards the bear. And the bear trying to get its prey, running towards the plane! They knew what was about to happen.

Suddenly bear stopped and stood up to see what was going on, like grizzlies do when they are confused. The plane was now inches off the ground and trying to get up, FAST. It was clear they were going to collide! Then just before they made impact, the bear dropped back down on all fours and the plane went over it with its wheels passing on either side of the bear!

Once they were safely back into the air, they circled around to see what happened to the grizzly. It was having a royal fit of rage and taking it out on the lunch bucket! Herman said after that they NEVER left the plane again without taking their guns!

This Story I Call "Being Drowned by a Grizzly!"

Herman and his crew were working a small river in the remote area of Alaska gold country. While a couple of men were working the sifter, Herman was running a rubber-tired front-end loader. He had backed away from the sifter when he stepped out of the cab and climbed down to the ground. Just as he turned around at the bottom of the ladder, a grizzly charged him from out of the brush! In Alaska prospecting, you ALWAYS carried a powerful handgun strapped to your chest, and a 12-gauge shotgun tied to your hip. Neither gun was ever allowed to have the safety on. Safety meant death in split second timing! Herman had both. He turned and fired the shotgun at point blank range into the bear. There wasn't time for a second shot. There never is. He went for his handgun and started firing upward into the bottom of the grizzly's jaws. This was putting cannon balls into the bears brain while he was chewing on you. The bear dropped dead, or almost dead, right on top of Herman, smashing him into the river and into the gravel on the bottom of the river. Notice that it's very hard to breath under water, under gravel, and under grizzly!

The crew, who also had their firearms in readiness, turned and began shooting the grizzly also. They thought Herman was in the cab, but when it was discovered that he was not there, the question was, "Where is Herman?" Someone said, "I think he might be under the grizzly!" A massive attempt was made to role the bear over but it was way too big. Then someone jumped on the front-end loader and rolled the bear over. Herman came up spitting water and gravel and gasping for air. After he got his wind back, he said that he looked to see if he had any parts or limbs missing, but he was intact, except he was very sore for a few days. Just another day in paradise!

#1 Quick Sale

It is common for a helicopter to land at your claim and offer to buy your gold at fair market value, thus saving you the expense of flying it out at $2,000 an hour. If you indicate in any way that you have even a trace of gold, they immediately start blowing you away, machine guns and all. Then they load up your gold and leave. Herman always met them at point blank range with an automatic shotgun pointed right at their heads. He would say, "Leave now or never, right now." They always left immediately. Just one example of the laws of survival in gold country, Alaska.

#2 Dark Cloud

It's been known for centuries that gold, or money, changes people for the worse. The best men with the best intentions can change when it comes to gold. They get a certain look about them that is dark. They start acting differently, sometimes becoming more quiet and more suspicious. But always dark. Sometimes they become very upbeat, but their upbeat words don't match the dark spirit that comes over them. Whether they are quiet or upbeat, they both have the same agenda; to shoot you in the back. When the timing is right, they strike out. They will kill the whole crew before it's over.

Herman said the best way to stop them is to expose it and confront them in front of everybody. Let everyone know that this man wants to kill us. Watch your back. Keep him in your gun sights. Make sure you do this in front of everyone, including the dangerous man in question. This usually clears it up very quickly. You can tell when the dark cloud goes away.

#3 Firepower

Three things are mandatory for backwoods Alaska:

#1 is a high caliber handgun tied or strapped to your chest, fully loaded, and never on safety. When the bears start chewing on you, you poke this gun under its jaws, pointed toward its brains and pull the trigger as fast as possible. It will blow the bear's brains out, and will splatter them all over your face, but it will stop the bear long enough for you to make your move to a safer distance, and then you make sure he is further disposed. This is also the same gun you will have to use when the man who becomes dark starts to carry out his murderous plans.

#2 You carry a 12-gauge shotgun, loaded with slugs, securely fastened to your hip. Never keep the safety on.

A bear will sneak up on you in the brush and he will get as close as he can get and still be unknown. Then when you turn around, he will charge full speed at you. He may not even growl. But you will hear the sounds of his charge. There will be no time to shoulder the gun or time to take it off safety. You have to spin around and shoot from the hip. If you're fast, you may get one shot. Seldom do you get a second shot. The old timer prospectors are very good at seeing the bear first and getting two shots at the bear.

Sometimes the bear will stand up on its hind legs to get a better view of your position. Shoot at the bears crotch. The slug will shatter his pelvis and hip bones, thus blowing out his hind legs. But he will still charge, even if he has to drag his back legs. Keep sharing the slugs in your shotgun with him, aiming for his head. If you fail to give him all your slugs, he will want the bullets from your handgun, as he starts chewing on your face.

#3 Beretta

The only gun that worth owning in gold country is a beretta. It's the only gun that will not jam up when working in water and sand environments. If you don't have a berretta, you ain't going. You depend upon your partner to protect himself and you, and he is depending on you to do the same. If he ain't willing to do it right, then he ain't got no business being there.

A Funny Story Involving a Hand Truck

My wife and I were out of town one weekend and we stopped at one of those membership only food stores and "everything else" store. While there I bought a blue hand truck with yellow plastic protectors. It was on sale. I took this hand truck to work with me and chained it to my workbench in the shop. A couple of days went by and I found out that Herman Nelson was coming down to install carpet on one of the yachts. He came in late that night and started his work right away. I knew I'd see him the next morning.

When I got to work, I found an interesting note signed by Herman Nelson, tied to my hand truck saying that I was a thief and he would be looking me up as soon as he came back that night. Herman didn't know that was my shop or my hand cart. I found it extremely funny, though I didn't know why he left such a note. I was looking forward to his arrival!

Later that day (Herman came in around 2:00 PM.) I went looking for him. Sure enough, he was manually packing rolls of carpet from his carpet trailer to the floor underneath the yacht. Those rolls are very heavy, so I called, "Hey wimp!" to him and went over to him. He dropped the carpet roll and said that if some thief hadn't stolen his brand-new hand cart, he wouldn't have to pack these rolls. I started asking him questions to dig further into his story.

Sure enough, he had been to the same store I was in last weekend and had bought the same identical cart. I hadn't told him my side of the story yet. So I said, "Can you show me where you found the no-good thieves stash of your hand truck?" He led me to my shop and pointed to the guilty hand truck. He had a few words about hanging around there to find this thief and rip his arms out very slowly.

By this time I could no longer keep a straight face. I was smiling like a dog eating grapes. He wanted to know what was so funny about it, so I told him the rest of the story. We both had a good laugh over it and we both went looking for HIS missing hand truck. Herman found it later that night. Just another day in paradise and another precious memory. I'm glad I wasn't the thief he was looking for!

The Anaconda Gold Claim

One of the mysteries surrounding the Alaskan gold country, has always been lost claims, or some creek loaded with color that someone finds accidently, but can never seem to find their way back to it again. Thus, they spend a lot of time always searching for the lost creeks, or lost mines, or lost claims. There are many such stories floating around any gold country. However, there are also real lost claims out there, but they are kept in secrecy for obvious reasons.

The anaconda gold claim is one such story. The facts surrounding it are well-known to every prospector. As time has gone by, the real facts are buried in superstition and folklore, and eventually all is lost but the lingering legends. But finding that claim is like finding a needle in all the vast backcountry of Alaska.

The known facts are these. The Anaconda Gold and Mining Co., in Alaska was a well-known and thriving company. They had everything needed to find gold; the right people with the right mindset and with a trained eye and lots of experience. That was the foundation that worked, and they found color on a regular basis. Their name became well-known in Alaska. But when the price of gold dropped to an all-time low, the company found itself too top heavy to function. So they shut down some of their operations that were less profitable and streamlined their personnel. Meanwhile, the price of gold continued to drop. Finally it became apparent that the company had lost so much money in capital and returns, they eventually went bankrupt. If the price of gold had held steady even for a few months longer, the story would have ended differently. The real game changer in this story was that the company had found a site that was offering the possibility of an unprecedented gold strike. But the investors thought it was just a scheme of the company to get more capital, even though the bottom had dropped out of the gold industry. In the end, the company went under and the investors suffered their own losses.

Herman Nelson was very familiar with all the facts about Anaconda. The many contacts he had in the prospecting circles also provided many not so well-known insights into the Anaconda operation, particularly pertaining to their last dig. Consequently he learned who was involved, and had an idea of just where it might be. But he also knew the foolishness of chasing down ghost gold stories, or "ghost gold" as it is sometimes called. But then one day something happened that changed everything and it set Herman Nelson on a full blown, all out, no holds barred, mission. If what he had been given was real, he had just found the Anaconda's last dig. He knew enough about it to keep his mouth shut. Over time, tiny "seemingly nothing" pieces of information had been found but they all pointed to several different places. THIS was truly the missing piece! Now he was certain.

Backing up a little in this story, let's cover just what happened that changed everything.

Herman was far up north making arrangements for his next gold season. It cost $2,000/hour to have your equipment flown in and you paid for both ways. You paid in advance. You had to buy the equipment up front from wherever you bought it, and at the end of the season you leave it all there. Nobody wants to pay that kind of money to have a bunch of equipment flown back out. It is always cheaper to leave it there, especially if your digging season produced no color (gold). Better to just leave it.

It was while he was up north making these arrangements when his normal pilot that he used didn't show up due to mechanical problems with his plane. So, in the pilots' cafeteria at this very remote airfield, he went to find a pilot. It is surprising to know just how many of these remote airfields are scattered all over back woods Alaska! Fortunately for Herman, he was well- known and much respected by almost everyone in these remote places. They all knew him on a first name basis.

So he approached a pilot and told him his story. (By the way, these pilots know each other very well and they do favors back and forth all the time. Don't think you're going to fool anyone up there! Claim jumpers will try, but as a rule its actually the pilots that protect the prospectors and miners.) The man agreed to take Herman out but on the condition that Herman paid for both of their lunches and listened to a story this pilot wanted to tell. Needless to say that was fine with him. (It was also customary. If a pilot does you a favor, you buy him lunch in exchange for saying thank you.) Lunch in back county "anyplace" is NOT cheap! He told me later, he had a gut feeling to talk to this guy and to trust him all the way. As with most people in far remote areas, their gut feeling means everything.

It seems this pilot had started out years ago trying to fly "bush pilot" in Alaska. But his first job offer came from a mining company that was expanding and needed pilots. So he hired on, and ended up flying for them full time. He did this for several years. Finally the day came when that company went under, so he went back to bush flying. He really liked it, but now he was getting old, and flying had lost its adventure long ago. He was thinking about heading back down to the lower 48. It seems he had family down there and he had made up his mind to go home. When Herman pressed him for the name of that compony, he said "Anaconda."

The lights were already coming on in Herman's head. They discussed that last prospective dig that Anaconda had done before they went under. (A dig is an area that's explored for gold, without making an official claim on it, or acknowledging your presence there.) He remembered it very clearly because he was the designated pilot for that project. (Herman told me later that he could hardly believe what he was hearing!) So, when Herman asked him what he wanted for those flight maps and logs for that project, the man said, "You can have them!"

Either the pilots were kept in the dark as to Anacondas finding, which they probably did for safety, or this guy was a very large bag of hot air! He was about to find out! The pilot took Herman out just as he had said he would, dropped him off, and came back a few days later as planned. When they landed back at the remote airfield, they visited for a while and then the pilot gave Herman the flight plans and logs from the Anaconda project. "Anaconda Gold and Mining Company" was stamped right on them. So it was all true! And here were the documents that would pull it all together. It was a day Herman said he would never forget!

But just as every step forward has its potential, it also has its drawbacks. There was a little upstart mining company just a few miles away from where the lost claim was located, and they were filing claims in that direction. If it turned out to be the actual site, then it was just a matter of time before the Anaconda claim would be discovered. The little upstart company had no idea of what they were about to discover if they continued much farther, but Herman knew what they were going to find. But when? And could he get there before they did and file his claim? Claims are very expensive and Herman didn't have that kind of money laying around. There was only one option; to get there as fast as possible, do a little panning to verify the gold, and file the claims. If it was the real site, there shouldn't be any trouble panning enough gold to pay for the claims.

All prospectors daily monitor the claims office and its daily business. If Herman filed too quickly, everyone else would be on it. So, for protection, you file several claims at once, completely covering the area of your "main" claim. This keeps everyone far enough away to protect your strike. But again, claims are very expensive. He knew his investors might rally to back him up, but he had already discovered someone in his investing group who couldn't keep their mouth shut. One word to the wrong person and Herman and his crew could never be seen again. It sounds unbelievable here in the lower 48, but in the back side of gold country that was daily reality. Herman knew it all very well.

That was the year I was supposed to go with him on this first expedition to verify the site. But there were some problems. First of all, nothing could be said to his investors. It was too risky at this point. Secondly, there was very limited cash available to start such a project. And, thirdly, the pilot had said there was no place to get in or out of the site except by flying. The ground was extremely steep, high and rocky. At the far end of it was a river that flowed very fast through a gaping gorge. Getting in and out was by far the most dangerous task that had to be dealt with first and it had to done on a shoestring budget.

I agreed to go and said, "Count me in, I'll be there." But when the time came for me to go, Herman called me saying, "Are you ready to live off beans and sweat?" At that point I had to tell him my condition. "I blew my back out," I informed him. "I've got two blown discs and two broken vertebrae and I'm scheduled for surgery. I can hardly move and won't be able to for quite some time!" To say that he wasn't impressed would be a serious understatement. But what could he do? What could I do? Nothing! Herman had to go by himself and this almost cost him his life. If he wasn't such a hard case anyway, he probably wouldn't have made it.

The helicopter flew into the designated area a few miles from where he actually needed to be. Because of the terrain, that was as close as he could get. It swept in with a long cable hanging from it. The cable was disconnected once the cargo was on the ground, and Herman waves the helicopter off. At the end of cable was a monster quad and trailer, loaded with all the needed gear to blaze a trail, camp out, and make emergency repairs. There also was a satellite cell phone, a couple of guns for protection and lots of ammo, plus food and first aid supplies. Herman would have to cut a trail for a couple of miles just to get to the rim of the canyon. Then he had to find a way to get down the face of the cliff and restart his journey to the "spot" that had been indicated on the flight map. Anaconda had built a very small airstrip at the site several years ago, but the vegetation had all grown back so that it was hardly recognizable from the air. After several days of trying to find an entrance into the forbidden area, it became obvious that the only way in was to drive a quad straight down the face of one of the walls. It wasn't a complete cliff and the quad would have to be anchored the whole time. And somebody would have to ride and maneuver it as it descended the face.

Once there, a clearing could be made, and a helicopter could be landed. But time was running out. The helicopter that landed him in that area was soon due to return to pick him up. The quad with its gear would have to be left behind and if he were not there, it would fly away, leaving whoever was left behind to die. That was the law of the country. It was hard. The land was hard. Those who dared to challenge it were hard. Soft men didn't make it there. Sometimes the aircraft might circle around for a bit looking for those who were supposed to be there, but usually that did not work. The fuel spent and the time to return was paramount. If a pilot spent too much time trying to play hero, it could cost him his life, as well as anyone else's who might be on that flight.

That season ended without any success. The tall timber and rock-faced cliffs made it impossible to land there. He had to return on time, but the view of the valley matched the terrain of the map. And far in the distance, when looking off the rim of the cliff, there could be seen what appeared to be "something" of a long-ago air strip. Herman had found his long sought-after prize. Next year would be the year to remember!

Herman's Last Trip

The following year I was supposed to go with Herman as he made his final call into the forbidden valley of Anaconda. The surgeon who did my first back surgery said my back would heal, and then after one year, I would be back for the last surgery. He was right.

Herman called me to see if I was still going with him on this do or die mission. The hardest thing for me to do was to say that I couldn't go that year either. I was suffering from severe back problems and was headed back into surgery for the second time. I knew the hard facts of the matter. If I were having any problems at all with my back, then being in gold country was totally out of the question forever. The rigors and hardships made it no place to be suffering a back injury. That was the saddest decision I ever had to make, but God was in it somehow. At the time I couldn't see where.

So, Herman had to go without me again. He had told me right up front that he wanted me to go as I was a natural for the job. My talents and endurance was in high demand in gold country. He said he knew if I went there would never be a time when the dark monster of greed would fill my spirit and heart. He knew I would stand behind him at all cost and he would never have any doubts that I would get his sons back to civilization if anything happened to him.

As I hung up the phone, I seriously struggled with conflicting emotions. I wanted that opportunity to go to the Alaska backcountry more than anything. But here I was lying in bed, and the only place I was going was the hospital. I not only felt like I had just let down my closest friend, but I had done it at the most critical time. I knew he was taking his two sons with him and he was depending on me to be there to ensure their safe return. But all I could see was "I let him down."

Neither one of us had any control over the circumstances involved. It was completely out of our hands. But there is something inside a man that says I am who I am, and I will not give in to the pressure to compromise, no matter what the price. My letting him down was also letting myself down. It put me into a position of not being trustworthy enough to keep my word. It was a matter of integrity. The battles and giants I faced after that were almost too much even for me. I had to call out to God for his strength during those following days of inner battles.

Herman went on that trip with his sons, into the forbidden valley. In my trusted place, he took a man who turned dark when the color started showing. Herman saw the change and knew from experience how things were going to turn out. He knew what he would have to do if the man didn't come back from the dark world inside of himself. After a few days of wondering if this man was going to kill him and his sons, Herman said it was time to confront the problem straight on.

They had faced all the normal problems of charging bears, flash floods, equipment failures, total exhaustion, 18-hour days and claim jumpers. But having to fight with your own men, for the survival of everyone there, is by far the most difficult battle of all. The confrontation was made in plain sight of every man to see and know. There was no doubt who to watch out for, or the consequences if that someone didn't come to his senses. (It wasn't the kind of company meeting you would expect in the lower 48; out there, there were some very tough men and some very fast guns.) If you wanted to do something stupid, you probably would. But rest assured you would be outnumbered, out drawn and out shot, hands down. It's a fast way to die slow. Every man out there would be watching you, trigger happy and ready. Get your head on straight or lose it. Any questions? I don't want to copy the WAY he said it. But that's sort of the message you have to get across loud and clear. It has a way of bringing men out of their dark world and back into reality. Fortunately for that man, it worked. He had shown his dark side to be a coward, in a place where cowards weren't welcome.

Herman later said, "If you had been there this would not have happened."

They had several mechanical problems. Herman called me about it and we got things back on track. If I couldn't be there physically, this was the next best thing. It worked for now.

They took lots of pictures, as they always do, being mindful not to capture any scenes that would tell too much about where they were. They also found a lot of color, depicted by happy smiling faces showing the "pan." But the time came to leave, and they had to leave early because the way out was straight back up the rock face they had come down. That was going to take some time, and a lot of work.

The man that had turned dark seemed to hold steady after the confrontation. But on the climb back out, his cowardice returned, and it sent Herman and his quad tumbling back down the rock face. As it turned out, the quad rested against a large rock with a tree growing out beside it and that saved all of them! Without that quad, somebody had to be left behind, which meant death. And Herman had only suffered a broken leg. He got back up with his broken leg, dragged his quad off the rock, got it to start again, and starts riding his rear wheels as he goes back up the steep incline. When he got back to the place where the man had lost his nerve and jumped off, Herman stopped and ordered him back on the front again, this time telling him to stay on! They were almost to the top when the man had jumped off. If the quad had continued to roll, it would have gone airborne, spinning in a free fall to the bottom again. He was very thankful for that rock! God was watching over them for sure. I asked him about his leg and he said exactly what I thought he would say. It only hurts till it quits hurting, by then I'll be home again.

But their troubles weren't over yet. They had come out the same way they went in, but the weather changed for the worse. Coming in, they had to use a bush pilot and his little beaver plane. It could barely land on the bare rock spot for them to unload their cargo. But now, just a few miles away from the pick-up spot, snow came in like a white out. It wasn't due for a couple of days, but as always in the back country, nature isn't always on your side. They kept moving as long as they could see, knowing there were places where if you went off the narrow path, you would become airborne all the way back to the bottom, without advance notice. When they reached the pick up spot, it was rather obvious no pilot would ever see them there, and if they did, there was no way for that pilot to land in the blinding snow and stop on top of that solitary flat rock. Herman said that if God brought them that far, he would see them home safely. The others had very serious doubts for very serious reasons. They waited and waited some more. When it came close to the pick up time, Herman called on his satellite cell phone trying to reach the pilot. It took a few tries but finally the pilot answered and said he was having some problems with visibility and wind. Many prospectors had been caught in the sudden weather change and they were all trying to get out. Herman told the pilot they would wait right there, just in case he had any notions about landing anytime soon.

Then they waited some more. After a few hours, the wind died down and the snow stopped. It pays to pray! However there was still no plane and it was WAAAY overdue!

The situation was rather un-nerving, but peaceful at the same time. Then they heard the crackling of the satellite phone. The voice said, "Your pilot is overloaded and on his way back to civilization. I've got a smaller plane, but I think I can find you. Want to try it?" Herman shouted, "If you land here with a kite, we're all getting on board!" A few minutes later the sound of the plane could be heard. The pilot circled a few times trying to get down and came in as slowly as possible, landing right on top of the flat rock covered with snow! Don't ever underestimate the abilities of the Alaskan bush pilots! When he first saw the plane, Herman was shocked at how small it really was. He told the pilot, "When you said small, you weren't kidding!"

They gladly left everything behind except color. They sat on each other's laps, got stuffed behind the back seat, and laid across the floor. He said his knees were pressed so hard against the dash, he may have left a dent in it!

Taking off was no small deal either! They were way overloaded, and literally had no runway. Herman asked, "Can you take off from this rock?" (Pilot) "It's easy. Launch yourself off the rock, go gliding down the brush-covered hillside, engine at full throttle, picking up speed. When you get your speed up enough or run out of room, whichever comes first, point things upward and don't hesitate!" The rest of the story is history.

I still can't make up my mind. Either the Alaskan bush pilots have a gift from God to fly the impossible, or they are totally insane and trying to kill everybody! But since their records are filled with the legendary impossible and with a very high rate of successes, I'm beginning to wonder. . .

Farewell to a Legend

Herman was a prospector from the old school. He grew up in Alaska in the prospector circles. It seems he worked with the best and the worst of them. Either way he learned very early and very well, the do's and don'ts of the prospector's life. He was a hard man on the outside, with his bushy white hair and beard. His eyes seemed to penetrate you and made you feel awkward if he stared at you. I found his judgment of people's character was uncannily accurate and he was always blunt and to the point. Some people were afraid of him. His speech was always clean, but hard and direct.

He didn't talk much unless he got to know you and liked you. Even then, a typical conversation sounded like you were about to kill each other. But in reality, you both were having a good time being together and discussing everything from prospecting, to God, to other ideas and concepts. He never liked idle talk, you had to be going somewhere with it or have something profound to say. That was Herman.

Herman was a Christian all the way to his heart and soul. He truly loved the Lord but had no respect for the modern-day soapsuds preachers or shallow stupid people who called themselves Christian. "They were as shallow as mosquito guts after you smacked it!" he would say.

Herman worked just as hard as his speech and character. At 70 years old, he was still in extremely good shape except for his knees. They were bad and hurt all the time, but it never slowed him down very much.

I loved Herman as a brother in Christ and also like a father. We became very close and had a lot of laughs and serious talks together. All of them are precious to me today.

His favorite pastime was installing carpet. Why he liked it so much I do not know. He didn't need to be doing anything if he didn't want to, but that was a business he had started many years ago, and he stuck with it even when he no longer had to.

I first met him while I was working at a shipyard, where they built mega luxury yachts. Herman did all their carpet laying for them. Needless to say, he was a perfectionist all the way. When we first met we hit it off right away and stayed close for the rest of his life.

If you're a prospector in Alaska, you can only work for a few months out of the year. But when you did work, you worked long 18-hour days nonstop. In the land of the midnight sun, that's a tall order. You stopped for absolute necessities and a few hours of sleep only. You had to be tough all the way to the bone. And Herman had no problem being tough. That was him all the way.

Behind that tough man's fearsome appearance and hard-core speech, there was a heart of gold. People who were acquainted with him simply would not believe it when you said Herman was a big teddy bear. They would make some wisecracks about him and avoid him like the plague. NOBODY wanted to make him mad or cross. If you were "straight," you would be okay, but if you wanted to be stupid, you'd best avoid Herman Nelson. He didn't stomach it much, and you knew it.

He was a riot to work with and there was never a dull moment when he was around. But you had to be tough to get in his inner circle, and there you'd see a whole different man.

When I first heard that he had passed away, I cried bitterly. It took two weeks to finally accept it, and even then, I took it very hard for a long time afterwards. I have never met another Herman Nelson. He was a dying breed of old-time prospectors. Today it's all about machinery and high tech, but to Herman it was grit, an eye for finding gold, more grit, and solid character. Wimps couldn't make it in his world.

Just how he got an eye for finding gold, nobody knows. He didn't know either. To him it was a matter of looking and knowing what you were looking at and knowing where to look. It was that simple. If you didn't know what you were looking for, you had no business being out there getting in somebody else's way, or sticking your nose in where it didn't belong.

In our many talks and visits, he shared many stories of his years of prospecting. he had pictures of most of them, but for a few there were only the scars. Either way, his stories kept you spellbound and were unforgettable.

He always kept a gold nugget on a chain around his neck. He said if he ever got stranded someplace, he knew he would have more than enough money to get back home. He showed it to me one day and I must admit, I wouldn't want that much gold hanging around my neck at any time! It was about one ounce of gold. However, considering the character of the one wearing it, I might feel sorry for anyone who thought they might steal it.

His faith in God was hard core because Herman was hard core, though inwardly he was a man of compassion. Few ever saw that side of him. Today I believe he is in heaven. I was told by his son, "Herman had gone out on a carpet job in Alaska, but when he failed to return, they went looking for him. They found him sitting on the passenger side fender of his carpet trailer. At first they thought he was asleep and just sitting there, but when they approached him, they found he was dead." It was later found that he died of a heart attack. There was no sign of struggle and his phone was still in his shirt pocket. It looked as if he got tired and sat down. His passing threw his family into a tornado of strife. It blew his family apart. The gold he sought for, to provide for his family, could not bring peace to their hearts. And when his steady hand of faith was removed, they fell apart.

I can never forget Herman, or his legendary experiences. He loaned me the photo album of his last trip saying he would pick it up the next month. But that return trip never came. When I found out about his passing, I made several attempts to contact his family because I supposed they would want the album back. But I could never get anyone to answer the phone. Then one day, out of the blue, I ran across his son! What a great time we had seeing each other again. It was then I found out about the sad news of Herman's family. I was told how they had turned everything upside down trying to find that album. It seems there is something in it that was very important to them, but as I went back through it, I could not see anything that looked important at first. Then it dawned on me! It was right there the whole time!

His son told me to keep the album. That is what his dad would have wanted. If the album showed up, it would start another massive war over who got it, and what could be gleaned from its pictures. As for the claims filed on the Anaconda claim, they expire every year. But since Herman had not actually filled a claim, it was just an experimental dig to verify what was actually there. So that site returned back into a mystery. I suppose that some upcoming gold company will someday discover it and the last page of the Anaconda Gold and Mining Company will be written.

UNDERSTANDING FORGIVENESS

Forgiveness of a simple offense is a simple matter. But for those deep destructive hurts that leave crippling scars, emotional handicaps, and haunting quirks that destroy us from the inside out, forgiveness becomes a process, not a simple action.

Applying the understanding of simple forgiveness to a complex problem doesn't work and leads to deeper despair. It's like learning to make paper airplanes, then trying to fly a jumbo jet. Both are flights, both are airplanes, but are two separate planets. We know that to be forgiven requires our own willingness to forgive others. People will sincerely try to forgive on a simple level, but often their attempts fail because simple forgiveness will not work where complex forgiveness is needed. Those who fail draw the conclusion that they cannot forgive, or that forgiveness doesn't work. Thus they are eaten up and destroyed from the inside out by their fears or bitterness. So, these brave hurting soldiers of the cross carry a deep hidden secret of bitterness and resentment. Sometimes their outward circumstances force them to live a double life. Their walk with God changes from knowing God and living right, to feeling violated and afraid of God. They forsake a religion of righteousness and purity and embrace a religion of works and sincerity, all the while convincing themselves and hoping that somehow God understands and will overlook their bitterness.

Some have been so damaged by their inability to forgive that their failures become darker and heavier than the original offense that started it. Some have been driven to extreme atrocities, breakdowns, and darkness so deep that suicide seems to be their only escape.

These tragic tales are often fostered by the misconception of what forgiveness really is.

Even well-meaning and sincere people who love us often try to help with the simple concept of simple forgiveness. Their sincere attempts to help become the very weapon that kills us. We say, "We have tried forgiveness and it doesn't work." Again, simple forgiveness will not work on complex issues. We sometimes blame God for the failure, thus plunging us into even deeper despair and darkness. Sincere people truly mean well, but by not understanding the depths of the darkness, or the answers to it, is a clear indication they have never faced the depths or the damage of the battles themselves.

The first step to understanding complex forgiveness is to first understand what forgiveness is NOT. Many have tried to forgive, but their understanding of forgiveness was based on simple forgiveness. Simple forgiveness says someone stepped on my toes; I need to get over it. And if I don't, I'm met with harsh verbal attacks on my maturity. While that may be the case in the simple forgiveness we teach children, it has no bearing what-so-ever on the tragic scars we are sometimes forced to carry. These are two separate worlds all together. Let us examine what forgiveness is not! It may reveal where some of our battles are coming from.

What Forgiveness is Not:

1. <u>Accepting the blame</u>: If you didn't do it, then you didn't do it. Forgiveness will not change that.
2. <u>Blaming others</u>: If what somebody did was wrong, then it is still wrong. Forgiveness will not change that.

UNDERSTANDING FORGIVENESS

3. <u>Justifying anyone's wrong action</u>: Forgiveness doesn't turn wrong into right.
4. <u>Demanding vengeance</u>: Forgiveness does not clear the way for retaliation. More is said about this later.
5. <u>Re-establishing trust</u>: Trust must always be *earned*, not forwarded or loaned. Forgiveness does not change that.
6. <u>Re-establishing communication</u>: Certain people are destructive to you, the values that you hold, and the people you love. To allow them to destroy you because you forgave is contrary to scripture and common sense. Avoiding them is not a sign of bitterness. It's them reaping from their own actions. Don't cast your pearls before swine.
7. <u>Justifying bitterness</u>: Two wrongs don't equal a right. What happened was wrong. Getting bitter over it is much worse. Bitterness is a clear sign of a lack of forgiveness, (or lack of a clear understanding of what forgiveness is not!) And if we find that forgiveness doesn't work, then we must go back to God and start over with what forgiveness really is.
8. <u>Erase what happened</u>: Forgive and forget is not always a reality and sometimes not even a possibility. Forgiveness does not erase the scars we must sometimes live with. Learn from the experience, adjust your own compass, and keep going forward, but don't repeat the experience. God can be selective of what he remembers. We are not God so we cannot do that. Forgiveness does not make us God. When we live with the scars, we can't erase what happened.

9. <u>Restore love</u>: Love is not a switch or a flashcard remedy. True love takes time. To resurrect love out of the ashes of pain, takes even longer. To love the offender is a process on our part. It takes time to heal and recover. Forgiveness doesn't change that.
10. <u>Forgiveness is not making or allowing myself to be the scapegoat</u> or the whipping post for anyone, at any time, or anywhere!

Complex Forgiveness

1. Complex forgiveness is letting go of *all of it*, by giving *all of it* to God.
2. This can only happen when we come to the realization that we can't take it anymore.
3. As long as you're willing to hang on to any part of it, then God will continue to let you suffer from what you refuse to let go of!
4. Anything we don't let go of, we will continue to be the victim of.
5. Once these are turned over to God, they become his battles, not ours! God never loses a battle!
6. No one can take us out of our father's hand!
7. However, this giving it to God, is **not** an instant act or experience. It is a process.

The Process of Complex Forgiveness

The parts of the process itself probably won't happen in rapid sequence. They can, but normally scars and healing take time. Blessed is the man who can settle it in his heart to go through with God as fast as possible! It may take time for us to turn these things over in our mind and count the cost! Then we must prepare our hearts to accept them and act upon them until they become a part of our lives. To rush through them because we agree with them in our minds, is not the same as acting upon them in faith and consistency from the heart. A wise king will count the cost of the battle before he charges, headlong, into the fray.

Keep asking God to help you at every turn of the road and every step. Also, deliberately place yourself under the mercy of God by means of prayer, reading scripture, obedience, and avoiding those things that trigger an internal war. This may not be possible at first. But setting time aside every day to practice these things will build results!

The darkness we have fallen into may be accidental on our part, or intentional on the part of someone else, but the road out must always consist of deliberate acts on our part. We must ask ourselves; do we want out, or do we want to rot here? Getting out and getting the victory will not be accidental. If we want to rot there, all we have to do is nothing!

1. We must first reach the place where we want to change. It is possible to be so embittered that all we want is revenge. At that point, darkness has become our refuge. We point the finger of blame and justify ourselves, based on their wrong. We blame them for our sad condition. This may be entirely true, but the real question is, "Do we want to live under the tragic fallout from the attack, or do we want to be delivered from it?"

    Like the prodigal son who "came to himself," he had to realize his emptiness and remember that his father's house had plenty. He wanted to change. But wanting to change is not the same as changing! He could have blamed a lot of things and perhaps been right in some of it. But his real deliverance would only come through his personal choice to act upon it!

We find that he arose and went to his father's house! We too must come to our ourselves, our desperate case realized, and change our course for the father's house! It is possible for us to walk in the sunshine and feel the warmth of God's love once again. But God kidnaps no one. We must want to go and we must go!

2. We must realize we can't do it on our own. We need God's help to change. If we could do it on our own, we would not still be there or suffered like we have. Asking God to help us change is vital.
3. If we were to be brutally honest with ourselves, we would have to admit there are things in our lives that God is not pleased with. Things that may or may not have anything to do with the original dark experience. However, we must ask God to forgive us of ALL our sin. God will not cut a shady deal on half sin. There are no discount coupons on forgiveness. It's everything or nothing. God is serious about it and so must we be.
4. Giving it all to God does not happen by us just by thinking about it. We must act upon what God shows us. Are you tired of living under the heaviness and darkness of the battle? Identify the things that trigger the battle within and avoid those triggers. And when we fall into those triggers ask God to help. Even if victory takes time, it is time well spent!

UNDERSTANDING FORGIVENESS

5. Accepting the blame is a common church jargon that is used by people who don't have a clue what they are talking about. It may sound good in religious zeal, and they even try to justify it by calling it humility. But, in the bitter world of darkness, accepting the blame is surrender to the enemy. It is surrendering your dignity for an act you did not do. It surrenders your self-esteem and your sense of right and wrong. And when you discover it was a terrible mistake to confess to something you did not do, it will destroy you when you try to set things straight. The same ones who said to accept the blame will stand in line to call you a liar, based on what you already "confessed to." You can probably guess the enemy of your soul will not accept any blame, and he will take full advantage of you when you do so for things you did not do.

    Remember, when you accept the blame for something you did not do, you are also accepting the blame for many other things that you had no knowledge of, but were connected to. The workers of darkness will heap things up that you didn't know existed!

6. Blaming others has some interesting effects that are hidden. Every person has a sense of justice somewhere inside of them. It's natural and healthy to see some terrible injustice get its reward. Pointing the finger of blame is to say they did it and need to be punished. This stems from that sense of rightness that we all possess. But the truth of the matter is, if they don't repent, they will be punished with an eternal punishment from God. They are not getting away with

anything. Even if they have hidden it from the whole world, they cannot hide it from God. This brings us back to that challenge of giving all of it to God. Are we willing to surrender our right of vengeance to Gods control? This is all part of "do you want to change? Do you want out?" You have to make a decision at this point. If you want to rot in darkness, do nothing. The things we don't surrender to God will become our tormenters in the future.

7. The thought of seeing someone burning in hell or even in the lake of fire, should make you sick. If you do not give your bitterness and desire for revenge to God, it will not keep them from going there. But it will take you with them. Like that king, you must count the cost of your actions before you make any hasty decisions. In counting the cost, it's YOUR cost!

8. Once we surrender our right to vengeance to God, it satisfies that inner demand for justice. There is a certain measure of peace that comes with that surrender. Now comes the next bridge we must cross. If we have truly given that to God, we must take our hands off! Giving it to God is putting it on Gods altar. Not everything we give to God is our best. Don't be surprised if he asks for your worst darkness also! When you decide to go back and "beat them up a little" because they deserve it, you are taking them back from God's altar, and telling God to go away. Is that what you want to do? The temptation may be great to rehearse the matter and point the blame once again. But remember, you surrendered that vengeance to God. If you go back and start

UNDERSTANDING FORGIVENESS

reliving the nightmare, you will also get all the darkness that went with it.
9. Forgiveness is the key that turns reliving the trauma, with all its heaviness, into learning from it, with all its peace.
10. It isn't that we will not remember what happened, but if we must face that trigger, and maintain the spirit of forgiveness! Remember to put things in the best light as we truthfully can. Don't make excuses for them, but consider other issues that *kindly* help us to understand them. They are hurting also. They may hide it, lie about it, and continue to blame you, but God's word says every man has a conscience. They would do well to start listening to it!
11. So, you have given them to God, then you stop blaming them, (remember pointing the blame = they did it= they need to be punished!) because you're letting God take care of it.
12. And when you are forced to face a trigger point, you sidestep it by putting it into a kinder and more noble light. This is God's way of protecting you from backsliding into the darkness again! Always take the high road!
13. By this time in your deliberate act of coming out of the pit, you have discovered that the more you keep yourself in the mercy of God by prayer, scripture and following God's leading, the stronger you are becoming and the darkness is fading. The load is getting lighter! Again it may take days or weeks to get to the next step. This is not an exercise in cognitive reading, but deliberately preparing our heart in coming out of the pit of darkness.

14. As we hold steady on this course, there are some things that are going to happen. The silent healing will have already started. Our faith is starting to live again and our hope is getting brighter and brighter. We are changing for the good! The sunlight is coming into full warmth. We may not be at the finish line but we can see it from here! Keep going forward! There will be setbacks. Triggers show up unexpectedly. You may fall back down, but God is still helping you. We may be cast down, but not forsaken. Get back up instantly and finish your climbing out of the pit. Standing close to the top is not the same as being out! Get back to taking deliberate steps out!
15. As we change on the inside, God is probably changing your environment. New friends, a different job, perhaps even moving to a different location. I have seen this so often and have recognized the pattern. It all depends on how far we have come in obeying Gods leading.

We will continue to heal by obeying Gods leadership. Nobody else is capable of leading you out. Some may encourage you, but don't shift your focus from Gods leadership to someone else just because they said something nice! Satan is good at sending someone with smooth sounding words that will detour you back into destruction. Stay focused on God and his word! Our hearts will begin to warm once again. By that I mean, we will eventually start feeling sorry for those who have hurt us. This opens the door for praying for them and our prayers are not forced or fake. We really mean it. This is a true sign of spiritual growth. Its learning to love again through God's love in us. Praying for our enemies is a prayer reserved for the victors!

UNDERSTANDING FORGIVENESS

Others can pray for them, but NOBODY can touch heaven on their behalf like you can! God is well pleased when we get to that point but that does not open the door for trust. Trust must be earned and that with great caution. It's possible to never be able to trust them again. That's a reality we must face and accept, even if they come to us and ask forgiveness. Don't let them into your safety circle.

They have to prove themselves for a long time before you will be willing to place your head on their chopping block again. You can put your head in the lion's mouth if you want to, but he has bitten you several times before. This is not bitterness, it's the reality of don't cast your pearls before swine! There are things people do that they will reap permanent damage from. It's a sad reality we all must face and be warned of. Understanding that principle has nothing to do with bitterness. God my reach that person, just as he has reached you. But remember, trust must be earned.

Finally, as you grow in grace, testify to others what God has done for you.

Simple forgiveness is great for simple offenses. But when the scars and trauma take over, simple forgiveness will not work. We must deliberately open the door to healing by our own hand, and that will take time. And if you meet someone who is struggling with some dark battle, share your victory with them! God will be much pleased, and so will you!

One step into Glory and you will know, it was worth it!

ABOUT THE AUTHOR

Robert Bryan was born in Kansas City, in 1956, to Marvin and Mary Bryan. The family suffered many hardships that ultimately ended with the divorce of his parents when he was about 13. It was then that he found himself living on the street.

At the age of 14, he found his dad who had remarried. They were a major influence to him for the good. His stepmom's family welcomed him with open arms and restored his confidence in people. His dad and "Mom" encouraged him to get back into school and continue his education, which he was happy to do. But race riots broke out at the school where he attended and his academic education came to a halt. The riots made it impossible for him to safely stay with his dad as their proximity to the school made no one safe. Robert was already having daily fights against the rioters who wanted him and several others dead. So, he returned to Jefferson City, Missouri where he stayed with extended family for a time. But when that fell through, he was back on the streets again until the age of 17. However, while living with his dad and stepmom, at the age of 15 he came to know the Lord. He felt a call to preach but had no idea how to go about such a thing. When he found himself back on the streets there seemed no possibility of going forward with his new found faith in the Lord. He supported himself by knocking on doors asking for any kind of work and his mechanical skills and self-motivation sustained him. He had to stay on the move during this time, but frequently stayed in town with his Granny.

Finding handyman work in town without having transportation proved a big problem. He did find a job as a busboy/dishwasher that paid 0.65 cents an hour plus a free lunch every day! But the job was only temporary, and again he was hard pressed when he lost that job. It was now December of 1973 and winter was on with all of its challenges. One day, seeking refuge from the cold, he went into a Navy recruitment office where he unknowingly enlisted into four years of service.

His enlistment into the U.S. Navy in January of 1974, at the age of 17, was the best thing that could have happened to him. He served until January 1978, spending a short time in Vietnam era combat on board ship. He achieved the rank of BT3 on board the USS England, DLG 22. He married Jovanna Boucher in 1976 and after his honorable discharge, they moved to Missouri for her to meet his family. His heart was clearly there, but each attempt to live in Missouri was always brought to an immediate stop.

He worked in the logging industry, operating heavy equipment, for 14 years, from 1979-1993, out of Aberdeen Washington. When that industry was shut down, he again returned to Missouri. It was while in Missouri that he was called to pastor a church in Burlington, Iowa, which he accepted.

He successfully pastored the Bible Missionary Church in Burlington Iowa from 1993-1999 until health issues forced him out of full-time ministry. While in Burlington he worked for a tree service doing high climbing and tree removal for the power company. He then moved back to Washington state once again where he spent some time in recuperation and much overdue rest and healing.

ABOUT THE AUTHOR

From 2001-2013 he worked at Westport shipyard in Westport, Washington where his mechanical/electrical/heating/high pressure boilers skills were in great demand. When the shipyard was sold to another company in 2013, he returned to school by attending Renton Technical Collage in Renton, Washington, where he graduated on the Dean's list in 2015 as a universal refrigeration technician at the age of 58. He later said, "Cramming a 3-year course into 15 months was the hardest thing I have ever done in my life!" He gives the credit to his wife who encouraged him and helped him every day, and also to God who strengthened him and provided for them during that time. He will tell you that "Living by faith does a lot for you in finding out who God really is! He is faithful, kind and very understanding!"

He worked for the state of Washington in Buckley WA. troubleshooting HVAC, mechanical/electrical issues until his official retirement in August of 2020.

He and his wife have been married for over 45 years. He still calls her "sweetheart" and "heart-throb." Together they have raised four children and they have 9 grandchildren who are making certain their parents experience the full adventure of raising children!

www.ingramcontent.com/pod-product-compliance
Lightning Source LLC
Chambersburg PA
CBHW060943230426
43665CB00015B/2044